Young Femininity

Young Femininity

Girlhood, Power and Social Change

Sinikka Aapola, Marnina Gonick
and Anita Harris

Consultant Editor: Jo Campling

First published 2005 by
PALGRAVE MACMILLAN
Houndmills, Basingstoke, Hampshire RG21 6XS and 175 Fifth Avenue,
New York, N.Y. 10010
Companies and representatives throughout the world

PALGRAVE MACMILLAN is the global academic imprint of the Palgrave
Macmillan division of St. Martin's Press, LLC and of Palgrave Macmillan
Ltd. Macmillan® is a registered trademark in the United States, United
Kingdom and other countries. Palgrave is a registered trademark in the
European Union and other countries.

ISBN 0–333–96511–6 hardback
ISBN 0–333–96512–4 paperback

This book is printed on paper suitable for recycling and made from fully
managed and sustained forest sources.

A catalogue record for this book is available from the British Library.

Library of Congress Cataloging-in-Publication Data
Aapola, Sinikka.
    Young femininity : girlhood, power, and social change / Sinikka
Aapola, Marnina Gonick, and Anita Harris ; consultant editor, Jo
Campling.
        p.   cm.
    Includes bibliographical references and index.
    ISBN 0–333–96511–6 (cloth) – ISBN 0–333–96512–4 (pbk.)
    1. Girls – Social conditions.   I. Gonick, Marnina.   II. Harris, Anita,
1968–   III. Title.

HQ777.A23   2004
305.23′082 – dc22   2004042106

10   9   8   7   6   5   4   3   2   1
14   13   12   11   10   09   08   07   06   05

Printed in China

Contents

Acknowledgements

We would particularly like to acknowledge Johanna Wyn, who introduced us to each other, and whose idea it originally was that we work together. Johanna's encouragement has been fundamental to us throughout the process. We also warmly thank the following people who have helped in various ways to bring this project to fruition: our editor Jo Campling, Tuula Gordon, Jade Bilardi, Janne Hiipakka, Anna Niemelä, Maria Pallotta-Chiarolli and Mary Napoli for the research she did.

We also appreciate the support of our colleagues in the School of Political and Social Inquiry, Monash University, at the Department of Sociology, University of Helsinki, at the Department of Curriculum and Instruction in the College of Education and the Women's Studies Program in the College of Liberal Arts at The Pennsylvania State University.

The book was written with the financial assistance of a Monash University Faculty of Arts Project Completion grant, the Academy of Finland Postdoctoral Fellowship, the Helsingin Sanomat 100-year-Jubileum Foundation stipendium and the Alfred Kordelin Foundation grant.

We also thank the Menzies Centre for Australian Studies, King's College, London, where we were supported as visiting scholars to work on the book during autumn 2001.

Some small parts of this book have been published in a different form as 'Not Drowning or Waving: Young Women and the Limits of the Third Wave Debate' by Anita Harris in *Outskirts: Feminism on the Edge*, May, 2001, and this material is used here with permission from the editors and publishers.

The authors and the publisher would like to thank the following people, institutions and companies for permissions to reproduce copyright material in the form of quotations:

A-lehdet Oy for a quotation from www.demi.fi; Australian Clearinghouse for Youth Studies for quotations from *Against the*

Odds: Young People and Work, edited by J. Bessant and S. Cook and from *Researching Youth,* edited by J. McLeod and K. Malone; David Higham Associates for a quotation from *Fathers and Daughters* by S. Sharpe; Dunmore Press Ltd. for a quotation from *At School I've Got a Chance* by A. Jones; Egmont Kustannus for a quotation from *Girls*-magazine; Elsevier Ltd. for a quotation from the article 'Friends or Foes? Interpreting Relations between Girls in School' by T. Gordon, J. Holland and E. Lahelma from *Genders and Sexualities in Educational Ethnography,* edited by G. Walford, copyright (2000); Farrar, Straus & Giroux for a quotation from *Going All the Way: Teenage Girls' Tales of Sex, Romance and Pregnancy* by S. Thompson; Finnish Youth Research Network for quotations from *Murrosikä ja sukupuoli. Julkiset ja yksityiset ikäjärjestykset* by S. Aapola and from the article 'Pikkutyttöjä vai puoliaikuisia' by S. Aapola from *Tulkintoja tytöistä,* edited by S. Aaltonen and P. Honkatukia; Gaudeamus/Oy University Press Finland for a quotation from *Nuorten kulttuurit koulussa. Ääni, tila ja sukupuolten arkiset järjestykset* by T. Tolonen; Lotta Haikkola for a quotation from her Master's thesis in sociology, University of Helsinki, *Ääni ja aikuisuus. Kansalaisuuden ehdot osallisuushankkeeseen osallistuneiden nuorten tulkinnoissa;* Päivi Harinen for quotations from her book *Valmiiseen tulleet. Tutkimus nuoruudesta, kansallisuudesta ja kansalaisuudesta;* HarperCollins Publishers Inc. for several quotations from 'Ophelia Speaks', edited by Sara Shandler, copyright © by Sara Shandler; Harvard University Press for quotations from *Raising Their Voices: The Politics of Girls' Anger* by Lyn Mikel Brown, copyright © 1998 by the President and Fellows of Harvard College; Hecate Press for a quotation from article 'I'm Wasting Away on Unrequited Love' by L. Hillier in *Hecate* vol. 27(1); Kylie Lewis for a quotation from zine 'Her Heroes Aren't Gone'; Pia Lundbom for quotations from her article 'Hei kaveri – millä välineillä äänestät?' from *Kyllä politiikalle, mutta . . . Nuoret ja eduskuntavaalit 2003,* edited by K. Paakkunainen; Moon Rocket Distribution for a quotation from girlzines.net; Anna Niemelä for a quotation from her Master's thesis in sociology, University of Helsinki, *Erilainen nuoruus? Varhainen äitiys, ikä ja elämänkulku;* Bengt Nordin Agency AB for quotations from *Fittstim,* edited by L. N. Skugge, B. Olsson and B. Zilg; Lilli Ollikainen for a quotation from her article in *Sisters Club*-magazine; Open University Press/McGraw-Hill Education for quotations from *The Company She Keeps: An Ethnography of Girls' Friendship* by V. Hey, copyright (1997) and from *Consuming Children* by J. Kenway and E. Bullen, copyright (2001); Orca Musikutbildning for a quotation from www.upsweden.com; Oxford University Press for quotations from *One of the Guys: Girls, Gangs and Gender* by J. Miller; Maria Pallotta-Chiarolli for quotations from *Girls' Talk*, edited by M. Pallotta-Chiarolli; Palgrave for quotations from *Growing Up Girl. Psychosocial Explorations of Gender and Class* by V. Walkerdine, H. Lucey and J. Melody; Research Centre for Contemporary Culture at University of Jyväskylä for quotations from *Naiseuden naamiaiset. Nuoren naisen diskoruumiillisuus* by T. Nykyri; Routledge/Taylor & Francis Books, Inc. for quotations from *Hopeful Girls Troubled Boys* by N. Lopez, copyright (2003); Rowman & Littlefield Publishers for quotations from the article 'I'll Tell You What I Really, Really Want: Girl Power and Self Identity in Britain' by S. Budgeon and the article 'Feeling Better with BRAVO: German Girls and Their Popular Youth Magazine' by M. Herrmann from *Millennium Girls*, edited by S. Inness; Ruckuscollective.org for a quotation from www.ruckuscollective. org; Russell Sage Foundation for a quotation from *Growing Up American: How Vietnamese Children Adapt to Life in the United States* by M. Zhou and C. L. Bankston III; Rutgers University Press for a quotation from *Pretty in Punk: Girls' Gender Resistance in a Boys' Subculture* by L. Leblanc; Sage Publications for a quotation from article 'Emergent Feminist Identities: Young Women and the Practice of Micropolitics' by S. Budgeon in *European Journal of Women's Studies*, vol. 8(1), copyright (2001); Salon.com for a quotation from www.salon.com; Seal Press for quotations from *Real Girl, Real World: Tools for Finding Your True Self*, edited by H. Gray and S. Phillips and from article 'It's a Big Fat Revolution' by N. Lamm from *Listen Up: Voices from the Next Feminist Generation*, edited by B. Findlen; Sumach Press for a quotation from the article 'Young Women and Disability' by A. Di Virgilio from *Turbo Chicks* edited by A. Mitchell, L. B. Rumble and L. Karaian; SUNY Press for a quotation from *Constructing Female Identities: Meaning Making in an Upper Middle Class Youth Culture* by A. Proweller, the State University of New York Press, © 1998 State University of New York; Jenny Svenberg for a quotation from her article 'Tack gud jag är lesbisk – om homosexualitet' from *Fittstim*, edited by L. N. Skugge, B. Olsson and B. Zilg; Taylor & Francis Journals (UK) for quotations from articles 'I'd Hate to Be Just a Housewife: Career Aspirations of British Muslim Girls' by T. N. Basit from the *British Journal of Guidance and Counselling*, vol. 24(2), 'The Bumpy Road to Womanhood' by K. Barron from *Disability and Society* vol. 12(2) and 'Standing Alone, Working Together: Tensions Surrounding Young Canadian

Women's Views of the Workplace' by L. Hughes-Bong from *Gender and Education* vol. 10(3); Thomson Publishing Services for quotations from the article 'The Waltz of Sociability: Intimacy, Dislocation and Friendship in a Quebec High School' by V. Amit-Talai and H. Wulff and from the article 'Inter-racial Friendship: Consuming Youth Styles, Ethnicity and Teenage Femininity in South London' by H. Wulff, both from *Youth Cultures: A Cross-Cultural Perspective*, edited by V. Amit-Talai and H. Wulff, and from 'Sexuality, Gender and Schooling. Shifting Agendas in Social Learning' by M. Kehily, from *Young People's Views on Sex Education: Education, Attitudes and Behaviour* by L. Measor, C. Tiffin and K. Miller, from *Young, Female and Black* by H. S. Mirza, and from the article 'The Workplace. Becoming a Paid Worker: Images and Identity' by S. Bowlby, S. Lloyd Evans and R. Mohammad from *Cool Places. Geographies of Youth Cultures*, edited by T. Skelton and G.Valentine; Kristina Thulin & Jenny Östergren for quotations from their book *X-märkt. Flickornas guide till verkligheten*; Warner Books, Inc. for the poem 'Black Beauty' by Latosha Renne Guy and for a quotation by Tammy Sue Lowe, both from *Girl Power* by Hillary Carlip, copyright © 1995 by Hillary Carlip; Young Voice for a quotation from *The Can-Do Girls* by A. Katz; Riitta Yrjänheikki for a poem by EmZii from www.geocities.com/taivaansteppaaja; and Elke Zobl for a quotation from www.grrrlzines.net.

Every effort has been made to trace all the copyright holders but if any have been inadvertently overlooked, the publisher will be pleased to make the necessary arrangements at the first opportunity.

Introduction

In this book we[1] work in the traditions of feminism and critical youth studies to ask questions about changing meanings of girls and girlhood and how these meanings are negotiated and lived by young women in late modern societies. In this period of rapid global change, new demands and opportunities have created changes in how girlhood is defined, the social expectations young women encounter and their performances of identity. Our approach to these issues is to analyse girlhood as something that is constructed socially, rather than merely as a stage of life fixed by biological processes and programmed psychological development. Such a perspective allows us to see girlhood as a site of both competing narratives and an experiential process grounded in historical, material and discursive contexts. Girlhood is something that is both individually and collectively accomplished through participating in the social, material and discursive practices defining young femininity. Thus, what it means to be a girl is constantly changing. Even in the same historical time-frame and social context, experiences and meanings of girlhood will shift because gender and age also intersect with race, class, sexuality, ethnicity, nationality, and ability. The various meanings and experiences of girlhood are not created in isolation, they inform each other. White, middle-class girls negotiate their identities against who they are not – male, black, working-class and so on. The same is true for girls of all races, classes and ethnicities.

Here are two examples which illustrate how this works. This poem by African American Latosha Renne Guy was written when she was 18 years old. In the poem she responds to social ideals of beauty which are based on white European features. As a black girl she cannot attain this ideal and thus is excluded from predominant definitions of beauty. In a series of comparisons she notes how based on these ideals her beauty will always be found lacking. However, she also resists the values attached to dominant versions of white femininity with their exclusive focus on looks and replaces these with what she considers the more important goals of contributing to the fight for rights of African American people.

Black Beauty

Little Black girl, they laughed at
you and called you black
tar black
but you smile
cause you won't give them the skin
off your back
Little Black girl
they called your hair
kinky and nappy
but with your own hair
you're content and happy
Little Black girl they said
your nose was too wide
but you never pay any mind
to what's on the outside
Cause this little black girl
is proud of what she is
and she won't budge, sell out,
compromise, or give in
This little girl is growing into a
Black woman
concerned with nothing less
than the betterment of her race
and she has much
more to think
about than
the features of her face.

(Latosha Renne Guy, African
American, in Carlip, 1995, p. 193.)

Reay's (2001) study of girls' social groupings in a British inner-city primary school provides another example of how identities are always formed in relation to others. Reay notes that there were four identifiable groups of girls in the third-year class she studied – the 'nice girls', the 'girlies', the 'spice girls' and the 'tomboys'. She suggests that being nice was coded as a specific formulation of white, middle-class femininity and thus had derogatory connotations for working-class girls. In focus group discussions with working-class girls all agreed that 'no one wants to be a nice girl'. Reay argues that for a majority of the working-class girls in the class, being a 'nice girl' signified an absence of the toughness and attitude that they aspired to (Reay, 2001, p. 159). Once again, we see that establishing oneself as being a particular kind of girl means negotiating with what one is not or does not want to be. Race, class, sexuality, ethnicity, and ability are amongst the factors which shape what it means to be a girl. Thinking about girlhood and how it intersects with categories of social difference is not simply then about adding on extras or special sections to a basic formula. Rather, girls become girls through their negotiation of raced, classed and sexed femininities.

In this book we trace the ways in which hegemonic discourses and social forces surrounding youth and gender provide definitions of various forms of young femininity and their intersections with class, race, sexuality, ethnicity and ability in late modernity. We suggest that these discourses structure young women's lives in increasingly complex ways. They also continue to create marginalized others whose lives, bodies, relationships and selves do not conform to the dominant forms of girlhood circulated by these discourses. One of the challenges we encounter in putting this book together is how to even write about girls and girlhood when we are also trying to use an analysis which understands them as identities and cultural constructions which are not coherent, stable and unchanging. We struggle with how to talk about girls' lives when doing so also creates the very exclusions we are attempting to redress. For despite our best intentions, it is never possible to capture the experience of all girls in a text. Thus, the book holds in tension the desire to understand and represent girls' experiences and the very real material conditions which shape them with the knowledge that claiming to be able to do so is a fiction. This admission is not, however, only about the limitations of what our own book seeks to achieve; it is also about an understanding of the relationships between the discourses of girlhood and the identities of girls. That is, if we are arguing that girls negotiate their gendered identities through discourses of femininity and other categories of social difference we must also acknowledge how our own work functions in the discursive field of girlhood as a fiction which creates girls as beings with specificity.

The idea that new meanings and opportunities overlap and compete with older understandings of girlhood is the driving force of our discussion. The key questions we explore in this book are as follows. How is girlhood defined within media, contemporary theory, and pedagogical and psychological discourses? What kinds of possibilities do these discourses surrounding femininity and youth create for girls in negotiating their own gendered identities, and what global socio-economic forces come to bear on this process? What are the strategies girls use in their efforts to find their way among traditions, new possibilities and challenges?

We investigate these questions using various methods. We analyse the discursive and material construction of girlhood under late capitalism, bringing together theoretical and empirical work from a range of different Western nations. We also examine how young women shape their identities, asking how girls from various social backgrounds and in different cultural contexts resist and adapt to the contradictory discourses surrounding femininity and youth as a lifephase in the Western world. We develop under-standings of young women's cultural productions, social practices and relationships to social institutions in order to explore the multi-farious meanings of sexuality and the body, friendships, family, school, work, citizenship and politics and personal and cultural identities for girls today.

While we have not aimed for comparative research in the tradi-tional sense of the concept, we have deliberately sought to juxta-pose various kinds of materials from different parts of the world in order to consider their similarities and differences, and to explore the construction of girlhood across a range of local contexts as wide apart geographically as Australasia, Europe and North America, but which can all be conceptualized as late modern Western soci-eties. The societies we concentrate on are in many ways very dif-ferent, but they also have some very influential similarities, namely a democratic political system, a market economy and a history of civil movements, including the women's movement. At the moment all of these societies are characterized by an intense process of restructuration and individualization; fundamental changes are happening in the structure of the labour-market, edu-cation, as well as the family and many other spheres of life. Per-ceptions of age phases, gender, nationality and ethnicity are being reworked in various ways in all Western societies. Systematic com-parisons and parallels have not been sought, but we analyse the gendered discourses that surround girlhood within and through national boundaries, and highlight variations as well as similarities within constructions of girlhood between and within particular countries such as Australia, Britain, Canada, Finland and the USA.

In our view, it is illuminating and inspiring to bring these per-spectives on girlhood together, to create a kaleidoscopic picture of young femininity; a picture that changes continuously as one moves through the various images. We present similar types of questions to widely ranging materials, and the combined result of our work has unique perspectives to offer.

A History of Constructing Girlhoods

Commonsense understandings present us with a view of girlhood as a universal, biological condition of female experience. This per-spective was popularized by those who initiated academic work about what it meant to grow up female. For them, girlhood was simply a physical and emotional stage of development along the linear path to female adulthood that all young women experience in more or less the same ways (see for example Hall, 1904). This model of girlhood has its foundations in scientific and particularly psychological frameworks, whereby experiences of growing up are supposed to transcend the individual and the specific. All girls are imagined to pass through the developmental tasks of youth in the same way. Differences of race, class, sexuality, ethnicity, and ability are not factored into these understandings of girlhood. As a result, the controlling image of girlhood tends to be that of the dominant social group, that is, white, middle-class, heterosexual, and able-bodied.

More recently, however, the frameworks of feminist and youth studies have introduced other ways of seeing girlhood and the transition to adulthood. They draw attention to the social, cultural, historical and political dimensions of how we define youth, femi-ninity and adulthood. For example, Lesley Johnson (1993) traces a defining moment of how current conceptions of youth emerged in the 1950s. Focusing on the Australian context, she argues that the notion of the self-determining, autonomous individual that is understood as the accomplishment of youth having reached adult-hood is a cultural ideal that emerged in response to economic and social transformations occurring all over the industrialized world. She also highlights the gendered implications of this notion of adulthood. Johnson (1993) suggests that it is a cultural ideal which, until the second wave of feminism, and perhaps beyond, did not include women. She argues that girls, no matter how old, never achieved adulthood using this definition, because rather than autonomy and self-determination, the requirements of mature femininity demanded dependence and a self who lived through relations with others.

Women's lack of status as adults was reflected in the language used at the time to identify female gendered persons. It was quite common to refer to any female as a 'girl', whether she was a child, an adult or even a senior citizen! One of the implications of this history has been the strong insistence by second wave feminists of the use of the terms 'woman' and 'young woman' as signifiers of seriousness, equal standing, and adult or mature status. However, more recently 'girl' has been recuperated by young feminists, who wish to reclaim, re-invent or invert its meaning. It can denote an identification with girl culture or feminine accoutrements and is also used as an informal form of address. In this text, we use girl and young woman interchangeably as much for stylistic reasons as for the political implications of the terms. We are not only interested in exploring the range of experience that may fall into the category, we also question the normative ways in which the category is constructed within the social contexts of schools, work, popular culture, and families. Because we are concerned with girlhood as a cultural construction, we do not consider it relevant to define this category according to certain chronological age-limits.

Some of the classic work of early feminist researchers focused on the nexus of adulthood and femininity that Lesley Johnson (1993) identified as the key problematic for girls growing up in modern times. They documented the ways in which young women were positioned unequally in relation to men, and how they were inculcated into femininity and subordination. 'Proper' girls were supposed to be heterosexual, chaste, submissive, attentive to their 'looks', family-oriented, professionally unambitious and compliant. These qualities were emphasized in young women's relationships to education, employment, media, the family, the church, romance, friendship and their self-esteem and body image (Griffin, 1985; Lees, 1986; Roman *et al.*, 1988). More recently, theorists grapple with the diverse range of experiences and meanings of girlhood, in a time where expectations of what a young woman is are changing radically. Seen as the beneficiaries of the second wave of feminism, young women are understood to have new opportunities that were previously only available to men. While this historical period is unique and important because of the unprecedented options for young women, it is recognized that these opportunities are not available to all young women in the same way or to the same extent. Moreover, it is also important to understand the broader social context in which these new options for girls have emerged as one that is also making new demands of them.

Globalization has changed the political economy of lives all over the world. It has created new forms of relationships between nation states, between citizens and states, and between employers and employees. Global labour markets have generated massive changes. Service and financial sectors, and technology and communications industries have replaced the manufacturing sectors that drove Western economies to the South where labour is cheaper. The result has been a greater division between the quality of employment available. For those who have the educational credentials and skills there is well paid professional and managerial work. For others who do not, jobs are limited to those which are poorly paid, often part-time, and without security. Globalization has also intensified the movement of people across borders as new markets and employment opportunities open and others shut down. Youth researchers note the significant disruptions to the circuit of production, reproduction and consumption marking the transition into adulthood (Furlong & Cartmel, 1997; Griffin, 1997; Wyn & White, 1997). The effect of such changes on people has been the requirement of continual self-invention and transformation in order to survive within the new social, economic and political system. Girls and women live this requirement in particularly gendered ways (Walkerdine et al., 2001). The neo-liberal incitement of individualism, rational choice and self-realization bumps up against discourses of femininity creating contradictory and complex positions for girls. Accordingly, a new phase of 'girls' studies' is needed; one which grapples with theorizing the changing conditions under which young women's diverse self-making occurs.

Work that begins to address these issues pushes the boundaries of the emerging field in what is perhaps an even more fundamental way than that which focuses on the absence of girls in youth studies and accounts for the differences between various girls' experiences. This new work draws on the insights of anti-racist, postmodern, and queer feminism to trouble the category 'girl' itself. Following from the challenge posed by feminists to constantly contest and re-create the category 'women', this work asks how the subjective and collective meanings of girls as categories of identity have been constructed (Driscoll, 2002; Gonick, 2003; Johnson, 1993; Walkerdine et al., 2001). Like the category 'women',

'girl' has been an important one in forming a politics of identity
with which to achieve political objectives. For example, 'girls' is a
category which has been invoked by feminists seeking to change
educational policies and practices in the fight for gender equity in
schools, in access to leisure activities like team sports and in
arguing for the dangers of certain media representations for young
women. In challenging 'girl' as a category, this work insists on the
need to investigate the material and ideological specificities of any
particular moment which constitutes girls as being one kind of
being or another. There are often differing definitions and as we
will discuss in more detail in Chapters 1 and 2, two such competing definitions form the basis of discourses of 'girl power' and
'Reviving Ophelia'.

The prevalence of these two contradictory discourses is also
reflected in the emerging literatures on girls. In some of this literature, the focus is on the sudden convergence of girls at the centre
of popular culture, social and economic policy, and public debate
about changing times. From this perspective, young women are
being hailed as the new success stories of contemporary times. The
entertainment and advertising industries favour what Hopkins
(2002) calls 'girl heroes'; feisty, sassy, attractive and assertive young
women who are celebrities, protagonists of TV shows, pop culture
icons and media idols. The success of girls has been met with much
anxiety about what this implies for boys. Such a concern pits the
interests of girls against those of boys, as if the success of one
always entails losses for the other (Epstein *et al.*, 1998). Governments, however, have responded with shifts in policies which
re-focus on the educational needs, body image, mental health,
and leadership for boys in light of the argument that young women
are outperforming young men in school and beyond in almost
every aspect of personal development. Many commentators and
researchers argue that the complex and rapid socio-economic
changes generated by globalization, de-industrialization and the
retreat of the welfare state have been more advantageous to young
women than young men (Chisholm, 1997). However, others
emphasize the need to examine more closely which girls are doing
better than which boys, suggesting that it is primarily upper and
middle-class girls who are outperforming working-class boys.
Moreover, girls' school achievements are not transferred to continued advancements in the work place or displacing men from the
highest and most lucrative positions (Epstein *et al.*, 1998).

Another body of work, however, suggests that young women are in deep trouble, at risk of causing harm to themselves or more likely to develop troublemaking and anti-social behaviours. Along with these new opportunities, there are more challenges in the lives of girls today than perhaps ever before. Whilst we hear about phenomenal schoolgirl success and the triumphs of girl power, we are also told of increasing incidents of girls' violence, self-esteem problems, and propensity for self-harm. The extraordinary popularity of the book *Reviving Ophelia* (Pipher, 1994), which argues persuasively that contemporary society robs girls of their voices and leaves them vulnerable, symptomatic and psychologically damaged, attests to the significance of this story of young women as in crisis.

The emergence of this literature in the latter part of the 20th century and in the early 21st century clearly marks a growing interest in girls across the disciplines and in the community as well. Girls, girlhood and third wave feminism are topics raised in a broad spectrum of texts taking up the themes of everything from self-esteem and resilience (*Urban Girls; Schoolgirls; Reviving Ophelia; Making Connections*), relationships to popular culture (*Tough Girls; Delinquents and Debutantes; Fashioning the Feminine; Daddy's Girl*), new definitions of feminism (*Manifesta; Talking Up; To Be Real; Third Wave Agenda; Listen Up; DIY Feminism*), to schooling and life chances (*The Company She Keeps; Young, Female and Black; At School I've Got A Chance; Growing Up Girl*).

Contemporary girls' studies, as we might label this new phenomenon, seeks to understand the gendered specificities of the already popular field of youth studies, as well as the meanings of generation and the impact of feminism in times of rapid social, economic and cultural change. It has a number of diverse reference points. These include the groundbreaking work by the original feminist youth researchers, for example, from the Centre for Contemporary Cultural Studies at Birmingham University, (see Chris Griffin's *Typical Girls?* (1985) and Angela McRobbie's *Feminism and Youth Culture* (2000)), the research on the intertwining of psychological, developmental and cultural elements of feminine identity, generated by Carol Gilligan (see for example *Making Connections* (Gilligan *et al.*, 1990)), and the reflections of the members of the Second Wave Women's Movement at the point of generational change. Contemporary girls' studies attempts to make central the constitution of 'girls' as a category through an examination of the diverse experiences of young women in their social worlds. It takes seriously as a subject of scholarly investigation the circumstances, opportunities and challenges in girls' lives today.

We argue that the representation of 'success versus crises' indicates important new formulations of growing up female that are unique to the late modern Western world. Young women are increasingly perceived as not simply being shaped by natural developmental forces or socially constituted as adjuncts to men. They are riding the crest of major generational and social change, and face a growing array of opportunities and challenges. However, biomedical models of adolescence and classic feminist understandings of the gender system continue to intersect with newer ways of understanding girls and girlhood as constituted through socially and historically specific discourses. This suggests girls' studies has reached a critical point in interpreting the meanings of girlhood. We argue that there is a number of competing discourses in circulation about girlhood, some of which are newly emergent, and others that have been common ways to interpret young women's experiences since they were first a subject of academic inquiry. Therefore, while we document new ways of understanding girls, we are also interested in how more traditional interpretations of girlhood have persisted and still take on significance in contemporary times. Ultimately, however, we aim to move the discussion about girls and girlhood beyond polarizing discourses. Our purpose here is to explore contemporary ways of interpreting girlhood, to identify the issues that confront young women into the new century, and to highlight their responses to new modes of growing up female. In short, we seek to answer, from a variety of perspectives, the critical question posed by Walkerdine, Lucey and Melody (2001, p. 11): 'Just how are girls' subjectivities created in the social spaces that open up for them in specific historical circumstances and social and cultural locations?'

How the Book is Structured

The book is divided into eight chapters, each examining the emerging narratives and material shifts in the constitution of contemporary young femininity, and young women's responses to them through an exploration of different aspects of girls' lives.

Chapters 1 and 2 explore the ways in which 'girlhood' is a contested and historically located term. We overview the ways contemporary girlhood under late modernity in the Western world is constructed within media and in youth and gender studies, as well as in cultural, pedagogical and psychological discourses. We trace the key debates about girlhood, focusing on two major current discourses: 'girl power' (Chapter 1) and the 'crisis' of young women's subjectivity (Chapter 2). We ask how they are constructed, how girls relate to them, what other discourses define girlhood, and how these can be understood in their cultural, economic and social contexts.

Chapter 1 'Girl Power: Representations of the "New" Girl' traces the development of girl power; the ways the concept is used, and the major stakeholders in the debate about girl power. Here we ask what is the relationship between girl power, feminism and consumption? In documenting and analysing the concept of girl power in popular and theoretical representations of various forms of the phenomenon, we raise some questions about the emphasis on the individual found in some versions of this discourse. We problematize the assumptions that all girls, no matter their racialized, class and ethnic backgrounds, have access to the social and economic resources to produce themselves in this way.

Chapter 2 'Reviving Ophelia: Girlhood as Crisis' explores an alternative discourse of girlhood, that of 'crisis', which runs alongside the concept of girl power. Here we analyse this other representation of girlhood within various texts, including again the multiple sites of popular culture, educational and feminist theory and the media. Here we also consider recent theoretical developments that seek to explain youth politics and identity in late modernity in terms of 'risk society' and individualization. We analyse the ways these discourses intersect with particular social issues related to girlhood – self-esteem, body-image, eating disorders, risky sexual behaviour, violence, alcohol and drug use – to produce girls as 'Poor Ophelias' (see Pipher, 1994).

In both these chapters, a critical look at the prevailing discourses of girlhood is deployed to move beyond the dual representations of today's young women as either 'strong and powerful' or vulnerable and 'at risk'. This dichotomy does not always reflect the multiple positions girls occupy in society and in their local environments. We analyse girls' various resistances to and accommodations of the dual discourses of 'crisis' and 'power' currently defining young femininity. We explore how their capacity to position themselves depends on their social, economic and cultural resources, and their desires and investments in particular versions of young femininity.

We then shift our discussion from discourses and narratives about girlhood to how the discursive and experiential aspects of contemporary girlhood are contextualized within broader economic and social forces of the twenty-first century. The structural constraints but also material resources by which girls make and can potentially transform their lives under late modernity are considered in these chapters, particularly those related to their possibilities in making educational choices and establishing themselves in the labour market, as well as their shifting positions in relation to the family.

Chapter 3 'Education, Work and Self-Making' addresses young women's relationship to education, employment and the economy. An overview is presented here of the kind of possibilities that are created for young women within an extended education system and limited labour market. In what ways do study-paths and occupational tracks still continue to be gendered in late modernity? How do girls make school-to-work transitions, and what kind of biographical stories can girls construct for themselves in late modernity? There are claims that young women today are better off than young men; for example, their academic success at least in some fields has exceeded that of young men. But why do they still rarely reach the highest positions of decision-making in society, and why do they continue to have difficulties in establishing themselves in the labour market? We analyse how globalization and the disintegration of traditional work patterns affects girls and understandings of girlhood in the Western world. We consider how global economic forces produce girls as both dependent and vulnerable, and powerful and autonomous.

In Chapter 4 'Girls and the Changing Family', the focus is on a social institution too rarely considered in youth studies, namely, the family, and girls' variable relationships to their families of origin as well as their visions of their future families. The sphere of the family has undergone considerable changes during the past decades, and family forms have diversified at the same time as traditional understandings of the family have been questioned. The life phase of youth in the Western world has extended from both ends in the past decades, creating a long in-between period, when young people's social status is unclear. In the economic sphere they continue to be strongly dependent on their families of origin, while continuing their studies and trying to get established in unstable labour markets. This is in stark contrast to their position as a special target group within the consumer market. Further, young people mature physically earlier than ever, and many of them lead active sexual lives from an early age. However, with increasing numbers of young people living at home longer, their sexual autonomy must be negotiated with parents or other guardians within the household. These, and many other aspects of the contemporary experience of youth cause tensions within their families: there is a constant negotiation about young people's rights and responsibilities. Girls' contradictory positions as 'dutiful daughter' and 'young adult in the family' mean they have to balance autonomy and dependence in their lives. Families can be a source of support and encouragement for young women, but they may also be spheres where stereotypical gender expectations are reinforced. We analyse the different meanings contemporary family life has for girls, and the various strategies young women use to negotiate power and dependence in their diverse family lives.

Chapters 5 and 6 focus on the meanings of friendship, the body and sexuality in the constitution of young feminine identities and social worlds. The relationship between constructions of girlhood and the ways in which girls across the Western world negotiate their identities and their relationships in everyday life is discussed. We explore the kinds of possibilities the discourses of young femininity create for girls from various backgrounds in negotiating their own gendered, embodied subjectivities and their social worlds.

Chapter 5, entitled 'Re/Sisters: Girls' Cultures and Friendships', explores the central role of social relationships and friendships in young women's lives. We explore some stereotypical assumptions about girls' friendships. In late modernity, young women's friendships are not only exclusive pairs focused on joint secrets, as is commonly believed, but take on many forms and shapes. Girls create personal relationships in various kinds of milieux, including the school, the neighbourhood, and around hobbies, and the activities girls engage with in their friendships are diverse. We are particularly interested in how different social groupings of girls are represented and how girls relate to these images and how their own friendships and subcultures challenge or utilize these representations. We explore the changing meanings of friendships for girls, and the contradictory ideals within them, such as continuance and change, equality and power. We analyse how relationships between girls are used to mediate their identity formation under late modernity, and how gendered meaning making is accomplished through friendship and girls' cultures.

Chapter 6 'Sexuality and the Body: Old Binaries and New Possibilities' takes up the ways girls construct their sexual and embodied subjectivities and how they create sexual relationships, trying to negotiate double morality and maintain their autonomy. The key 'tasks' of adolescence – achieving sexual, physical and emotional maturity – are shown as deeply gendered and gendering experiences. Some girls, even in late modernity, face the difficult task of balancing being attractive (to men), yet maintaining their reputation and avoiding sexual abuse/harassment. Other girls negotiate their sexual identities through same-sex relationships which often entails being confronted by homophobic strictures on the expression of this desire. Concerns are rising in the Western world over issues such as girls' eating disorders, sexual coercion and body image problems, but also over girls' increased sexual freedom. This is often played out in particularly complex ways for girls whose families have immigrated to the West. We look at the ways girls in their diversity draw on and challenge these discourses and how they make meaning of their bodies and cultural practices surrounding sexuality and embodiment. How do young women negotiate their agency in the sexual sphere: what kind of practices are seen as 'good/bad', 'risky/safe', 'traditional/modern'? To what extent are new expressions of their sexual relationships taking place? What kind of relationships do they form in relation to their bodies, and what kind of embodied activities do they engage in that bring them pleasure?

In Chapters 7 and 8 the discursive and experiential aspects of contemporary girlhood are contextualized within broader political and social forces of the twenty-first century. The focus is on the different ways young women place themselves within the broader discourses defining citizenship, political choices, social change and young feminism.

Chapter 7 'Politics, Citizenship and Young Women' pursues the questions concerning young women's position in society in the context of politics and citizenship. Ambiguous social status and economic uncertainties create anxieties but also opportunities for understanding the ways girls politicize their experiences and construct themselves as citizens. The gender-neutral discourses of (neo)liberalism, choice and personal freedoms seem to be very influential among young people today, and this has consequences for their relationship to politics. Further, an emphasis on young people's social debt and increased surveillance of their activities has in many cases placed them on the margins of civic life. However, young women are also challenging traditional conceptions of political engagement and youth rights and responsibilities. What kind of new spaces might there be for young women to speak out, and what strategies might they draw on to politicize girlhood? We look at the gendered, classed and cultured nature of the construction of youth citizenship and ask how young women might redefine active citizenship in 'girl-centred' ways.

In Chapter 8 'Feminism, Power and Social Change' we look at young women's multilayered relationship to feminism. It is here that we see the complex ways that they analyse challenges and opportunities presented by changing times. They are often depicted as the beneficiaries of second wave feminism, but with no clear agenda themselves about how to proceed with a social movement in times that do not support collective action. While a 'generation debate' has come to characterize this problematic, often constituted in terms of young women being insufficiently 'political', we examine here how young women themselves draw on feminist strategies and resources in new ways. These are not always comprehensible through a traditional framework of political analysis, but represent important new ways that young women negotiate the contradictory discourses of individualism, power, crisis and risk that are so prominent in their lives.

Interwoven throughout the book are 'intertext' commentaries by young women addressing various dimensions of their lives. The material has a range of origins and forms including interview extracts from our own and others' various research projects, published work by young women from anthologized texts of their work, girls' web-pages and weblogs, zines, artwork, poetry and other expressions of cultural and political creativity, reflection and activism. Our intention in including this material is to create the possibility for an engagement with girls, their voices and lives that moves across and between different texts, representations and expressions. Such a reading disrupts the notion of 'girlhood' as a monolithic category rather than one that is highly contextual, relational, contradictory, changeable, and diverse.

In including texts by young women, we do not claim to have developed or co-authored this book with young women and we acknowledge that even in selecting the material for inclusion in the inter-texts we are shaping our discussion of young femininity from the point of view of youth researchers. We do not contend that in including these texts we are presenting the 'authentic voices' of girls or attempting to capture the truth from girls themselves. Neither do we suggest that the material we include covers a comprehensive sample of young women, or that any of it should be perceived as typical or representative of the views of all young women across the Western world. Debates about hearing and representing the voices of young women have highlighted the problems inherent in these stances: the dangers of generalizing from specific populations; the impossibility of obtaining the 'facts' behind narratives of experience; the entitlement young people have to keeping their stories to themselves (see for example, Mahoney, 1996). Rather, the intertexts are intended to add a complexity of layers for thinking about young women's lives in such a way as to continually exceed the frame of reference of both our text as authors and any of the writings of the intertexts. They are meant to serve as pesky perturbation to any reading of contemporary meanings of girlhood as coherent, contained and fully comprehensible.

Note

1. As writers, we constitute a multi-local and multi-disciplinary team, each located on a different continent – Europe, North America and Australasia – and representing a different research background. Anita Harris works in Australia, and has a background in political science and sociology, Marnina Gonick is a Canadian who works in the USA and specializes in gender, education and cultural studies, and Sinikka Aapola, a sociologist and youth researcher, works in Finland.

   We see our multiple geographical locations and professional backgrounds as a strength that we have been able to utilize in many ways. We have been able to draw from a great variety of sources and discussions touching on girlhood both globally and locally in our writing process.

   While we have our differences, we do have important similarities as well; we have all been active in gender studies, and share a long-term interest in qualitative methods and in topics that relate to girls and young women, ranging from representations of female adolescence to girls' friendships, young women's family relations to questions regarding ethnicity, girls' schooling experiences to sex education and many other themes. And although our geographical locations are widely scattered, and the countries we live in have very different histories and cultures, we are nevertheless all located in countries which can be conceptualized as Western societies.

Our cooperation has a long history. We first started working together on a joint project that later took the form of this book in 1995, by corresponding with each other over email. Marnina and Sinikka had met while conducting doctoral studies at the Ontario Institute of Studies in Education, and Anita was later introduced to them by Johanna Wyn, who happened to be a visiting scholar at OISE at that time.

In 1998, we arranged to meet in person in Montreal, Canada, at the World Congress of the International Sociological Association. It was there that we first presented together, and worked intensively to create the basis for the first preliminary draft for a joint book on Western girlhood.

Until early 2000 we continued to work on our book proposal, and finalized our conceptual framework by linking the two contrasting discourses of girlhood to neo-liberal concepts of the subject, as well as decided which aspects of girls' lives we would focus on. Our efforts were finally rewarded by a contract to publish this book towards the end of 2000. We could then apply for funding to actually write this book, and gradually we worked towards a finished text, in a constant dialogue.

In November 2001, we three met again at the *New Girl Order? Young Women and the Future of Feminist Inquiry* conference in London, where we merged our individual efforts on the book into a panel presentation on the discourses of 'girl power' and 'reviving Ophelia'. We continued writing, commenting and rewriting the text in order to be able to bring our ideas to readers in the most inspiring way.

In the course of these years, our cooperation has also manifested itself in a joint article on girls' sexuality (Harris *et al.*, 2000), as well as in research visits by some of us to each other's universities, dozens of international telephone conferences and hundreds of emails. The end product is a truly collective piece of work in the sense that the framework has been created together, and that we have all contributed to the discussions in each chapter.

CHAPTER 1

Girl Power: Representations of the 'New' Girl

Introduction

In the media, popular literature, television, movies, academic conferences and special issues of feminist journals, there has been an incredible proliferation of images, texts and discourses around girls and girlhood beginning in the early 1990s. The result has been a growing complexity in the ways in which young women are represented and their lives understood by both themselves and others. In the next two chapters, we try to make sense of this phenomenon by suggesting that it symbolizes both a certain kind of cultural fascination with girls and a contemporary anxiety about them. We suggest that two competing discourses are currently circulating, albeit in a range of different forms and expressions, across late modern Western societies, which organize and give shape to this dual conception of girls and girlhood. These are 'girl power' and what we are calling 'reviving Ophelia' after the popular text by American psychologist Mary Pipher (1994).

In identifying 'girl power' and 'reviving Ophelia' as dominant discourses we are not suggesting that these are the only existing ones or that they will remain in their current form and relationship to each other, unchanged and dominant forever. Rather, we are interested in them as a collection of statements and ideas that are currently producing influential networks of meanings about girls and girlhood. Studying these discourses, and others like them, enables us to think and ask questions about how certain meanings of girlhood become common sense and 'authoritative'. Since discourse shapes how we come to think and produce new knowledge and facilitates shared understandings and engagements, knowing more about how 'girl power' and 'reviving Ophelia' operate, allows us to attend to the relationship between the current cultural fascination with and anxiety about girls and how these meanings are lived by girls. However, even as discourse facilitates thought and actions it also works to constrain them, as it sets up the parameters, limits, and blind spots of thinking and acting. All discourse must be seen, therefore, as both enabling and constraining. As a result, we must also ask what the 'girl power' and 'reviving Ophelia' discourses leave out, marginalize or prohibit from being included in the issues and debates surrounding what it means to be a young woman in these times and places.

Our interest, then, is not to explicate the veracity or falsity of the claims made under the rubric of one or both of the 'girl power' or 'reviving Ophelia' discourses. Ours is a rather different kind of project. We want to investigate the contemporary 'conditions of possibility' that enable 'girl power' and the rescue of Ophelia – two seemingly contradictory discourses – to circulate as powerful post-modern truths about girls and girlhood. We want to ask how these discourses are involved in the formation of complex and non-unified subjectivities for girls. And further, how these discourses are circulated in the public sphere and how they are lived by girls of various racialized and classed backgrounds. Moreover, we pose certain questions about the political consequences for the forms of subjectivities made available to girls through these discourses.

We suggest that while these two discourses may be read as symptomatic of transformations of gender and its meanings, they also suggest something about the ways in which gender is being re-coded and re-worked along familiar binaries.

Girl Power and the Riot Grrrl Movement

'Girl power' is a complex, contradictory discourse used to name a range of cultural phenomena and social positionings for young women. Associated with a new take-charge dynamism, this discourse re-writes the passivity, voicelessness, vulnerability and sweet naturedness linked to some forms of raced and classed girl-hoods (and as we will discuss in the next chapter, to the 'Reviving Ophelia' discourse). Celebrated by some for creating more expansive forms of femininity and critiqued by others for the way in which it is formulated around an individualism fraught with neo-liberal ideals, the meanings and implications of girl power continue to shift and change depending on the context and purpose of its articulation. What is clear about it, is that 'girl power' raises important questions about the relationships between feminism, femininity, girls and new subjectivities.

At the time of this writing, 'girl power' has thoroughly entered the English lexicon. The concept of 'girl power' has also become widely used in non-English-speaking countries. Within the Nordic countries, for example, 'girl power' has been used in a staggering range of contexts. 'Girl power' has come to denote anything from girls-only soccer or golf tournaments to theatre plays on young women's lives and to international educational exchange programmes for girls. The term has also been used by young right-wing women politicians to promote their voting campaigns. However, the origin of the term is usually traced back to the early 1990s, in the US to a loosely formed movement of young, mainly white and middle-class women, a large proportion of whom identified as queer, who gathered in Washington DC and Olympia Washington in the United States and who called themselves 'Riot Grrrls'. With their roots in punk rock music and their motto 'Grrrls need guitars,' the riot grrrls reclaimed the word girl, using it strategically to distance themselves from the adult patriarchal worlds of status, hierarchies and standards (Hesford, 1999, p. 45). Its usage also marks a celebration of both the fierce and aggressive potential of girls (the 'grrr' stood for growling) as well as reconstitution of girl culture as a positive force embracing self-expression through fashion, attitude and a Do It Yourself (DIY) approach to cultural production.

Bands such as Bikini Kill, Bratmobile, and Heavens to Betsy exemplify this combination with their mixing of a girlish aesthetic with all that is most threatening in a female adult: rage, bitterness and political acuity. Many grrrls used their bodies to convey this ironic melding of style with political expression by, for example the juxtaposition of gendered signs (for example '1950s dresses with combat boots, shaved hair with lipstick, studded belts with platform heels' (Klein, 1997, p. 222)) and through writing politically loaded words such as 'rape', 'shame', and 'slut' on their arms and stomachs (Japenga, 1995, p. 30 as in Jacques, 2001, p. 49). By most accounts the movement was a response to the sexism, elitism and violence of local masculinist punk scenes where exclusionary practices meant that girls were considered less than full members of the scene (see Chapter 6 on this topic). In contrast, the 'girl power' of Riot Grrrl encouraged young women to see themselves, not as the passive consumers of culture, including that of the punk scene, but as producers and creators of knowledge, as verbal and expressive dissenters. Their critiques address their own and others' experiences as women as well as their experiences of race, sexuality, class and other forms of embodiedness. As a result, Riot Grrrl is viewed by many who study young women's cultures as exemplary of what is being called 'youth feminism' (Garrison, 2000, p. 142). The movement's inauguration was in August 1991, during the week-long International Pop Underground Convention in Washington, DC, where 'Girl Day' opened the gathering.

> Girl's night will always be precious to me because, believe it or not, it was the first time I saw women stand on a stage as though they truly belonged there. The first time I had ever heard the voice of a sister proudly singing the rage so shamefully locked in my own heart. Until girls' night, I never knew that punk rock was anything but a phallic extension of the white middle class male's frustrations. (Rebecca B, quoted in *Girl Germs* 4 (1991).)

A year later, a three-day national Riot Grrrl Convention was held in DC comprising a number of educational workshops on topics such as violence against women, fat oppression and unlearning racism (Jacques, 2001, p. 47). Riot grrrl, or as it also became known, grrrlpower, quickly spread around different parts of the world, including to the UK, Europe and Australasia. Young feminist punks and young women involved in related music and DIY cultures developed transnational networks to forge their political and cultural agendas. This networking has been made possible through new kinds of media such as zines and the internet.

In addition to regular face to face meetings, gigs, workshops and conventions, the Riot Grrrls network through zines, which are self-written and designed photocopied publications they hand out and mail to other girls. The writings take up a full range of themes and styles: angry, supportive, advice-giving, on issues like relationships, harassment, mental, physical and verbal abuse, and rape. Cartoons, photographs, collage, and text which are often autobiographical are typical zine content. Zines, according to Green and Taormino (1997), 'originate from a need for expression, a need girls have to discover the truth about themselves and their lives. Through zines, we can see young women uncensored and free to discuss their realities' (Green & Taormino, 1997, p. xiii). Hesford (1999) suggests that zines are 'paradoxical feminist writing spaces' because of the way writers negotiate with and appropriate the discourses of dominant culture and liberal feminism. She argues that these feminist autobiographical writings are critical sites for the construction of social identities, noting how they may be marked paradoxically by the interplay of dominant and counter-hegemonic discourses (Hesford, 1999, p. 45). Importantly, the purpose of these media has been to create an inexpensive, self-produced site for expression for those without access to or interest in mainstream forums. Zines are often attempts to forge new communities beyond their locales. The capacity to build a global grrrl movement through these media is critical to many zine creators.

Girls are also turning to cyberspace and the creation of e-zines as an alternative site for self-expression. In comparison to print zines, online zines have the advantage of limited production and distribution expense after the initial investment of a computer, which is of course an expense out of the range of possibility for some. However, the material is accessible to anyone with a computer and modem and thus facilitates networking, community building and dialogue (Ferris, 2001, p. 55). The opportunity to post one's website, without having to go through corporate, mainstream, commercial, official – and even – adult channels, makes a difference for shifting the locus of political activism, as well as who can produce politicized cultural-technological objects. However, despite the opportunities opened up by using what has been a male-dominant internet to communicate about feminist issues it is important to recognize that, 'this expansion of discursive space does not necessarily, nor easily, translate into shifts in dominant public discourse' (Hamilton, 1999, p. 131 as in Ferris, 2001, p. 55).

Washington D.C. Riot Grrl Manifesto
RIOT GRRL IS . . .
BECAUSE we need to accept and support each other as girls; acknowledge our different approaches to life and accepting all of them as valid.
BECAUSE we seek to create revolution in our own lives every single day by envisioning and creating alternatives to the status quo.

In the wake of the Riot Grrrls, numerous all-girl rock bands were born, amongst them the enormously popular Spice Girls from Britain, and the slogan 'girl power' began to be bandied about in forums beyond the Riot Grrrl milieux. T-shirts with pro-girl sentiments like 'Girls Rule' and 'Girls Kick Ass' started to show up at malls. Jacques (2001, p. 49) argues that the messages on these shirts bear a direct relationship to the words the riot grrrls wrote on their bodies. However, she points out that while T-shirts have a long history as a conveyor of political slogans, it is important to remember that Riot Grrrl was deliberately anti-consumer culture. 'Writing on oneself with a marker is not only a political, feminist action (first in choosing to "deface" the feminine body which is ideally a flawless object; second, in drawing attention to issues of women's oppression through the words), but displays the classic do-it-yourself ethic of punk' (Jacques, 2001, p. 50). Thus, in buying a trendy T-shirt, whether or not its slogan is meant to be ironic, any critique of capitalism is, by definition, lost in its (mass) production.

With the proliferation of the term, the meanings of 'girl power' and what girls who embrace it could and should do with it did not remain static, nor did it get taken up with the same political and social intentions of Riot Grrrls by others who claimed it. Coverage of Riot Grrrls quickly appeared in American mainstream magazines such as *Seventeen* (1993), *The New Yorker* (1992), *Newsweek* (1993), *Rolling Stone* (1993) and *Time* (1998). A similar trend occurred elsewhere, as the mass media attempted to grapple with this new, intriguing and saleable phenomenon. For the Riot Grrrls the coverage brought objectionable incursion. Not only was there a rush to categorize the movement whose members defied that there were strict definitions to be had, but, there was also a permutating and re-articulation of the girl power message.

> The revolution starts inside you . . . Stop Girl Competition and Jealousy. You don't have to take shit from anyone . . . Be who you want, say what you want . . . No, we are not paranoid. We are not manhaters. No we are not worrying too much. No we are not taking it too seriously . . . We are not a band, not about violence, not about man-hate, not a fashion statement, not some elite club. You don't have to be a punk. You don't need our permission. There are no rules. No leader. Everygirl is a Riot Girl. (DC Riot Girls, Winter 1993.)

While the riot grrrls themselves clearly saw their movement as attached to a liberatory social and political agenda, the mainstream media opted to present a different message altogether. A *Rolling Stone* article concluded, for example: 'Riot grrrls' unifying principle is that being feminist is inherently confusing and contradictory and that women have to find a way to be sexy, angry and powerful at the same time' (France, 1993). Here in a bizarre twist, it is feminism that is seen to complicate what is assumed would otherwise be an easy and straight-forward transition from girlhood to woman. *Newsweek* took a somewhat different stance to dismiss the serious-mindedness of the movements' politics (Chideya, 1993). In doing so it draws on hegemonic discourses associating youth as a time when rebellion is expected, but is also expected to be in most respects temporary (Driscoll, 2002, p. 205). 'There is no telling whether this enthusiasm or the Riot grrls catchy passion for "revolution girl style" will evaporate when it hits the adult real world. Most of the grrls are still in the shelters of home or college – a far cry from what they'll face in the competitive job market or as they start to form their own families' (Chideya, 1993).

As soon as the coverage began, a US-wide 'press block' was invoked in 1992–93 by some participants in order to prevent the possibility of colluding with 'exploitation, misquoting, and such' (Spirit, 1995). The block was also meant to preserve the original intent of the movement. According to Kathleen Hanna (Bikini Kill singer), 'we weren't doing what we did to gain fame, we were just trying to hook up with other freaks' (quoted in Greenblatt, 1996, p. 25). The articles multiplied anyway, revealing more about their authors' lust to 'uncover' a potential new trend than about the movement itself. The disruptive nature and threatening intent in the girls' voices and actions were ignored, while attention focused on their clothing and their appearance (Godfrey, 1993). In the wake of this, the movement itself began to splinter over how to address the exposure. For example, debates ensued over ownership and defence of the ideology, terminology, websites and appropriate media, including a heated debate about the use of urls containing the word 'grrl' versus 'grrrl'.

> So much stuff has been said about what riot grrrl is, actually what some misinformed people have said. I'm sick to death of defending riot grrrl every time I turn around. I don't even know why it should be defended. Riot Grrrl is NOT what Seventeen, Newsweek or the LA weekly make it out to be or any other media thing. The media attention has taken riot grrrl and twisted it and distorted the name to mean little if anything of importance. . . . Riot grrrl is about emotions, feelings, not fashion, or hating boys, it's about us, grrrls. It's real and a threat because it goes against the patriarchy as anything is a threat that goes against the patriarchy. (Dawn, 19, in her zine 'Function', Seattle, USA.)

The antagonistic relations with the media and subsequent blackout response from some Riot Grrrls raises larger questions about the complicated relationships between subcultures and the politics of incorporation (Hebdige, 1979) on the one hand and the politics of commodification and representation on the other. As Jacques (2001) succinctly states, the dilemma the Riot Grrrl movement faced was one of reifying an opposition between preserving authenticity but risking elitism, or reaching a wider audience but 'selling out'. She says, 'for a political movement that wanted to reach alienated girls, the media black-out strategy closed Riot Grrrls off to girls in smaller centres and risked defining RG as an exclusive, insular movement' (Jacques, 2001, p. 48). The contradiction of the situation was not lost on some Riot Grrrls: 'The mainstream media – what seemed like the best medium for communication, the best way to spread "girl love" – had failed us.' Yet the author also recognizes that this exposure inspired many more girls 'to question, challenge, create, demand' (Spirit, 1995). This opposition between 'authentic subculture' and 'mainstream sell out' continues to echo in different versions of the girl power debates.

Selling Girl Power, Selling Feminism?

Now I see Spice Girls and supermodels and sparkly slogan shirts – their version of lame 'girl power' is so far away from our original vision of 'grrrl power'; co-opted, watered down, marketable, profitable – all style and not a fuck of a lot of content. I walk through the mall and I see a chain store clothes shop is selling me some 'girl power' in the form of furry winter jackets. (Kylie, in her zine 'Her Heroes Aren't Gone', Australia.)

Despite the objections of Riot Grrrls, the lid was off the can and certain aspects of the 'girl power' phenomenon became ubiquitous, entering mainstream cultural arenas through an incredible range of products and services. In the media, the term 'girl power' was used to headline almost any newsworthy event or phenomenon that involved women, from career advancements and girls' educational achievements to gendered crime rates. Community organizations and government departments also picked up on the terminology and aspects of the ideology; as Susan Hopkins notes (2002, p. 3): ' "Girl power" has . . . been appropriated by liberal educators and bureaucrats as a ready-made empowerment plan for girls.' For example, 'Girl Power' was the name given to a 1997 US Health and

Human Services Program for a public health initiative designed to help keep young females 'healthy, smart, and strong'. 'Girl-power takes the stage', was the headline promoting an American Sesame Street musical production entitled, 'When I grow up'. The trailer goes on to say, 'if girls follow their dreams and work hard, they can do whatever they want'. In an all girl scene the mini-women sing about their larger than life dreams: to become an astronaut, a language teacher, a lion tamer, a train engineer, and a surgeon. A Swedish sports organization describes its activities in the year 2001 and announces: 'This year the "Girl Power"-project has continued – the goal of the project is to get more young girls to become leaders or active in the organization. The most concrete activity has been the "Motion workshop" which has included gymnastics for children.'(Translation from Swedish by Sinikka Aapola) Thus, despite the popular slogan, this project has not extended much beyond the traditional understandings of young women and their involvement in sports as limited to the field of gymnastics. Another Swedish project, 'Grrrl Tech', is directed at 13–30 year old women. The goal of the project is to introduce girls to the male dominated sphere of computers and new media. Funding for the project comes from the regional government, the Swedish Savings Bank foundation as well as local Universities (www.grrltech.nu). Girl power positions young women as feisty, ambitious, motivated and independent. Inevitably, from the early days of the circulation of this discourse, it became not only a catch-phrase for educational programmes, but a successful marketing tool for the culture industries.

The Hollywood blockbuster contenders of 1999 saw a fierce competition for recognition as the ultimate in girl power authority. The *Houston Chronicle* (Davis, 1999) called Charlie's Angels the latest archetype of 'girl power', while the Associated Press head-line (1999) states: Forget Charlie's Angels the year's ultimate girl power movie is 'Crouching Tiger, Hidden Dragon'. Although critic Gina Arnold notes an interesting aspect of 'girl power' as trend, when she says that while the West's fascination with it is quite recent, in Asia female cartoon heroines and martial arts movies featuring non-animated women action heros are not a new a phenomenon at all (Arnold, 2001, p. 1). Girl power was also hailed, in 1999 by *WIN Magazine* (Wilder, 1999) as the music industry's new buzz word with an international array of performers heralded as title holders. Every female pop artist, from Madonna to Avril Lavigne, has been attributed with girl power.

G: One thing I think is a bit fucked up is that as soon a girl in Sweden chooses to rap, things are immediately turned into feminism.

C: – So . . . ? Isn't that what you'd expect?

G: No, I mean that it looks more as just a strategic move. They don't go out with it initially, so it looks more as some marketing team has been thinking 'hmmm, she is a girl . . . ok, then it has to be Grrl Power, that will make some sales'.

(http://www.upsweden.com/acts/showacts.php?act=khumalo&lang=eng)

And in television, shows like Buffy the Vampire Slayer, Xena: the Warrior Princess and Sabrina the Teenage Witch have also won popular attention for their representations of the 'new girl'. 'Western storytelling', a writer for the popularized *Psychology Today* insists, 'hasn't seen their ilk since the legendary female fighters of the Celts' (Ventura, 1998, p. 62). As Hopkins (2002, p. 1) argues, the 'cute but powerful girl-woman' has become a pop culture icon: she is an 'heroic overachiever – active, ambitious, sexy and strong'.

But it is perhaps the British all-girl band the Spice Girls that is most (in)famously associated with the popularization of the girl power motto. The band was enormously successful, reaching their peak in 1997 and disbanding soon after. Their first compact disc sold over 50 million copies worldwide in one year (Lemish, 1998, p. 165). In their lyrics, Emma (Baby Spice), Geri (Ginger Spice), Melanie B. (Scary Spice), Melanie C. (Sporty Spice), and Victoria (Posh Spice) call for equal rights and advocate that sisterhood is powerful. In contrast to the media's response to the messages of the Riot Grrrls, the Spice Girls' message was celebrated. The *Village Voice*, for example, waxed eloquent about how the Spice Girls, 'have done the seemingly impossible: they have made feminism, with all its implied threat, cuddly, sexy, safe, and most importantly, sellable' (Press & Nichols, 1997, p. 10). But the hyper-sexualized and highly stylized marketing of the girl power of the Spice Girls raised cries of outrage from some feminists, producing a series of striking questions about the relationship between feminism, femininity and commercialization. 'Can anything feminist be so predominantly popular (even for a short time?) Can feminism be a mass-produced, globally distributed product? And can merchandised relations to girls be authentic?' (Driscoll, 1999, p. 178).

The Spice Girls' 'girl power' does not involve knowing who you are on the inside, but whether your Wonderbra should be lace or leather.

(Ariel Federow, USA)

(http://students.washington.edu/ruckus/vol-1/issue-4/gal.html)

Interview:

Shelley: Do you think that kind of Spice Girls' 'girl power' is real power?

Shayne: No. I don't agree with it because it's portraying them as thin, beautiful, talented. I mean everyone is talented but they are just portraying them in a way – well obviously not everyone is going to just disregard it and laugh it off. For some people, it will actually have a strong effect. I mean like with eating disorders and to what extent it encourages girls to attain that. I think it is very dangerous. (Shayne, Britain, quoted in Budgeon, 1998.)

The question 'Is girl power feminist?', posed by Driscoll (1999, p. 174) and many others, would have been absurd to the early Riot Grrrls. But, in a context where girl power is also equated with the emergence of teenage girls as a powerful economic force, the contest over its continuing proliferation of meanings guarantees only that it is a question whose answer is not at all obvious. Recently, the spending power of 12–17 year old British girls has been estimated at 1.3 billion pounds. In Australia, 11–17 year olds' collective income is AUS $4.6 billion, and in the US, young women aged 8–18 are deemed to be worth US $67 billion (see Barwick, 2001 and Brown, 2000; Cuneo, 2002, and Nikas, 1998). Much of this discretionary income is guided towards girl power products. As trade journals tell advertisers, to capture the shopping power of Generation Y, they need to understand that 'the new trend is about Girl Power – a celebration of femininity and individualism' (Nikas, 1998, p. 20). Even the mainstream media have entered the fracas over the question of authentic girl power versus its commercial potential, when for example, the *USA Today* printed an article noting the launch of yet another teenage version of a woman's magazine, in this particular case *Teen Vogue*, accusing it of 'hawking fake girl power' (Vanderkam, 2003). And in the *Time* magazine issue of July 1, 1998 whose cover reads, 'Is Feminism Dead?' girl power is evoked in a number of the articles as a marker of both the successes of feminism and a sign of its demise. For example, a story written by Ginia Bellafante (1998) suggests that, ' "girl power", that sassy, don't-mess-with-me adolescent spirit that Madison Avenue carefully caters to', is evidence that women's struggles for liberation have indeed changed women's lives for the better (Bellafante 1998, p. 58). And while indirectly critical of the marketing campaign targeting girls, another article by Nadya Labi (1998) in the same issue of *Time* mentions Buffy, the Spice Girls, Alanis Morrisette, and others as exemplars of the pervasive and lucrative dimensions of girl power commerce (Labi 1998, pp. 60–62). What is not in question, therefore, is that girl power is a marketable concept that many are anxious to tap into. The scheme of girl power and marketing was given a six page feature article in the December 8th 1997 *Fortune* magazine. The piece celebrates the conspicuous consumption of teenage girls with a very patronizing tone. 'If you want to sell to the girl-power crowd you have to pretend that they're running things, that they're in charge' (Munk, 1997, p. 136 as cited in Taft, 2001).

> Want to know the dumbest thing I've ever heard of? Girl Power. If you haven't heard, it's this attempt to wrest feminism from muscly gay girls who don't shave and to give it to cute models who have everything. Here's actually an explanatory quote from the analytical text Girl Power, coauthored by Posh, Scary, Sporty, Baby and Ginger Spices: 'Feminism means skipping a date and going out with your friends instead.' Ah, I thought feminism was saying 'I'm not asking you to find me desirable, because I'm smarter than you and could bench press your house, which coincidently is the size of my sauna'. (Emily Carmichael, 15, USA (Carmichael, 1999).)

The discussion of 'girl power' in feminist circles is also far from unequivocally resolved. Some embrace the phenomenon for the mainstreaming effect it has had, bringing feminism into the lives of young women through music and film and television characters. For example, Debbie Stoller, former zine writer, current editor of *Bust* magazine, says of television characters Xena, Buffy and Sabrina: 'these characters all share a common strength: the ability to leap over sexist stereotypes in a single bound.' She argues that these shows 'are hinting that there's a wellspring of untapped girl power out there, with the potential to change the world if it could only be released. You go, girls' (quoted in Projansky and Vande Berg, 2000, p. 15). Others agree, suggesting that 'the feminist underpinnings found in the Girl Power pop culture icons are helpful, if not critical, for young girls as they negotiate and navigate toward womanhood' (http://www.rohan.sdu.edu/~hofmans/GirlPower.html).

However, other feminists claim the crass commercialism and commodification of girl power has voided it of any feminist content it might have once had. Jessica Taft, for example, argues strongly on the dangers of young women's embracing of the concept. She suggests that because girl power is presented as the gentle, non-political and non-threatening alternative to feminism, it functions as a way for girls to identify girl positive feelings with a non-political discourse and to think about girlhood in cultural ways rather than as a space for social and political action (Taft, 2001, p. 4). Moreover, girl power's popularity is credited to its very lack of threat to the status quo for the ways in which it reflects the ideologies of white- middle-class, individualism and personal responsibility over collective responses to social problems. The result is a redirecting of attention away from the 'degradation and economic exploitation of women worldwide . . . and the commercial enterprises largely responsible for the continuing gendered and racialized exploitation of labourers globally – the very enterprises producing girl power products for western consumption' (Ono, 2000, p. 165).

> I personally don't like the words 'grrrl' and 'riot grrrl' . . . Why should we/I as a European girl tag myself with a word/movement that is over ten years old and happened in the States, I think we need to create our own new movements and terms that are well defined instead of using a term that is so old and has been fucked with in the media. (Riikka, high school student, Finnish-Italian-Swedish-Russian, manager of *Ladybomb* distro; www.grrrlzines.net/interviews/ladybomb.htm)

In a completely different context Sarah Projansky and Leah Vande Berg (2000) provide a very interesting analysis of the television show 'Sabrina The Teenage Witch'. In a nuanced account of the program they show how it presents a girl power that is at once empowering through numerous references to gender equality, anti-homophobia and anti-discrimination. At the same time, they argue that its girl power is contained by narratives that centre whiteness and emphasize beauty, heterosexual male attention and a feminine responsibility for others (2000, p. 16). The show which premiered in the US in April 1996, centres around events in the life of sixteen year old Sabrina Spellman, who lives with her two aunts. They are all witches. Sabrina's is a world in which an independent young woman is encouraged to 'use her strength, self-confidence, and magical powers and where she is accepted and loved for who she

is, even when who she is takes her across binary gender and sexuality boundaries' (Projansky & Vande Berg, 2000, p. 27). They also
suggest, however, that like a typical sit-com the narrative structure
of the show is one of problem-complication-confusion-resolution.
In the series it is Sabrina herself who causes the problem and the
escalation of the problem by using magic in questionable ways to
fulfil her personal desires.

The narrative structure of the series thus provides a gloss that
predominantly defines 'Sabrina's independence as problematic and
responds to it by supplanting it with repetitive lessons about sub-
limating self and prioritizing responsibility to others' (Projansky &
Vande Berg, 2000, p. 32). If magic stands for girl power, then the
series promotes a message that the appropriate use of girl power
is it to maintain and enhance a normative femininity. Moreover, the
series' feminism is also rendered problematic by Projansky and
Vande Berg for the way in which it celebrates consumer capitalism,
co-opts cultural difference and leaves unquestioned the privilege Sabrina is granted by virtue of her magical special status
(Projansky & Vande Berg, 2000, p. 33). Their very strong conclu-
sion is that the popularized feminism promoted by girl power,
maintains rather than undermines gender, race, and class hierarchies (Projansky & Vande Berg, 2000, p. 36).

Catherine Driscoll (1999, p. 186) however, argues for an understanding of girl power that does not position it as 'either it is or it
isn't' feminism. She suggests, instead that the mixed messages – 'if
you're with my sexiness, you're with my politics' – of the girl
power message expounded by pop icons like the Spice Girls,
might have interesting effects on the circulation of the label 'feminism' and even on dominant understandings of what girls want.
She suggests that the Spice Girls generate dialogue about feminism
in a massively popular field. They talk about how what they say
and do may or may not be feminism and about the relations
between politics and popular culture. Driscoll (1999) states that
while the Spice Girls may not produce revolutionary change,
groups like them do create a shift in the dominant paradigms of
cultural production directed to girls. She notes that these shifts
might be indebted to the impact of other girl culture forms
(such as the Riot Grrl), but that the embracing of popular rather
than avant-garde cultural production inflects further possibilities.
'Spice Girls' fandom might demand less dramatic changes to
girls' positions within established political and social systems
than does participation in the Riots and resistances of some other

forms of girl culture. But, the Spice Girls do call for significantly changed relations to the lives of girls as they are' (Driscoll, 1999, p. 188).

Girl Power and Race

Whichever perspective on the multiple forms of 'girl power' one takes, it seems the phenomenon clearly signals a shifting mode of youthful femininity. That is, the view of girl power as collective and individual empowerment and the one that sees girl power as com-mercialized exploitation that furthers a neo-liberal agenda both suggest a new articulation of girls and girlhood is being pro-nounced, as well as new forms for thinking about how girls' lives might be lived. Angela McRobbie (1996) advises that in undertak-ing an investigation of changing forms of femininity that have emerged in cultural forms, it is necessary to 'pay attention to the space of interracial, interactive experience and to exploring the processes of hostility, fascination and desire which penetrate and shape the nature of these encounters' (McRobbie, 1996, p. 39). In the increasingly mixed-race British context of youth cultural media, where images of friendship and intimacy between girls from dif-ferent ethnic backgrounds and mixed-race heterosexual couples are increasingly being used in advertising campaigns and other cul-tural products, McRobbie suggests that the effect is the production of 'a new vocabulary of inter-racial desire which extends the notion of shared cultures of femininity' (McRobbie, 1996, p. 41). Thus, while it may be clear that a new articulation of young femininity is evolving, it is also crucial to explore how it positions different girls in relation to the texts of girl power. Does girl power, for example, address all girls in the same way? What kinds of inclu-sions and exclusions does girl power engender? Is a shared culture of femininity produced by girl power? And/or does girl power reproduce existing social hierarchies and divisions? In this section of the chapter, we are particularly interested in the inter-discursive space created where the cultural forms of girl power meet and intersect with the discursive space of race.

One entry-point into this inquiry is to revisit the question of the origins of the 'girl power' concept. Although most of the dis-cussion on origins, as we have already seen, starts with the Riot Grrrl movement, hints of a different lineage are suggested by others who trace girl power to other sources. For example, according to

Laurel Gilbert and Crystal Kile, the authors of *SurferGrrrls*, the grrrl in Riot Grrrl, is at least partially derived from young African American women's phrase of encouragement to each other popular in the late 1980s 'You go girl' (Gilbert & Kile, 1996, p. 5). Relatedly, others suggest it is not the white punk music scene but rather Black hip hop music that spawned and supports the changing modes of femininity understood as girl power. One African American girl strongly asserts, 'I remember growing up to the flavor and stylings of teenage female rappers like Salt 'N Pepa, McLyte and Queen Latifah and seeing "girl power" served up constantly as a spicy dish of independence, pride and assertiveness throughout hip hop music. For me girl power is in no way a particularly nineties thing, and it certainly does not have a White girl's face' (*Hues* (1998), 8).

Starting from this point of departure, it seems 'girl power' is very much entangled with the question of inter-racial fascination and desire. The girl power phenomenon is not unique in its cultural appropriation and re-articulation of images and discourses of black women's strength, power and agency to serve a mainly white middle-class young women. According to the British study by Simon Jones, *'Black Culture, White Youth'* (Jones, 1988) there is a long history of relations between white subcultures and black culture and music. He claims that black expressive culture, in particular music, is a resource as well as a source of envy and admiration on the part of young whites. This is because of its strength of feelings, its cultural richness, its ability to offer and confirm to young black people a sense of their own identity.

Black youth have had to be incredibly resourceful in seeking out positive reflections of themselves in mainstream culture and in producing their own images to counter the mainly negative ones that exist. It is possible to see how young white women have encountered similar challenges. Looking for ways of disrupting limiting discourses of femininity and youthful subjectivities and replacing them with competing ones that offer newer more expansive opportunities for being young and female, it is possible to see how the powerful, agentic discourses of black femininity would be extraordinarily attractive. Moreover, McRobbie (1996) argues that through the strong identification with aspects of black culture, young white people may also dis-identify with racism. Using the example of the British film 'The Commitments' (1991), she argues that music, fashion and style make available a symbolic language for popular anti-racism (McRobbie, 1996, p. 43). This, certainly, seems to be the case for the Riot Grrrls, where, as we have already seen, an anti-racist politics infuses their feminism.

The cultural politics of race may also be a feature of the media response to the Riot Grrrls. Alison Jacques (2001) advances a very provocative idea, when she connects the media's fascination with Riot Grrrls to the fact that in late 1980s North America, rap music was gaining widespread popularity. She suggests that it is possible that young, angry white middle-class women were thought to be preferable to, and perhaps less threatening than, angry black men. All the sensational coverage of girl power resulted in a shifting of public attention. Simultaneously celebrated, dismissed as youthful rebellion, and fostered as a source of commercial interest through its marketization, girl power's feminism and anti-racism was rendered more ambiguous in the process.

It is also important to consider how those popular media forms that took up the discourses of girl power represented the relationship of this changing mode of youthful femininity to race and anti-racist politics. In a detailed study of the television series 'Buffy the Vampire Slayer', Kent Ono (2000) makes the case that despite the liberating images of girls in the Buffy text, debilitating images of and ideas about people of colour are conveyed in it through a re-establishment of neo-colonial power relations. With no person of colour playing a significant character in the series, Ono argues that marginalized characters serve a pedagogical function by affirming contemporary racial, gender, sexual, class and ability hierarchies. The media valorization and glorification of girl power ignores, de-centres and marginalizes people of colour. Moreover, the vampires that Buffy and the other slayers eliminate in every episode of the show are often depicted in racialized terms. For example, as the vampires descend into evil something about them becomes darker, their clothes, their faces and their surroundings. Thus, Buffy's girl power may be seen to come through an associated villainization and demonization of people of colour (Ono, 2000, p. 164).

Ono (2000) argues that popular media discourse about girl power and Buffy forward a problematic understanding of power and liberation when race is taken into consideration. The idea of liberation and empowerment is linked to a certain kind of violent aggression deployed by white females. In order to promote this as a liberatory aggression, racial hierarchies of people of colour are relied upon: liberation and empowerment are gained through images of white women murdering people of colour. Ono (2000) concludes that the proliferation of discourses about feminism into the popular, corporate domain comes with great risks and expenses. That is, the most socially marginalized within society become the scapegoats in the process of popular culture's championing of its version of white liberation (Ono, 2000, p. 180).

A somewhat different relationship between girl power, race and anti-racist politics is played out in the television series 'Sabrina the Teenage Witch', mentioned above. Like the Buffy series, all the central characters in Sabrina, are white. The one recurring non-white character is Quiz Master, played by an African American, and he is portrayed drawing on a long tradition of stereotypes of African Americans. For example, he wears outrageous costumes, has a clownish manner, and is completely incompetent as a Quiz Master. Despite, the lack of non-white characters, Projansky and Vande Berg (2000), argue that this does not mean that Sabrina and her aunts have no access to racialized cultures. On the contrary, they are constantly bringing them into their lives through the use of magic. In the process, whiteness is repeatedly re-centered and cultural references with specific meanings in particular social contexts are re-coded as objects of pleasure for Sabrina and her aunts. The magical crossing of national and race boundaries, can be seen as occurring in ways that articulate a tourist identity and neocolonial position for the family of witches (Projansky & Vande Berg, 2000, p. 33). Projansky and Vande Berg (2000) conclude that multiculturalism is represented in the series as a form of privileged consumption which Sabrina and her aunts access while completely oblivious to the class and race politics which makes this access possible for them. In this instance, girl power is the magical force that facilitates a willful ignorance, the result of which is the maintenance of gender, race, and class hierarchies.

Living Girl Power

In this last section, we close the chapter by considering girls' engagements with girl power and what it both enables and constrains in their lives.

> Do something anything out of the norm for girls to show that you resist the stereotypical guidelines of what girls should do or be or act like . . . anything that ever was/is exclusive to boystown has had all previous rights removed. The world is yours. (DC Riot Girls, Winter 1993.)

If someone says in Finland there ain't girl energy/
fuck it, soon they will need a kit of emergency/
they can fuck themselves/
'cause here comes the girl who don't care about anyone else/
She's got a lot of girl power with her/
be careful, watch your back sir/
this time music ain't Spice Girls' bubblegum pop/
Just simple and rhymy Finnish hiphop/
I speak it loud and i speak it clear/
you other people have much to fear/
what is that in your eye, is it a tear/
I say what i know and feel/
I'm not faking, this is so fucking real/
everybody gets a part of my rhymes/
you can't win, you can try a million times
(EmZii, 14, an aspiring rap-mc, Finland, in her web-page www.
geocities.com/taivaansteppaaja/omabiisi8.html) (Translation from
Finnish by EmZii.)

We link these engagements with a series of questions about the relationships between girl power discourses and the coinciding rapid
social, cultural and economic changes taking place in much of the
Western world in this same time period. In particular, we are interested in further investigating girl power as an expression of what
Ulrich Beck (1992, p. 87) has called a 'social surge of individualization' emerging within the context of the rise of neo-liberalism.

Neo-liberalism is a form of Western liberal government that
reconstitutes the welfare state and relations with its citizens. Desta-
bilizing the post-war focus on state-building (through the development of social programmes and a contract between employees
and the State), neo-liberalism promotes a social world where the
individual is fully self-responsible. 'However apparently external
and implacable may be the constraints, obstacles and limitations
that are encountered, each individual must render his or her life
meaningful, as if it were the outcome of individual choices made in
the furtherance of a biographical project of self-realization' (Rose,
1992, p. 12). Individualization thus involves an increasing tendency
to self-monitoring, so that 'we are, not what we are, but what we
make of ourselves' (Giddens, 1991, p. 75). Under these conditions
contemporary gender identities and relations become emblematic,
representing in a kind of idealized form the possibilities of a self
cut loose from tradition and required to make itself anew.

Clearly, some aspects of the girl power phenomenon can be read as assisting in the production of the new self-inventing, neo-liberal subject. For example, in Budgeon's (1998) British study this linkage was a strong feature in the talk of the young white, middle-class women she interviewed. Self-determination was a recurring theme and especially evident as an ideal to which the young women aspired. Similarly, the young women often asserted the importance of inner strength, authenticity and being true to oneself (Budgeon, 1998, p. 122). As Budgeon suggests, these articulations of identity as choice and self-determination are linked in Britain to processes of individualization. In her reading of girls' engagements with and construction of the message: 'Being a young woman means being whoever you want to be', Budgeon takes a very positive stance. She suggests that the value of self-determination and individuality offers girls a powerful position from which to evaluate cultural rep-resentations of ideal femininity and to challenge and reject aspects of the available models femininity that did not suit their own visions of themselves and their futures.

But what of working class girls, Valerie Walkerdine and her col-leagues ask (Walkerdine *et al.*, 2001)? What happens to these girls when the value of self-determination and individuality becomes the new cultural ideal of femininity? More specifically what happens to working-class girls who encounter a 'girl power' that tells them they can be what they want in a labour market that cruelly sets limits on any ambition, together with an education system that classifies them as fit for certain kinds of work depend-ing on their academic capabilities? Walkerdine and her co-authors highlight the contradictions of the experiences of British working-class girls in a context where the future has been declared to be female. This declaration was made in response to the news that in the 1990s young women were outperforming their male cohorts at both the primary and the secondary levels of education. Young women were doing better than young men on standard achieve-ment tests and they were also now more likely to enter higher edu-cation (Budgeon, 1998, p. 115). Walkerdine, Lucey and Melody (2001) show that even these successes should be scrutinized for their differing implications for working and middle-class girls.

Reay (2001) suggests that although prevailing dominant dis-courses identify girls as the 'success story of the 1990s', her study in an inner city London school shows that, particularly when the focus is on the construction of heterosexual femininities – it is pre-mature to assume that girls are doing better than boys (Reay, 2001,

p. 156). In the school where her study takes place, some of the girls have grouped themselves using the identifying names of the 'spice girls' and the 'girlies'. According to Reay, the 'spice girls' interaction with the boys appeared to transgress prevailing gender regimes, while the 'girlies' followed a more conformist behaviour pattern. Yet, the spice girls were, for much of the time, also active in constructing and maintaining traditional variants of heterosexuality. For example, Reay shows how their espousal of girl power did not exclude enthusiastic partaking of the boyfriend/girlfriend games. There was much flirting, letter writing, falling in and out of love and talk of broken hearts. However, they also operated beyond the boundaries of the 'girlies' more confomist behaviour in their interaction with boys. Rating the boys was their favourite playground activity. As one explained, 'you follow the boys around and give them a mark out of ten for how attractive they are' (Reay, 2001, p. 158).

Reay (2001) theorizes that the 'spice girls' adherence to so-called girl power allowed them to make bids for social power not contemplated by the other girls. However, their 'girls with attitude' stance – the 'doing it for themselves' in ways which ran counter to traditional forms of femininity resulted in them being labelled at various times by teachers in the staffroom as 'real bitches', 'a bad influence' and 'little cows' (Reay, 2001, p. 160). Reay (2001) concludes that the espousal of girl power by the girls in the group produces mixed effects. On the one hand, it garners them power in both the male and female peer group, and provide spaces for them to escape gender subordination by the boys. On the other, the teachers' responses exemplify the limiting effects of such attempts to seek out empowering places within regimes alternatively committed to denying subordination or celebrating it.

This kind of contradictory effect may also be seen in a recent article featured in the *New York Times* Style Section. The article is entitled, 'She's got to be a macho girl' (Kuczynski, 2003) and describes a 'new' trend of girls who pursue boys. These girls are said to call boys on the phone, ask them out and sometimes even initiate sex. The teens and experts that Kuczynski calls on for commentary all agree that girls now grow up encouraged by parents, teenagers and peers to strive for more power and achievements than girls of decades past – but each somehow makes that sound like a bad thing, when it comes to relationships and sex. One 18 year old comments, 'I think with feminist thought being pushed upon girls from a young age, that some people put a premium on girls' dominating different areas of life.' And a counsellor at a Tennessee mental-health centre opines that the sexual revolution has 'bitten women in the butt'. It seems like girl power may be encountering something of a backlash, the effect of which is a repositioning of girls within familiar binaries of 'good' and 'bad' girls and their attendant meanings around sexuality, femininity, power and agency. However, while girl power girls are rendered socially problematic, other forms of femininity currently available for defining girls and girlhood are represented as equally undesirable. It is the discourse of the vulnerable girl that we shall discuss in the following chapter.

Conclusion

Girl power is a concept with various meanings and uses which shift depending on the context. Its pervasiveness as a discourse articulating emergent forms of femininity is perhaps due to the way it lends itself to multiple interpretations. It represents a feminist ideal of a new, robust, young woman with agency and a strong sense of self. At the same time as it has become a marketing slogan looking to attract the lucrative teen girl market. Its appeal to young women who have grown up as a matter of course with many of the social changes fought for by a previous generation of feminists is not hard to imagine. It offers them an image of young femininity which is about possibility, limitless potential and the promise of control over the future. Embedded in the concept is a sense that a life of success and happiness is within reach of girls who learn the skills and/or have the characteristics necessary for continual self-invention. The constraints of gender, race, class, sexuality, disability and ethnicity on this bright future is covered over by the suggestion that an individual can overcome all with the right attitude and drive.

The incredible attraction to girl power, on the part of the media, social institutions and girls themselves, must therefore be situated as an effect of the neo-liberal process of individualization. The concept resonants in today's world in ways it never would have in previous times due to the neo-liberal fashioning of a new subject and the changing relations of subjectivity and femininity.

CHAPTER 2

Reviving Ophelia:
Girlhood as Crisis

Introduction

In this chapter we trace and analyse the second discourse that we have identified as currently shaping public discussions of girls and girlhood in Western societies, which we are calling the 'Reviving Ophelia' discourse. It is extremely interesting and important to note that the 'Reviving Ophelia' discourse emerges into mainstream attention at the very same moment as the 'Girl Power' discourse, in the early 1990s. However, unlike 'Girl Power', the 'Reviving Ophelia' discourse is quite homogeneous, in that it has not elicited obvious competing stakes in its possible meanings or rival interests in the conditions of its circulation. It also appears that the Reviving Ophelia discourse has been a more dominant feature of North American discourses of girlhood than in other regions. The co-existence of the two discourses does, however, raise some intriguing questions. For instance, how is it that these seemingly opposite discourses emerge simultaneously? Do they, in fact, represent different forms of subjectivity available to girls? And if so, what are these? What is their relationship to each other? And perhaps most interestingly, what differing and similar formulations of the cultural ideals of personhood, individuality and agency do girls encounter and engage with through these discourses?

It is Mary Pipher's 1994 book *Reviving Ophelia: Saving the Selves of Adolescent Girls* that furnishes the name for this discourse. The book's multiple-month stint on the *New York Times* best-seller list not only launched public awareness of this discourse, its success also highlights an intensification of the cultural fascination with girls in Western societies. Pipher adopts Shakespeare's character Ophelia from Hamlet as the symbol of what she claims is a new crisis of girlhood. According to Pipher, in the story of Hamlet, Ophelia is the obedient daughter who kills herself, drowning in grief and sorrow when she cannot meet the competing demands of Hamlet and her father (Pipher, 1994, p. 20).

However, Pipher is far from the first to avail herself of the character of Ophelia to represent moral and social concern about girls and girlhood. For example, in the nineteenth century Ophelia was used to represent hysteria, which was at the time believed to be a real organic disease, transmitted genetically and associated with presumptive but unidentified changes in nervous tissue. Hysteria became a major focus of scientific study with girls and women as its major target. According to Georgianne Ziegler (1997, p. 71), during this time when photography became in vogue, young women in insane asylums were posed as Ophelia in photographic portraits. Her persona also exists in other forms. Nineteenth century and early twentieth century artists were obsessed with interpreting and defining her character. Sometimes she is portrayed as an innocent, young girl, the Victorian stereotype of what it is to be ladylike. Others portray Ophelia with strong sexuality. Still others portray her as some sort of magical being or saint. There are also several portraits of visibly neurotic Ophelias. Ophelia also seems to symbolize the adolescent girl that the very influential educationalist and psychologist G. Stanley Hall, established as the normative form of girlhood. Writing at the end of the nineteenth century he declared in his encyclopaedic publication 'Adolescence' (Hall, 1904), that adolescence was a turbulent and chaotic phase of life, and an archetypically feminine phenomenon. However, while boys were expected to pass through this phase into full adulthood, girls would remain forever in adolescence. They would be forever dependent on the 'support of a strong arm' i.e. in need of a husband – in order to cope in life (Hall, 1904, pp. 624–5). Clearly then, *Reviving Ophelia* engages a discourse that has a long tradition in Western societies and is thus able to tap into a resonating concern about the vulnerability of girls and the potential dangers they face growing up.

Saplings in a Hurricane

In the above-mentioned book Pipher (1994), a PhD and practising therapist, draws on her young, American female clients' experiences when she claims that 'something dramatic happens to girls in early adolescence'. Using language that mirrors the drama she claims girls live during this phase of their lives, Pipher draws on a series of metaphors to convey her sense of the vulnerability of young women. 'Adolescent girls are like saplings in a hurricane. They are young and vulnerable trees that the winds blow with gale strength' (Pipher, 1994, p. 22). Elsewhere in the book, girls are compared to 'planes and ships that disappear mysteriously into the Bermuda Triangle. Just as planes and ships, so do the selves of girls go down in droves. They crash and burn in a social and developmental Bermuda Triangle' (Pipher, 1994, p. 19).

The crux of Pipher's argument is that due to pressure from American culture adolescent girls are coerced into putting aside their 'authentic selves' splitting what was, in their younger days, a healthy and united individual, into true and false selves. This pressure to be someone they are not, Pipher claims, disorients and depresses most girls. At puberty 'girls become "female impersonators" who fit their whole selves into small, crowded spaces. Girls stop thinking, "Who am I? What do I want?" and start thinking, "what must I do to please others?"' (Pipher, 1994, p. 27). Pipher lays a good portion of the blame for girls' withering sense of self flatly at the feet of the media, calling to task a 'girl hostile culture' and its ability to crush their self-esteem. 'American culture has always smacked girls on the head in early-adolescence' (Pipher, 1994, p. 15).

> I stare hard into my eyes, searching.
> There is this saddened look on this girl's face – like she is in pain.
> I feel ashamed at what I look at
> I am disgusted with this worthless girl – this failure.
> Tears of fear slowly start to creep up into her eyes
> But she has to hold back – has to stay strong.
> I am hoping to see a figure which is perfect and beautiful,
> With every single bone and organ visible
> Protruding sharply through a pale paper-thin layer
> But come to find a different girl
> Now with all this excess flesh
> That which suffocates this poor girl
> I am disgusted and feel empty inside.
>   (Anonymous, 14, USA (1999).)

Pipher (1994) cites a range of studies to support her conclusions that while adolescence has always been hard, it is harder now because of the cultural changes of the last decade. She says, girls are having even more trouble now than they had ten years ago. For example, 'studies show that girls' IQ scores drop and their math and science scores plummet. They lose their resiliency and optimism and become less curious and inclined to take risks. They lose their assertive, energetic and 'tomboyish' personalities and become more deferential, self-critical and depressed. They report great unhappiness with their own bodies' (Pipher, 1994, p. 19).

> Reviving Ophelia
> The lily weeps and cries tonight.
> The silence drowns and keeps,
> Each broken heart that passes here
> In search of easeful sleep.
> I dreamt this dream a thousand times.
> I dreamt I saw your face.
> The sickly palour, robes of white,
> The heart that you must hide from sight,
> That daylight can't replace.
> You dreamt this dream once before
> And still I do revive,
> And try to draw from memory,
> And through your eyes I try to see,
> But you did not survive.
> (Clara Ho, Kingston, Canada (Ho, 1999).)

While Pipher's book raised the profile of this emerging concern about girls, the foundation for the success of the book was actually laid quite some time before. Approximately ten years earlier, in 1982, Carol Gilligan published *In a Different Voice: Psychological Theory and Women's Development*. In this highly influential and much quoted book, Gilligan makes the claim, that girls undergo a 'crisis in self-esteem' in adolescence from which they never fully recover. Gilligan suggests that adolescence is perhaps an especially critical time in women's development because to connect her life with history on a cultural scale, she must enter – and by entering disrupt – a tradition in which 'human' has for the most part meant male (Gilligan, 1982, p. 4). This poses a problem of connection for girls that is not easily resolved. Gilligan's book sought to address this problem by accenting the positive value of girls' moral reasoning, which in the psychology traditions of Freud, Piaget and Kohlberg was rendered either problematic or non-existent. Gilligan

critiques the meta-narratives of psychology which assume that
there is a single mode of social experience and interpretation. In its
place, Gilligan argues for the need to expand concepts of identity
and moral development to include the experience of inter-
connection and an ethic of care. This kind of inclusion, argues
Gilligan is critical for creating the necessary social and cultural
shifts to contain young women's self-esteem crisis (Gilligan, 1982).

The study has been critiqued for the way in which it uses the
experiences of, primarily, privileged white girls to claim a different
voice that positions all women in identical and essentialized ways
(Spelman, 1990). In concentrating on the differences of women's
moral reasoning from men's, Gilligan (1982) elides the differences
that may exist between women and the way in which these differences may be shaped by the social categories of race, class, sexuality, and ability. Beyond the limitations of this ground-breaking
study, however, has also been the way in which the text has been
taken up by others. Within the study of psychology, girls went from
being invisible to being vulnerable (Baumgardner & Richards,
2000). And the vulnerability discourse soon traversed disciplinary
boundaries and the walls of the ivory tower and spread in multiple directions.

Amongst the numerous studies and popular explorations of the
theme of girls' vulnerability which followed Gilligan's book, was
a report by the National Council for Research on Women for the
Ms. Foundation called *Risk, Resiliency, and Resistance: Current
Research on Adolescent Girls* (Shultz, 1991). There was also a more
critical take on the status of girls: an American Association of University Women Educational Foundation report, *How Schools Shortchange Girls* (1992), which has also been very influential in setting
feminist research agendas in the field of education in the US. It was
a scathing report on the ways in which the American education
system continues to provide less than equal educational opportunities and outcomes for young women. The report revealed a dramatic gender gap in self-esteem. And it linked this self-esteem
problem to the reduced participation of girls in math and science
in high school, even for those girls who did well in these subjects
in earlier grades. The survey does distinguish between girls of different backgrounds, noting that African American girls retain their
self-esteem during their adolescent years more than white or Latina
girls. And according to the study it is Latina girls who are the most
likely to suffer from the self-esteem crisis. This was followed by
Failing at Fairness: How America's Schools Cheat Girls (1994), a book

written for a popular audience by academics Myra and David Sadker, which reported on the many forms of discriminatory practices against girls in schools, including the fact that teachers were more likely to respond when boys called out than when girls did.

At the same time, journalist Peggy Orenstein's *School Girls: Young Women, Self-Esteem and the Confidence Gap* was published, and became the New York Times notable book of the year for 1994. The book presents a year-in-the-life of 14 year old girls in two California schools, and explores the girls' relationships to their schools, families, young men and themselves. Written as short vignettes about the lives, families and schools of different girls, the book draws readers into the trials and tribulations of issues such as eating disorders, suicide, violence, conflicts with friends, parents and teachers, and sexual harassment.

Taking Issue with the Vulnerable Girl Thesis

These texts and Pipher's all share a view that the girls' self-esteem crisis is a consequence of a girl-hostile culture that denies them expression of their authentic selves in adolescence. This explanation, of a culture that 'smacks girls on the head' in early adolescence focuses attention on the social factors existing outside girls themselves, and over which girls are presumed to have little or no control and few resources with which to fight back. Pipher does contextualize this culture as emerging out of sexism, capitalism and lookism – all of which she identifies as girl-hurting 'isms'. However, the omission of racism as a debilitating social ingredient in girls' lives is curious, particularly in the US context, where race continues to be the single most important factor in determining the life chances of young people. This very serious omission can only be explained by assuming that Pipher's study is not directed at young women of colour and that it is really only concerned with exploring the experiences of young white women. The suggestion seems to be that either white girls are vulnerable to cultural influences in a way that young women of colour are not, or that the lives of young white women are assumed to represent all of American girlhood.

The idea that young white women are encountering these features of American culture only as they enter adolescence also bears further questioning. Feminist researchers have done some very convincing work showing how gender, class, race and sexuality are negotiated by children as young as pre-school aged (see for example, Davies, 1989; Walkerdine, 1990). This is not to say that young women may not be confronting meanings of gender, class, race and sexuality in ways and with implications that they may not have done at an earlier age, but that identities and identity formation are much more complex than Pipher's study recognizes.

> As a woman who loves herself in the mind
> I know I deserve everything
> And I should get it.
> As a girl who hates herself in the body
> I know I deserve nothing
> And I should get it.
> It froths.
> I feel my blood hurtling.
> But I can't stop looking at myself.
> And I can't stop hating myself
> Sometimes I just cry.
> (Charlotte Cooper (1999), 18, USA.)

Other factors that Pipher draws on to account for the vulnerability of girls' 'authentic' selves, move away from the social towards the very well travelled territory of biology and developmental psychology (see introduction). Here it is girls' own bodies that work against them. 'Everything is changing – body shape, hormones, skin and hair. Calmness is replaced by anxiety. Their way of thinking is changing.' (Pipher, 1994, p. 27). This equating of young women with their bodies, at the mercy of their hormones, signalling the loss of rationality seems very closely related to the disease of hysteria which, as we have already seen, was also thought to befall young women at this time in their lives. The representation of adolescence as chaos feeds into many of the demeaning cultural stereotypes about girls and young women. In the following quote, girls' behaviour and emotions are presented as though they are beyond the bounds of comprehension. Pipher (1994, p. 20) says, 'girls become fragmented, their selves split into mysterious contradictions. They are sensitive and tenderhearted, mean and competitive, superficial and idealistic. They are confident in the morning and overwhelmed with anxiety by nightfall. They rush through their days with wild energy and then collapse into lethargy. They try on new roles every week – this week the good student, next week the delinquent and the next, the artist. And they expect their families to keep up with these changes.'

As Baumgardner and Richards (2000) comment, what these kinds of statements make clear is that the book is about girls but it is for adults, particularly the parents of adolescent girls. This leads them to raise the interesting question of whether Ophelia is a girl movement for adult women rather than for girls? This possibility is lent weight by the writings of adults who have framed research and investigations of girls' vulnerabilities around their own youthful experiences of feeling silenced. For example, Peggy Orenstein (1994, p. xxvii) writes in the Introduction to *Schoolgirls*, 'It was not until I saw how these vibrant young women were beginning to suppress themselves that I realized how thoroughly I too, had learned the lesson of silence, how I had come to censor my own ideas and doubt the efficacy of my actions.' Similarly, in researching *Between Voice and Silence: Women and Girls, Race and Relationship*, Jill MacLean Taylor, Carol Gilligan and Amy M. Sullivan (Taylor *et al.*, 1995, p. 11) found that 'girls' voices frequently encouraged women . . . in part because they . . . recall a voice and a world of relationships that had become a lost time for women – a time of clarity and courage at the edge of adolescence.' And Judy Mann (1994, p. 191), author of *The Difference: Growing Up Female in America*, writes, 'when I talked to adult women about this book, many of them described their adolescence with painful recollections that invariably had to do with a sense of lost self, a silencing of their voice, a loss of self-confidence and of identity.' This focus on adult women as the real beneficiaries of the girl movement is problematic both in terms of its political efficacy for young women, and for its tendency to commercialize the Ophelia crisis to create an adult (and therefore wealthier) market for books, programmes, workshops and the like. Janie Victoria Ward and Beth Cooper Benjamin (forthcoming 2004) also suggest that the political allegiances between women and girls have been left behind in this new focus on the particular and unique situation of girlness, categorized and explained by older women. Many young women themselves do not identify with the Ophelia image and do not find the 'silence and loss' framework meaningful (see for example Baumgardner and Richards, 2000).

I resented how 'experts' in their 40s and 50s immediately swooped onto the scene and brayed to the nation's teenagers about how we were supposed to feel. Adults – clearly suffering from a case of amnesia about their own high school days – don't like to admit that sex, drugs and violence are as much a part of teen life as they a part of adult life. (Lillie Wade (1999), 19, USA.)

A final factor that Pipher (1994) identifies to account for the increased vulnerability of young women in adolescence further exposes the limits of who she is addressing as 'the' American girl. She claims that the crisis of young girlhood is further exacerbated because 'American girls are expected to distance themselves from parents just at the time when they most need their support. As they struggle with countless new pressures, they must relinquish the protection and closeness they've felt with their families in child-hood' (Pipher, 1994, p. 27). The underlying assumptions here are of a certain normative family and relations with family members that omit the violence, abuse and discrimination that some girls encounter in their families. (This issue is explored further in Chapter 4.)

> Mary Pipher really hits the spot when she says that adolescent girls are like Ophelia . . . the book started to make me think [about] the question that seems to ring in every girls mind. Who am I? Really? Well, we can figure out what society expects us to be. Skinny portrayals of women. Sexy but tough. Seductive but not slutty. Gorgeous but natural. Strong yet dependent. Looking at these, I can honestly tell you that I definitely don't achieve these. Which leads me to be even more confused. I know what they want me to be, but I don't know what I am . . . I may not know I am who I am. (Bryna Windwalker, 1995.)

The Emergence of the Mean Girl

Although the Ophelia image still has enormous currency, we can document a new manifestation of the crisis discourse in the form of the 'Mean Girl', who has begun to eclipse the vulnerable girl in the public attention and in the media. The mean girl has been dubbed by the *Washington Post* as the 'Teenage Crisis of the Moment' (see Kantrowitz, 2002, p. 50). A huge and growing cultural industry has also blossomed around this issue. Popular books on the market at the time of writing this include the best-selling *Odd Girl Out: The Hidden Culture of Aggression in Girls* (2003), by Rachel Simmons, Rosalind Wiseman's *Queen Bees and Wannabees: Helping Your Daughter Survive Cliques, Gossip, Boyfriends, and Other*

Realities of Adolescence (2002), Sharon Lamb's *The Secret Lives of Girls: What Good Girls Really Do – Sex Play, Aggression, and Their Guilt* (2002) and Emily White's *Fast Girls: Teenage Tribes and the Myth of the Slut* (2002). Although most of these texts depict the Mean Girl as powerful rather than vulnerable, she is still a girl in crisis who requires work and adult intervention to bring her back on to a path for successful development.

In Finland, the phenomenon has been commented on by Sanna Aaltonen and Päivi Honkatukia (Honkatukia & Aaltonen, 2001), who have traced the discourse of the 'Tough Girl' into the late 1990s, when the media, popular culture as well as researchers and politicians started to comment on girls' 'new toughness'. In August 1999, the biggest newspaper in Finland, *Helsingin Sanomat*, published a cover story about a troupe of 'tough broads' from the suburbs, who were described as: 'girls who smoke, drink and tease those younger than themselves. On the train they terrorize everybody with their idle talk, and if their voice is not enough, they threaten to get you. And sometimes they do. Girls' behaviour has changed from the early 1990s . . . Now the fists will fly, when girls roam the city in their own gangs, not caring about other people and without shame.' (*Helsingin Sanomat* Supplement, August 1999; translation from Finnish by Sinikka Aapola). The concern expressed about the rise of this behaviour is that gender roles have become blurred with girls starting to take on roles more typically expected from boys.

In the US Meda Chesney-Lind and Katherine Irwin (forthcoming 2004) argue that the image of the middle-class, white mean girl, like the vulnerable girl, has serious consequences for lower class girls of colour. They suggest that the mean girl is the new kind of 'bad girl', previously depicted as a gang member and criminal, an image steeped in class and race stereotypes. They write (forthcoming, 2004), 'in contrast to the Latina or African American gang member growing up in the hood, the bad girl of the early 2000s was white, middle class, suburban, and has a promising future.' The shift in public attention to a different kind of bad girl meant that young women in general, and their apparent predilection for aggression, became a focus for concern and surveillance. This engendered an increased regulation of the so-called 'queen bees', but, more disturbingly, an increased criminalization of the 'acting out' behaviours of poor girls of colour. Chesney-Lind and Irwin note that since the emergence of the mean girl, criminal justice agencies have changed their practices in two significant ways. First, girls' status offences have been re-labelled as violent offences, and second, girls are now being arrested for 'crimes' (for example, schoolyard fights) that would have been ignored ten years ago. Although these changes appear to respond to an image of all girls as increasingly aggressive, it is young women who lack the resources to stay out of view of the criminal justice system who are targeted. Spiralling arrest rates for girls of colour have been the consequence.

Furthermore, the focus on privileged girls' self-esteem or aggression at the very moment that circumstances are deteriorating rapidly for less advantaged young women is troubling. This suggests that first, the success of middle class young women is of tremendous importance to late modern times, and second, that the individualization of problems and solutions has become a preferred way to interpret barriers to girls' opportunities. Chris Griffin (1997) notes the rise of speciality schools and residential programmes that cater to the troubled children of the wealthy, that promise to address these problems of self-esteem, 'acting out' or aggression. Such institutions, which may draw on Ophelia or Mean Girl discourses, offer middle-class parents quick-fix programmes that will set their children back on the track for success. As Walkerdine, Lucey and Melody (2001, p. 185) write, middle-class girls who encounter problems with emotional well-being are offered any number of expensive therapies to keep them on a path for achievement. For less privileged girls, outward manifestations of low self-esteem are more likely to bring them into the sphere of the criminal justice system than to private and attentive health care (see Chesney-Lind and Irwin, forthcoming, 2004). These girls are more likely to be positioned as a population to be dealt with by the police or courts of law. Their emotional and behavioural problems attract stigmatizing institutional interventions rather than assistance (see Harris, 2004). Furthermore, so long as the key issue for girls today is identified as primarily a psychological one, the underlying structural causes of their emotional, attitudinal and behavioural dispositions and the material differences between girls and the interventions offered to them are unlikely to be addressed.

In spite of these problems with the Ophelia discourse and its spin offs, this proliferation of publishing produced a range of programming responses in North American schools, communities, and religious organizations to address these newly defined needs of girls to overcome their vulnerability, and, more recently, their aggression. A small sampling of these kind of programmes include,

'The Ophelia Project' which started as a small grass roots volunteer organization in Erie Pennsylvania and is now spreading across the US, with paying members and a national team of volunteers. Promotional materials for the Tampa Bay Florida chapter of this organization draws on Pipher's language and metaphors of the need to rescue the 'authentic but lost selves' of girls. 'We are looking for awareness opportunities, pilot schools, interested community members who want to help girls preserve their "true selves".' The organization also provides programming focusing on relational aggression among girls (www.opheliaproject.org/index.shtml).

A related programme which also illustrates the way in which this discourse has resonated, been taken up, and culturally institutionalized is 'The Ophelia Project Video' which was created for 'Positivity Theatre for Youth', a LaPointe Wisconsin based theatre company. The video is a workshop tool that presents a series of scenarios of pressures that are considered typical of the kinds that girls encounter as they grow up. Workshop participants work with trained facilitators to discuss the video's contents and its relationships to their own experiences as girls (www.sunshineproductions.us/clips.html).

Local high school groups have also been created with this discourse acting as the catalyst and foundation for their existence. An interesting example of one such group is the Sutherland High School's 'Ophelia Club' where girls can share experiences and how they overcame them. The goals of the club include: 'reaching out to the community, for girls to socialize and support each other, and there is an emphasis on strength and empowerment.'

Programmes have also emerged in Europe. For example, in Sweden, a group of women theatre professionals produced a project in 2001 which was inspired by Mary Pipher's book. One of the three plays that was generated was entitled 'Property', written by 24 year old Lisa Ydring. The play features two characters, Ofelia and Mette; Mette who lashes out, and Ofelia who uses silence, eventually asking that her tongue be operated on. The play was controversial. One commentator writes, 'there is a certain limit. . . . Girls' anger and loss . . . is seen as too brutal and aggressive' (Attling, 2001).

> . . . how much less traumatic could early adolescence have been if I'd been taught women's studies as a child? How liberating that could be! Perhaps the struggle for a sense of self that is so much a part of

girlhood would be less traumatic. Maybe the popular metaphor for teenage girls would not be self-destructive Ophelia from Hamlet but rather Katharina from Taming of the Shrew. I know I'd rather be a 'shrew' than the crazy ex-girlfriend who drowned herself! (Naomi Sheridan (2001), 17, Yukon, Canada.)

All the media attention, publishing and programming has certainly provided increased and sorely needed spaces for girls to celebrate their girlhood. More spaces for young women to critically and collectively examine changing discourses of femininity are clearly desirable (Gonick, 2003). But, what kind of girl and girlhood does the Ophelia Movement produce? Which girlhoods does it recognize as worthy of celebrating or mourning? It seems that while the Ophelia movement also produced high visibility for a particular kind of girl and girlhood, it has done so by using very monolithic representations of girls. That is, girls are represented as simply victims of society. The movement has spawned what Jennifer Baumgardner and Amy Richards (2000, p. 179) call 'a veritable cottage industry' out of the fertile soil of girls' failing self-esteem. *Reviving Ophelia* begot *Ophelia Speaks: Adolescent Girls Write about their Search for Self* (1999), a compiled collection of original pieces contributed by girls of various races, religions and socioeconomic backgrounds, between the ages of 12 and 18 and edited by Sara Shandler when she was a teenager herself. For parents of adolescent women there is *Surviving Ophelia: Mothers Share Their Wisdom in Navigating the Tumultuous Teenage Years* (2001), by Cheryl Dellasega, and *Ophelia's Mom: Loving and Letting Go of Your Adolescent Daughter* (2001) by Nina Shandler, Sara Shandler's mother. The concern Baumgardner and Richards (2000, p. 185) have with the Ophelia industry, is that girls are being labelled victims of society and, by implication, passive dupes – whether or not they feel themselves this way.

> What is it about girls that everyone is writing books like Resuscitating Ophelia about how we have no selves, and my friends think they're fat, and aren't eating lunch, and boys are saying 'Yeah she's hot, but did you hear about her and those two juniors and she's really messed up and don't fuck her, you'd feel bad if you messed her up more,' and everyone is deeply, deeply concerned, except people trying to take our money and even they try to pretend? Just what is up with girls, anyway? (Emily Carmichael (1999), 15, USA.)

Ironically, the movement may be contributing to the proliferation of the girl-damaging media images through its own mass-marketing and subsequent cultural references to the figure of 'Ophelia' as a typical troubled contemporary girl (Projansky & Berg, 2000, p. 14).

> It's hard to imagine a book called 'Hamlet Speaks.'
> (Sara Shandler (2000), USA.)

Girl Power, Reviving Ophelia and New Subjectivities

We want to conclude this chapter by returning to further explore what the two discourses of Girl Power and Reviving Ophelia suggest about the different forms of subjectivity available to girls. How do we explain their co-existence? What are their relationships to feminism? And, perhaps most interestingly, what formulations of the cultural ideals of personhood, individuality and agency do girls encounter and engage with through these discourses?

To begin to address these questions, we will take a brief detour to return to the 1950s and to Lesley Johnson's (1993) analysis of the changing nature of women's relationship to modernity. Johnson suggests that the 1950s were an extremely significant moment in that women were for the first time recognized as subjects within discourses of modernity. This was, she argues both a feature of women's crucial role in the processes of modernization itself both as labour and as consumers – creating and being created as a new demand for new forms of technologies and new forms of cultural goods. And the fight for this recognition was, she suggests, also a significant part of the feminist agenda of the time.

While there are many ways we could talk about the two discourses we have identified we want to explore them as signifying another important and new phase – this time in the fashioning of girls into certain kinds of subjects in the late twentieth and early twenty-first century. Girls are as, Angela McRobbie (2000), has observed, now perhaps for the first time recognized as one of the stakes upon which the future depends. Thus, we want to link the discourses of 'girl-power' and 'reviving Ophelia' to shifts in the modernization project, and specifically those shifts that have brought about an intensification of what Beck (1992, p. 87) has called a 'social surge of individualisation'. Referring paradoxically to both 'individualism' and the obligation 'to standardize your own existence' in line with the imperatives of the labour market and governmental agencies (Beck & Beck-Gernsheim, 1995, p. 7), individualization involves an increasing tendency to self-monitoring, so that 'we are, not what we are, but what we make of ourselves' (Giddens, 1991, p. 75). Under these conditions, contemporary gender identities and relations become emblematic, representing in a kind of idealised form the possibilities of a self cut loose from tradition and required to make itself anew. This form of individualization has been linked to shifting relations between citizens and the state – from a focus on state-building (through the development of a contract between employees and the State during the post-war period) to concern for making the individual responsible. Like in the 1950s these changes also bear some relationship to shifting feminist agendas. Third Wave Feminism, with its 'Do It Yourself' ethic, raises some interesting tensions between making itself intelligible to a new generation of young people and normalizing these discourses of individualization and individual responsibility. (See Chapter 8 for a further discussion on this subject.)

Both 'girl power' and 'reviving Ophelia' discourses emphasize young female subjectivities as projects that can be shaped by the individual. Both encourage young women to work on themselves, either through the DIY self-invention and 'girls can do anything' rhetoric of girl power, or through the self-help books and programmes that are available to transform girls in crisis. Idealized girl heroes are now on display in popular culture and for sale in the girl marketplace. New, powerful identities can be created by purchasing the right products and having the right look. Difficulties and problems can be resolved through therapy and self-esteem workshops. Girls' subjectivities become worthy of surveillance, regulation and monitoring by adult authorities and girls themselves. As Ward and Benjamin (forthcoming 2004) write, 'In the world of programming, resources and attention are directed increasingly toward the girl herself', in what they describe as a 'girl fixing' agenda. They note that with the ushering in of the Mean Girl phenomenon, we see an even more narrow focus on the girl, and sometimes her parents, as the site for work and change. Both the discourses of girl power and girls' vulnerability individualize the process of forging an adult female identity in a late modern world.

We explore this dynamic further in the chapters that follow, by looking at how the discourses of girl-power and reviving Ophelia are manifested through the institutions and social relationships shaping girls' lives.

Conclusion

The Reviving Ophelia discourse has done much to bring to public attention some of the serious problems, struggles and disadvantages girls continue to encounter because they are female in a world that was never designed for women. In drawing attention to issues such as low self-esteem, rampant eating disorders, depression and high risk behaviours, Reviving Ophelia's importance rests in the ways it leads to an understanding of how individuals internalize structural inequalities. It demonstrates that despite the many gains made by women legally, financially and socially, the barriers to full equality have still to be completely dismantled. These inequalities are literally manifesting themselves on and through girls' bodies, psyches and spirits.

However, despite the alarmed concern for and increased attention to girls that has been generated by the very successful circulation of Reviving Ophelia, there are some very problematic effects of this discourse. We demonstrated how the discourse builds on the already prevailing image that girls who are deserving of social sympathy and concern are those who are white and middle-class. It presents girls who due to their racialized and classed positions are actually comparatively quite privileged, as hapless victims. In doing so, it further marginalizes girls who are socially, economically and politically disadvantaged. Central to our concerns about the effects of this discourse is the way in which it individualizes social problems. The solutions to the endemic of Ophelias at risk is for girls to do further work on themselves. Through therapy, programmes, and support, girls are encouraged to work out for themselves a personal solution to the social problems that could be threatening their lives.

CHAPTER 3

Education, Work
and Self-Making

Introduction

This chapter examines the impact of rapid socio-economic change
on young women's engagement with education, work and livelihood. Traditional education-to-work transitions for youth have
undergone radical revision under the sway of global economic
and social forces that have re-structured economies and labour
markets. Specifically, de-industrialization and the globalization of
economies have re-shaped the ways that youth engage with education and the workforce. Young women are ambiguously placed
within this new scenario. As we will go on to explore, many of them
have reaped the benefits of the 'feminization' of the labour market,
as well as the social changes brought on by feminism, both of
which have enabled them to take up rewarding positions in the
new economy. At the same time, however, it is a large number of
young women in particular who have been deeply affected by the
rise in youth unemployment and have negative experiences of the
new emphasis on training and skilling. In this chapter we will consider this contrasting situation, and reflect on how it complicates
debates about young women's high achievements in education and
the enduring effects of girl power at the level of work. To what
extent do young women enjoy new choices and take opportunities
to lead a more flexible work life, and how do the new discourses
engage with young women's identity work in the spheres of education and employment?

The New Economic Context of Education and Work

Material and ideological changes to growing up as a girl have been felt very keenly in relation to the new economic context of education and work. We have already seen how emerging opportunities and new kinds of constraints for young women have been borne out in the competing discourses of girl power and crisis that circulate in popular culture and society. The sphere of livelihood and economic autonomy has seen some of the most fundamental shifts in young women's outlooks and life chances. The industrial and economic transformations ushered in since the 1970s across the Western world have been the backdrop to new positionings of young women within the world of education and work. What have these transformations consisted of? There are several distinctive features which distinguish contemporary economies from simple industrial models by which capitalism has adhered to until now.

Specifically, mass scale manufacturing, which formed the backbone of the industrialized world, has diminished dramatically. In its place has come the expansion of industries such as communications, service and technology. This phenomenon is known as de-industrialization, which has had significant implications for the labour market and in particular, the availability of non-specialized, secure work for early school leavers. The emergence of these new industries has occurred on a global scale. Increasingly, management, shareholding, manufacturing bases and service outlets of corporations are disseminated across the world. Advances in technology that allow communications and financial movements to occur instantaneously have combined with loosening of regulations around trade, ownership and production to speed up this process of economic globalization. Processes and places for production have become more obscure, diffuse and flexible, as multinational companies shift manufacturing off shore and devolve labour management on to sub-contractors in search of cheap workers (Klein, 2001).

These new economic conditions have re-shaped the labour market as well as education and training. Specialized and constantly changing skills are required in many of the developing industries such as communication and technology. Other sectors, such as service, do not necessarily depend upon training and qualifications for successful execution of the work, and yet due to fierce competition, these are increasingly required of prospective employees. This competition is generated by the contraction of available work for low skill or unskilled labour, which was once in demand within traditional industries. While de-industrialized economies still require unskilled workers, the conditions under which they are now working makes employment at this level insecure and demanding. With a retreat of state regulation and economic rationalist policies within employment and industrial relations, unskilled workers in the new economy experience little job security, wage protection, occupational health and safety provisions, or opportunities for career development. The greatest increase in job availability across the de-industrialized Western world has been in part-time, casual, short-term, and temporary work. As nation states increasingly pin their economic fortunes to global market trends over which they have little control, employers depend on flexibility and mobility, and workers experience insecurity and uncertainty. This, in turn, puts increasing pressures on the educational system to meet the sometimes conflicting expectations of the state, as well as those of private employers, who require a steady flow of graduates meeting their specific job requirements, and, those of the students, who put their hopes of success in attaining educational credentials that will prove valuable in the ever-changing labour market.

This is why the general processes of social and economic change affecting the labour market have been followed by large-scale reorganization of educational systems that have taken place in most Western countries over the past decades (see Arnot *et al.*, 1999). In Australia, Europe and the USA there have been similar political developments since the 1980s, representing on the whole a move to the right, with a growing emphasis on individualization and differentiation rather than equality, and on free market thinking rather than welfare ideology. These developments, although far from monolithic, have resulted in wide processes of restructuring of education internationally, with tendencies towards a centralization and marketization of schooling, as well as towards closer links between schools and industry, even if the reforms have been quite varied on the national and local levels (Gordon *et al.*, 2000b, pp. 23–6). Education has always been seen as an important site for promoting national interests, and even more so in the prevailing political thinking. Schooling is seen as one of the main vehicles to improve the chances of national economies in the ever-intensifying climate of financial competition, via translating the demands of the labour-market into viable and effective study programmes.

As we have already seen, these changed conditions have been accompanied by the expansion of narratives of individualization and choice, whereby knowable trajectories and traditional support structures have been replaced by an emphasis on the individual and his/her personal strategies for 'making it'. The ideas of good personal choices and flexibility have become central to one's ability to manage under these circumstances (see Beck, 1992). Economic insecurity and risk are now imagined to be best addressed through individual resiliency and a capacity to change and adapt to a volatile educational and labour market. Individuals need to be prepared to return to education to re-skill themselves, to negotiate wages and conditions through private arrangements, to change career paths when necessary, to manage livelihoods without a 'job for life', and to take personal responsibility for their economic security. Therefore, individuals must balance risk alongside opportunity. These 'individual' processes of young people are, however, highly gender-specific, as well as deeply affected by their social and ethnic backgrounds.

Changes in Youth Transitions

The socio-economic changes and educational restructuring described above have had a pronounced effect on young people. It can be claimed that education in late modern society is the singular most important social institution shaping children's and young people's everyday lives and identities as well as their understandings of their future life chances. Its crucial importance to future life chances also comes at a time when in many countries educational systems are facing devastating budget cuts and reforms from governments. Many post-secondary institutions have responded by raising tuition fees to levels that are increasingly unattainable for many students. While it is vital to focus on the future effects of education for young people, as we shall do later in this chapter, it is also important to see the extended years spent in schooling as a central part of the contemporary process of growing up. It is not only the official level of schooling, but even the students' intense and long-time participation in the informal and physical levels of school, where friendships are formed and antipathies developed, differentiations between students created and renegotiated, that has a profound effect on their lives (see Gordon *et al.*, 2000b). The experience of schooling also continues to be highly gender-specific, as has been argued by generations of feminist educationalists (see Kenway *et al.*, 1998; Arnot *et al.*, 1999). In recent years, young people's schooling experiences have become more and more characterized by individualization, specialization and marketization (see for example Järvinen, 2003). Schooling is being increasingly framed in terms of choice and consumption, which means, among other things, heightened competition between schools for prospective students (Kenway & Bullen, 2001).

> I decided to go to Brunsdon Heights because they have got everything set out, like there is a big hallway and they have got what is down that hallway, like it says technology and maths. It's a smaller school and you won't get lost. And they've got tennis courts and basketball courts and they have got a big gym and they've got good stuff. At the other end of the school they have got a primary school and they use their oval as well. (Girl, 12, Australia, quoted in Kenway & Bullen, 2001, p. 133.)

Youth transitions to adulthood have generally become much more complicated, as the traditional markers of growing up are no longer in place. The most basic of these, that is, the capacity to leave school and find satisfactory, ongoing work, is the experience most notably absent in the new youth transition process. This brings into question the usefulness of relying on a 'transition' model to explain young people's circumstances and opportunities (see for example Dwyer & Wyn, 2001).

It has been well-documented that the new economy has seen the erasure of the full-time job market for young people and youth unemployment has emerged as a key issue facing de-industrialized economies. Early school leavers, or those who complete minimum levels and do not engage in further training, are particularly vulnerable to un- or underemployment. There is a new emphasis on skills, education and qualifications. Engaging in education beyond the compulsory years has become essential to young people's job prospects regardless of their gender, and many new training and education programmes now exist to shape youth pathways in radical new ways to accommodate this change (see Furlong & Cartmel, 1997). Welfare and state support for unemployed early school leavers has been cut back right across the Western world, or tied directly into training, although there may not be real employment outcomes from this process. Thus young people are encouraged, and sometimes coerced into education, and they often experience employment as a risky business, as there are no guarantees in terms of economic security (see also Wallace & Kovatcheva, 1999, p. 88). The expansion of the higher education system, the new emphasis on lifelong learning, and pressure to constantly upgrade their skills effectively requires them to get more education to compete for fewer jobs in an ever-changing labour market. Staying on in school and gaining further credentials has become enormously important, although there are no real safeguards for job security.

This scenario leads to unpredictability about personal and professional futures, and as we shall see in later chapters, places new demands on families to provide for children into their adult years. The requirement to exhibit good personal choices and flexibility is felt particularly keenly by youth, who may experience this situation as both enhancing opportunities and freedoms, but also the cause of deep anxiety. Du Bois-Reymond (1998) describes many youth today as living out 'choice biographies' (see Beck, 1992); in other words, they have more options before them, but are obliged to bear the burden of responsibility for making the 'right' choice. Large-scale Australian research suggests that young people work hard on themselves to become flexible and resilient choice-makers in unpredictable times (Dwyer *et al.*, 2003).

> I am only 20 and I already feel that I haven't succeeded because I have not managed to make something out of my life. I should have studied, travelled, found a course in life. At least I should have decided what I want to do. Sometimes I feel really anxious and totally worthless. I compare myself to my sis, for example, who had a job, an education and children by the time she was 22. There's only one year left for me to do that. When I feel like this, unsuccessful, I get totally apathetic and cannot do anything. In that way it becomes a vicious circle. It feels like the pressure to perform paralyzes me. (Lena, 20, Sweden, quoted in Thulin & Östergren, 1997, p. 139, translation from Swedish by Sinikka Aapola.)

De-industrialized socio-economic circumstances have significantly raised the stakes for correct choices, but these are not always accounted for in narratives of a smorgasbord of opportunities or new freedoms for individual pursuit of personal preferences. Consequently, whilst youth enjoy greater flexibility in imagining their life trajectories, they must also bear the material and psychological weight of the responsibility of self-realization with far fewer structural supports than were in place for previous generations. For many, this is a welcome freedom, whilst for others, it causes considerable stress and challenges. Walkerdine, Lucey and Melody (2001, pp. 2–3) argue that this pressure on young people to become responsible for their own destiny is at the heart of the invention of the 'new' girl. As we have suggested, the discourses of Girl Power and Ophelia offer young women ways to become their own projects. This emphasis on making oneself is particularly significant in the context of work in a de-industrialized global economy, where responsibility for livelihood is now squarely at the feet of individuals.

Young Women and New Transitions

Widespread debate has occurred about the gendered experiences of these new processes of transition in terms of the economic options now available to youth and their capacity to see themselves as 'choice biographers'. So far, this has been mainly expressed as an issue for young men and the future of masculinity (see Heath, 1999). Specifically, the loss of traditional, unskilled manual work has been seen as primarily a concern for young working-class men who are now deemed to be 'left behind' or without an identity in a rapidly changing world. Much is made of the 'feminization' of the labour market, meaning that jobs growth is occurring in areas where women dominate, for example, service, sales and communications, while manual labour is on the decline. This has another meaning as well, though; that the kind of worker that the new labour market prefers, the expressive, well-groomed, mobile negotiator, is based on a model of femininity (see Adkins, 2002). The nexus between masculinity, physicality and employability has been broken, and the ability to gain work, especially if one is without qualifications, seems connected to more traditionally feminine skill sets. These economic changes, together with the successes of feminism in improving gender equity in education and work, are often represented as damaging to young men and unproblematically advantageous for young women. The notion of a 'genderquake' (Wilkinson, 1994), brought about by the changes in the economy combined with the mainstream impact of feminism, is perceived to privilege young women to the detriment of young men.

It is our intention in the next section to examine how young women have been affected by these changes, and how new discourses of girlhood offer them ways to position themselves within a new world of education and employment. How do they balance risk and choice in education and the labour market? We suggest that they have been constructed rather homogeneously and simplistically as the only beneficiaries in the new economy, and that closer examination reveals that many girls suffer considerably in these circumstances. We suggest here that the picture is much more complex than the simple image of girls 'outperforming' boys suggests (see also Arnot *et al.*, 1999; Kenway *et al.*, 1998). To some extent, many young women have enjoyed the benefits of a changed labour market and many exhibit the resilience and flexibility required of those who will be successful. However, there are some young women for whom the experience of gaining a livelihood is a much more difficult process than ever before. We want to explore now the range of experiences of young women managing these new global economic forces, and reflect on the more straightforward stories of young women's unilateral privilege and power, or desire for professional success, traditionally defined.

There is a number of ways in which young women are perceived to benefit from new socio-economic processes sweeping across the de-industrialized world. These are in the areas of the re-structured labour market, the current emphasis on skilling and training for flexible employment, and becoming a successful 'choice biographer' negotiating one's path in the midst of a confusing web of choices in all spheres of life. Let us look at each of these more closely.

Jobs Growth and Career Aspirations

The first way in which young women benefit in the new economy is through the expansion of 'female' sectors of employment and the contraction of large scale manufacturing. Put simply, growth in jobs has occurred in traditionally female industries, for example, telesales, retail, service and communications. Even though unemployment and youth unemployment in particular have risen dramatically in recent times, there has been an expansion in some types of work where women tend to be found; specifically casual, temporary, part-time and short-term employment. At the same time, women have also gained access to higher professional positions from which they have previously been excluded, due either to formal or informal discrimination. Male-dominated areas such as law and medicine have become much more open and attractive to female graduates. Due to feminist advances in industrial regulations and policy, fairer pay scales and work place practices are now in place to make non-traditional professional work accessible to women. However, as Walkerdine, Lucey and Melody (2001, p. 7) point out, the creation of a new sector of elite super-professionals in finance, multi-national management and technology has also been responsible for the movement of women into the professions. As men move upwards into these prestige positions generated by globalization and de-industrialization of national economies, women have now stepped in to fill the ranks in formerly high status professional sectors.

Opportunities for young women in the new economy have not just come about due to economic shifts. Social and political forces have also had a big impact in changing the 'female role'. Feminism has had an enormous effect on young women's life plans, and career and work now feature as desirable and important elements in their planning for the future. Several studies have demonstrated how young women plan for the future in ways that are very different from previous generations. For example, large-scale survey research by Wicks and Mishra (1998) indicates the importance a majority of young women today place on securing paid work in good jobs. Both Bulbeck's study (2001) and the US National Longitudinal Surveys quoted by Hakim (1991) reflect how significant this emphasis is. Each contrasts contemporary aspirations with those of young women of the late 1960s and early 1970s, and suggests that the imagined trajectory of a lifetime of fulfilling paid work is a very recent development in young women's aspirations. Young women are often perceived to be the beneficiaries of the restructured labour market because their aspirations match work place opportunities. Job growth appears to be occurring in industries and under conditions where women are commonly found. The glass ceiling on some professional positions has been at least cracked, if not entirely broken, and young women are entering worlds of work that were previously only for men. Further, unlike even a generation ago, many of them are imagining and organizing their lives around the idea of a career, and in this way are entering into the new economy with enthusiasm and a sense of entitlement to participation.

Skilling and Training for Flexible Employment

In my opinion, people can make it by getting a good education and then finding a good job. It takes a while to get where you're going. But, eventually you get there. It's better than just sitting at home and staying stagnant and not doing anything. Even if you get your bachelor's, from there you go on, you do another two or three years, or four years for a doctorate degree. But you still get there. (Tina, 21, Antiguan American, USA, quoted in Lopez, 2003, p. 159.)

The second way in which young women are positioned as powerful and successful is in their relationship to education, skilling and training. As we have seen, the path towards a satisfying job currently wends its way through various educational requirements. Credentialing, and in particular, post-compulsory qualifications, have become critical if young people are to compete for work in the new economy. This emphasis has created widespread changes to youth policy, and particularly unemployment payment provisions, which now tend to be linked to training programmes. The need to stay at school, gain 'transferable skills', get qualifications and succeed in education is communicated to young people through these policies and through their experiences in employment. Overwhelmingly, it is young women who are seen as heeding this message and as a consequence, performing very well at school and then going on to higher education.

Research right across nations that have undergone de-industrialization demonstrates that girls' educational achievements particularly in the past two decades have been considerable. They have gradually improved their qualifications and reduced boys' lead in examinations overall, and even exceeded boys' achievements in some subjects (see Arnot *et al.*, 1999, pp. 20–1). Although there are national differences, the same trend has been discernible in most Western countries: young women's participation and success in post-compulsory and further education is not just keeping pace with young men's, but exceeding it (see for example Lagree, 1995; Furlong & Cartmel, 1997; Wallace & Kovatcheva, 1999; Järvinen & Vanttaja, 2001). Girls' improved achievements at school have often been attributed to educational policies and practices promoting equal opportunities that have been applied particularly since the 1960s. However, these programmes have not been as effective as has been believed in eradicating gender discrimination from schools or promoting equality between the sexes (Kenway *et al.*, 1998; see also for example Palmu, 2003, on the problematic construction of gender in school materials). Also, as Madeleine Arnot and her colleagues point out, such educational policies and procedures have shifted considerably during the years according to changes in government, and their effect on girls' school performance in nation-wide contexts has not been proved (Arnot *et al.*, 1999, p. 150). They claim instead that the massive changes in girls' education and girls' own educational aspirations have been interlinked with the general processes of social and economic change, and particularly with the reformulation of gender ideologies and feminism (Arnot *et al.*, 1999, p. 150).

As Lähteenmaa (1995) argues, high-achieving schoolgirls respond well to the need to get qualifications and skills for good work prospects. This phenomenon of the high-achieving schoolgirl who is 'outperforming' young men is not always celebrated, however. Her appearance has also ushered in a 'what about the boys?' debate, which tends to simplify the issues around gender and academic achievement by presenting a homogeneous category of successful young women who are denying opportunities to an equally homogeneous but victimized category of young men (see Epstein *et al.*, 1998; Yates, 1997). As many critics have pointed out, this debate can be seen as a form of backlash against feminist endeavours in general, and it has also served to conceal differences within gender categories, such as race, ability, class and culture, and to avoid analysis of the longer-term relationship between educational success and secure, satisfying work (see Heath, 1999; Kenway *et al.*, 1998; Arnot *et al.*, 1999). We will explore these issues further in a moment.

The ideologies regarding girls' education in the twentieth century have switched along two opposites that can be conceptualized as the 'gender differentiation model', which has emphasized girls' preparation for domestic futures, and as the 'equality model', advocating for equal educational opportunities for girls and boys (see Arnot *et al.*, 1999, pp. 35–6 and 83–101). However, the change in these ideologies has not only been in one direction, but different governments have had very different goals in relation to gender values over the years, despite feminist attempts to promote gender equality. Similar types of negotiations regarding the goals and practices of girls' education have taken place in many countries, while there have been some national differences (see for example Kenway *et al.*, 1998; Lahelma, 1993).

It is true, however, that young women's increased commitment to and participation in education has resulted in many of them achieving good, high-status jobs. At the same time, young women's new aspirations and achievements are sometimes seen to be universal, as though all have equal access to power, autonomy and success. This may not be the reality for many girls, and may not even be desired by some who are using circumstances of risk and choice to develop other life trajectories, with less emphasis on a successful professional life. There is also a need to consider the emotional issues behind as well as the costs of educational and academic achievement for girls and young women.

Balancing Choice and Risk

It is perhaps in the balance of choice and risk that young women are most often seen as successful in managing the uncertainties of the economy. Walkerdine, Lucey and Melody (2001, p. 3) suggest that girls, perhaps more than anyone else, are imagined to possess the skills of self-invention that are so necessary to survival in the new economic system. The combination of rationalist and neo-liberal rhetoric with feminist discourse has meant that young women are often spoken about as feisty, independent and powerful, in control of their lives, able to make choices and 'be whatever they want to be' (see Harris, 2004; Wyn, 2000). Catchphrases like 'girls can do anything' and the broader discourse of girl power that underlie them abound in advertising, public policy, non-government programmes for girls, curricula, and popular culture, as we saw in the opening chapters of this book. Possibility, choice and self-invention have become central to ways in which young women are able to think about their identities and futures within the new economy, and this is strongly encouraged by the market and the state.

For example, McRobbie (2001, p. 1) argues that young women's capacity for self-made economic success is heavily promoted by New Labour in Britain, as well as by media and advertising interests, because they have been invested in as 'standard bearers for the new economy'. She suggests that the promotion of the idea that it is young women who have risen to the top in the new, supposedly meritocratic education and employment systems because of their superior capacity for self-making conceals some more critical issues; that it is young women's labour that is required by the new economic order, and their hearts and minds that must be won over to its agenda. This message of self-invention, choice and flexibility has been taken seriously by many young women who sit at the intersection of feminist discourse and economic reality. For example, some research suggests that young women are more optimistic and confident about their economic futures than young men (Rattansi & Phoenix 1997; Katz, 1997; Rudd & Evans, 1998; Miles, 2000; Lopez, 2003) and more flexible and resilient in the face of change and disappointment (Krüger, 1990; Lähteenmaa, 1995; Chisholm, 1997; Dwyer & Wyn, 2001).

> I want to go to university, don't want to end up in an office. I want to do something creative, have a family too, but not too early, don't know if I'd like children. I don't want to become dependent on a man, I want to work. Work has to be fun. (Annika, 16, German, middle-class, quoted in Herrmann, 1998, p. 228.)

To some extent, then, global economic forces help young women become powerful and autonomous. Many of them do well at school and go on to higher education and successful careers. There are certainly more young women participating in the labour force and in post-compulsory schooling than ever before, and there is a great deal of support for the idea that girls can be resilient, flexible and self-actualizing. The professions have opened up enormously for them, and their capacity for pursuing prestigious careers and enjoying large incomes is unprecedented. However, it would be inaccurate to suggest that these opportunities are equally open to, or equally valued by all young women. As Walkerdine, Lucey and Melody (2001) have found in the UK at least, class background is still a key indicator of future success for girls.

> I started working as a research assistant at an investment firm because my aunt worked there. She actually spoke for me ... My first job was at the brokerage firm and my friend's job was at our local supermarket. My friend is still at the supermarket! We're the same age, went to the same high school and college, had the same upbringing and she's still a cashier at that supermarket! I'm sure that if my aunts didn't have those kinds of jobs I would have been a cashier too, because I didn't know where to start or where to go. (Yvonne, 21, Dominican American, USA, quoted in Lopez, 2003, p. 154.)

Upper- and middle-class young women, with considerable resources, networking opportunities and social capital provided by their families, can make the most of new opportunities. Without these support structures in place, though, many other young women struggle to find a livelihood and a place in the new economy. For example, Froschl, Rubin and Sprung (1999, p. 7) have found that 'the difficulty in progressing from secondary school to adult life is exacerbated for young women with disabilities'; which is in part due to discrimination and lack of opportunities in the labour market, but also a direct result of disconnection from significant social capital and networks which are increasingly important to securing a future. They say (p. 7): 'Young women with disabilities are being systematically programmed out of the after-school experiences essential to later jobs, careers, and education'. Similarly, Doren and Benz (1998) have found that young women with disabilities are more likely to experience poorer post-school employment outcomes if they have had no job experience in high school, if they come from a poor family, and if they have no personal networks to help them find work. Further, membership of the cultural majority remains a significant element of achieving educational and economic success. High achievement, both academically and professionally, is connected not only to class but racial and cultural values and resources. For example, both Fordham (1996) and Folds (1987) discuss how educational success for African American and Indigenous Australian young women respectively involves 'acting white'.

In the next section, we interrogate further the notion that young women in general are the winners in a re-structured labour market by looking at the class- and culture-differentiated effects of economic change upon them.

Labour Market Marginalization

Although some young women are well-positioned to take advantage of new work opportunities and flexible conditions, a large number has been marginalized by the re-structuring of the labour market and lack the social and economic resources to participate in satisfying and enduring ways. Marginalization is a particular problem for working-class young women who seek work directly out of minimum-level schooling. Although once secure work for the unskilled and unqualified was available, the industries in which such work existed have now more or less disappeared. There is considerable evidence to suggest that it is uncredentialled young women, more than young men, who have been hardest hit by the loss of traditional unskilled work opportunities (see Chisholm, 1997, p. 111; Dwyer & Wyn, 2001, p. 132; Walkerdine et al., 2001, p. 212). Unlike their more privileged counterparts, these young women are not being retained by the education system, and are not being groomed for professional careers. Although there is a new emphasis on training and credentialing, some young women still leave school early, and with only minimal qualifications are seriously disadvantaged when they seek work. As Chisholm (1997, p. 111) argues, they 'are most likely to enter and remain in the most vulnerable, insecure and poorly paid sectors of the labour market.' Without the educational qualifications that have become so important to securing work, and without the fallback of the traditional industries, such young women find themselves in and out of the welfare system, in unsafe, insecure and exploitative work situations, and at the fringes of the formal economy.

> I started off and it was alright then my boss started getting really bitchy ... She pushed me into a hot rack and I had a burn mark from that ... I wasn't getting paid overtime. I was supposed to work from 6.30am until 3.30pm with an hour for lunch. I was lucky to be out by 4.30pm ... I haven't been able to get work since then, there is basically nothing in this small town. I go around and ask everyone in all of the shops and everything. There aren't any jobs. (Kylie, 20, countryside, Australia, quoted in Dale *et al.*, 1998, pp. 192–3.)

The work that is available to this group of young women tends to be short-term, casual and/or part-time, and may not bring in a living wage or any job security. Further, this work is more likely to be unregulated, and to be lacking basic protections and rights such as adequate breaks and minimum wage. However, because even insecure and poorly paid work is in demand, young women are reluctant to complain about inadequate conditions for fear of losing their jobs, and hence exploitation is rife. Research has found many instances of such exploitation in the form of harassment, bullying and unfair dismissal (see for example Bessant & Cook, 1998).

The expansion of the service sector has provided the greatest opportunities for young women who are early or minimum level school leavers, but it is in this industry that exploitation is often at its worst. Unskilled positions in the service sector are some of the only places available to vulnerable young female workers, but they tend to become trapped in deadend jobs with no chance for promotion, wage increase or improved job security (see Walkerdine *et al.*, 2001, p. 67). The prevalence of young unskilled women in this sector has been noted with concern by many, for the majority of them are trapped at the lowest levels with no clear way to move up (see for example, Furlong & Cartmel, 1997, p. 30; Wyn & White,

1997, p. 109; Wooden, 1998). The growth in service and the disappearance of manufacturing has had a particular impact on some young unskilled women more than others. For example, in Anglo countries, those of non-English speaking background are particularly disadvantaged due to the emphasis on English language proficiency in the service sector, alongside the absence of public provision of adequate language programmes (Gregory, 1993). Racism is also closer to the surface in these industries, when employees are chosen according to their ability to best represent the image the company wishes to project.

> I think [my employers] believe that they [Pakistani Muslim women] don't look as professional as somebody else, I mean when they show you the uniforms and the pictures that they have in their magazines . . . it's like their way of doing it, she has nice little earrings, normally a bobbed hairstyle, perfect make-up, it's always the same sort of colours, they've got their ideas of the colours of shoes and tights they prefer too. They've got their idea of the image they are looking for and Asian girls don't fit it. (Young woman, Muslim, Pakistani, Britain, quoted in Bowlby *et al.*, 1998, p. 237.)

It is not just the restructuring of education, the labour market and the shift in industries that have affected young women's work opportunities in the new economy. The forces of de-regulation and the globalization of economies have also created new challenges for the structurally disadvantaged. Global competition has created new pressure on local economies, which are becoming increasingly stratified in order to compete with off-shore productions and the international search for the cheapest possible labour costs. The movement of work opportunities downwards from the formal economy into the informal and criminal economies has meant uncredentialled young women are also being forced outside the protections and conditions of the formal economy, in order to find work.

One example of the growth of the informal (and sometimes criminal) economy is the garment industry, where workers are often paid below-minimum wages to cut and sew clothing for subcontractors of multi-national corporations. The vast majority of garment workers are young women, often without proficiency in the dominant language and having newly migrated, with few skills, qualifications, opportunities or knowledge of their rights (see Nutter, 1997). Outsourcing, sub-contracting and sweatshopping are all modes by which this labour force is hidden and exploited. Similarly, the harvesting, processing and packing of crops has emerged as a growth sector where young vulnerable women are employed and paid the very least (see Ige, 1998). They constitute a significant proportion of the seasonal migrant farm workers who work for tiny incomes and under conditions that incur health risks, lack safety protections and insurance guarantees, and require long hours of physically demanding labour. The global economic order that has contributed to the rapid growth of the north/south wealth divide and consequent mass migration is especially exploitative of young women.

While these may be the most dramatic examples of the ways the new economy exploits the vulnerability of uncredentialled young women, there are in fact few alternatives for those who are without qualifications or skills. The welfare systems in de-industrialized countries have contracted, and unemployment provisions for youth are harder to come by. Young women are especially vulnerable to precarious livelihoods, attempting to survive through occasional state support, and short-term prospects in the formal, or more likely, informal or criminal economy (see Sweet, 1998, p. 7). For example, much cited research has pointed to young women's survival through prostitution, which has taken on the dubious status of a desirable career option for many young women in post-Communist countries, who are struggling under the marketization of the economy (see Bridger & Kay, 1996).

Challenges of Education and Training

It is not just the restructuring of the labour market that has reduced viable work opportunities for most young women. The much-vaunted emphasis on skilling and training for flexible employment has created its own challenges for many also. Thus far, we have looked at two experiences at the extremes of the labour market; the benefits gained from new opportunities and flexibility at one end, and marginalization and competition for poorly paid and exploitative work at the other. What happens in-between these two extremes, where the majority of young women probably fit? What about young women who have some advantages and resources, such as qualifications, but little social leverage, networks or capital?

We have already examined the shift in the new economy towards credentialing and skilling as prerequisites to obtaining work. For young people, and young women in particular, further education has now become almost compulsory in order to be competitive in the job market. Young women have responded quickly to this new demand, and are found in colleges and universities in far greater numbers than ever before. Thus there are many young women now in education who may previously have left school and gone directly into secure, low skilled work. Training and qualifications have now become essential to a pathway towards such work. However, the way in which training translates into good employ-ment outcomes must be closely scrutinized. The rhetoric of 'lifelong learning' and the importance of education for all young people is not necessarily matched by expanding opportunities in the labour market. Without other kinds of resources and support, many young women find that credentials do not lead to glittering careers, or even basic employment success (see Krüger, 1990; Wallace, 1994; Dwyer & Wyn, 2001, p. 131). This is particularly the case for young women who are not fluent in the dominant lan-guage (see Gregory, 1993). Put simply, the fact of young women's presence in higher education does not articulate into satisfying, secure work for all. For example, Wallace and Kovatcheva (1999, p. 120) suggest that in spite of young women spending more time in education, they tend to be found in 'feminized' educational areas that then lead to low paid jobs. Chisholm (1997, p. 112) has found that what she describes as 'credential inflation' has more of an impact on young women, because they are concentrated in fewer employment sectors, and hence face greater competition from one another.

Most young women find themselves obliged to train and become credentialed for work in the new economy, but tend to be limited to work in the emergent sales, service and communications indus-tries. Remaining in education is not necessarily a personal prefer-ence, but a consequence of the new demands of the service sector for 'qualified' young women (see Furlong & Cartmel, 1997, p. 35). Both education and career 'choices' are actually primarily dictated by the reduced employment opportunities of the contemporary labour market. Whilst the young women who train for and are employed in these sectors are also told that 'girls can do anything', their choices are in fact delimited by their lack of resources on the one hand and the diminishing youth job market on the other. At the same time, enduring ideas about appropriate race and cultural roles also cut across the broader discourse of young women's opportunity. For example, Lopez (2003, p. 56) refers to several studies that demonstrate how US schools 'socialize White and Black girls to occupy dominant and subordinate positions in the larger society'. Similarly, Mirza (1992) has found that young Afro-Caribbean British women are perceived in schools as inappropriately aspirational. Further, trying to achieve educationally can often mean 'whitewashing' one's identity in order to get the same opportunities as the dominant culture in schools, universities and colleges (see Fordham, 1996). Chances for success are dependent on matching an homogeneous image of a high-achieving young woman, which is characterized by whiteness, or at the least, distancing oneself from a minority identity.

> . . . you know you are different because you are like the only person that is Hispanic here [Best Academy]. But you don't see people like pointing [you] out because you are different. So, I would say that knowing you are Hispanic is just enough. Don't change because, you know, maybe by coming here, you like figure out that you have to change because you are the only one, and you don't want to be the only one. But I would [say], just don't change. Be yourself. (Beth, Puerto Rican, young woman at privileged private girls' school, USA, quoted in Proweller, 1998, p. 117.)

Increasingly, training is also filling the space between school and work for those who do not find employment quickly. Compulsory youth training schemes have become a common accompaniment to, or replacement for, unemployment provisions and other forms of welfare provided to young people who are marginalized by the labour market. These have been criticized for failing to provide real work opportunities, for reproducing gender stereotyping, and for misleading youth about their prospects (see Furlong & Cartmel, 1997, p. 32; Wallace, 1994, p. 46; Heinz, 1995). There has been considerable criticism of vocational training for young women with disabilities in particular; as Froschl, Rubin and Sprung (1999, p. 6) argue, 'In addition to being channeled into historically female fields . . . women with disabilities often feel pressure . . . to pursue a career in disability-related fields, such as social work, rehabilitation counseling, or special education'.

It is also the case that unrealistic expectations are often cultivated by training schemes, such that young people, and young women in particular, imagine exciting careers or even just the guarantee of work upon completion of a course, when these are not the outcome (see Jones & Wallace, 1992, p. 42; Gregory, 1993, p. 26). The strength of the narrative about girls' opportunities and unlimited freedoms, and the ways in which this is linked to the idea of young women doing well in further education, make adjustment to the realities of the job market difficult for many who participate in such schemes. For example, Bates (1993, p. 25) has found that young women who reluctantly train in areas they do not enjoy come to see their work as 'the right choice for them', in spite of having very few choices at all. Making informed choices about good training options is also often a difficult process when support is minimal and information is conflicting and confusing (see Fine & Weis, 1998). Finding and choosing appropriate and useful training that sets one on a track for prospects can be a matter of luck in access to resources and support.

> When they talk about confidence and liking yourself . . . you do things you think you wouldn't do. Even coming on the course, I didn't think I would come back. I went and saw my case manager and asked if I could enrol myself in a course. The one I was going to do was a retail skills course. I went to the [accommodation and youth support agency] info session on the types of courses, then decided to change. (Jann, young woman, countryside, undertaking job and course preparation training, Australia, quoted in Angwin, 2000, p. 102.)

Roker's (1993) research with successful middle-class girls in private education demonstrates how career success is in fact a matter of intricate planning on the part of the school and family, for whom the young woman's future becomes a project in itself. Good outcomes are the result of the enormous resources and economic and social capital at her disposal, as well as her capacity to take advantage of elite networks for employment and education opportunities beyond the immediate youth job market. It is not surprising that both Roker (1993, p. 135) and Yates (2000, p. 157–8) have found that privileged young women express the idea that individual effort is the key factor in career opportunities. However, the pressures of the 'choice biography' also come to bear on those who have, in reality, very little choice about their educational and employment pathways. Bates' (1993) research suggests that this narrative remains powerful even with those who do not have the other resources to become successful in the new economy. It is no wonder that even disadvantaged young women often speak of opportunities being open to all, and success being dependent on effort alone (see Rudd & Evans, 1998).

Ideas of girl power, freedom, choice and individualism translate easily into the economic context, in spite of the very real structural limitations of the new economy that differentially affect young women's educational and employment opportunities. These concepts are offered to all young women to take up, and as a consequence, lack of success must be attributed to personal failings and lack of effort. The power of new narratives of girlhood are realized in young women's grappling with the late modern economy. The self-inventing subject, who is girl-powered, resilient and flexible (or can be forged thus through therapies, self-help books and workshops) is a seductive position for them. To successfully make a project of oneself is to be richly rewarded in this economy. However, those who are unable to make the 'right' choices, who in fact lack the resources and structural opportunities to prevail as choice biographers, must bear the burden of personal failure.

Success Without Work?

> You've got to challenge yourself. At the end of the day you have got to have belief, you've got to get what you want for your full potential, not for anyone else – this job – it's your one and only chance to make sure you're happy. (Girl, 13, Britain, quoted in Katz, 1997, p. 12.)

New education and employment opportunities offer many young women different pathways towards success than those available to previous generations. However, to what extent are these pathways more limited than they first seem? The pressure to make good choices in a restructured labour market is one effect of these opportunities, for the risks of failure are also considerable. These pressures are felt by both those who are privileged and others who are marginalized, albeit in different ways and with different consequences. It is no wonder that research has found that employment and lack of money are the main causes of stress for young women (Holmes & Silverman, 1992; Brown et al., 1998). The need to succeed professionally is also a new development in young women's lives. One emerging phenomenon that responds to this is young women's valuing of other priorities in life apart from work. At the same time that employment and training options are open to them like never before, many of them are questioning whether this is the only track towards happiness and fulfilment in life. For example, Dwyer and Wyn (2001, p. 31) have found in their large scale longitudinal Australian research that young women place a higher priority on developing personal relationships (87%) and family/home life (93%) than on careers (76%). Three quarters of them also emphasize health and fitness issues. They say 'evidence such as this demonstrates how a narrow preoccupation with just the two dimensions of study and work in the lives of young people leaves out so much of what really counts in their lives and gives a false picture of the choices they are making and the reasons underlying them'. This development is important because it suggests that the ways in which young women are offered success, choice and achievement may appear to be empowering, but experienced as limiting.

> you get the feeling that if you don't go out and do this BIG JOB to make you all this money, you're nothing! If you just stay home . . . everyone's saying, 'what a loser!' (Sandra, working-class, countryside, Canada, quoted in Hughes-Bond, 1998, p. 286.)

While the importance placed on relationships, community, leisure, spirituality and so on can be interpreted as a sign of dissatisfaction with limiting notions of adulthood and power based on economic grounds, it can also be seen as a manifestation of individualization. A focus on personal growth and relationships, and attention to health, appearance and well-being, are all ways of regulating and working on the self even in its most private aspects. This prioritizing of the self – psychologically, physically and in relation with others – is consistent with a discourse of self-invention and self-surveillance that locates the chance of a good life with the individual and their personal effort. As Walkerdine, Melody and Lucey (2001, p. 8) argue, in the absence of secure work, a focus on personal transformation is 'a means to keep at bay loss of status and poverty in this changing world', whilst also suggesting that such effort is the best way to stave this off. Other youth researchers have argued that personal style and attention to both health and appearance have become important ways that young people do their identity work at a time when employment is receding as a site of self-making (see for example, Miles, 2000; Ball *et al.*, 2000). In other words, this is not a 'choice' between two equally available options, but a prioritizing of one in light of reduced opportunities to achieve the other. The meanings of a shift in focus from work to personal life for young women is thus worth watching closely.

Conclusion

This chapter has explored the effects of the new economy on young women's education and labour market opportunities. Young people's experiences of education have become more and more specialized and individualized, as well as increasingly characterized by marketization and the logic of consumption. Youth transitions from school to work have changed radically since de-industrialization, and in particular, since the collapse of the youth job market. For some young women, the new economy and the accompanying narratives of opportunities and flexibility have meant career developments and choices that were unthinkable a generation ago. For many others, however, the absence of traditional kinds of work for unskilled youth, the compulsory nature of training, and the lack of secure work in the new job sectors, have led to enormous economic difficulties.

Analysing more closely where a diversity of young women fits into this new economic picture means that ideas about girls 'outperforming' boys in education and grabbing the best of the jobs in the new labour market must also be scrutinized carefully. Whilst young women are participating in higher education in greater numbers, they are not all finding more rewarding or secure modes of livelihood as a consequence. Many young women are advantaged by flexibility and the opening up of the professions, but as Walkerdine, Lucey and Melody (2001) suggest, due to their class location, these young women would have succeeded anyway. More troubling is the situation for young women who are experiencing insecurity and poverty as a consequence of de-industrialization.

The narrative of choice biographies in relation to education and employment tends to devolve responsibility for work on to the individual, and hence disregard the structural conditions that make opportunities in the new economy a highly selective experience. At the same time, many young women are at the vanguard of efforts to re-think meanings of achievement beyond work, and open up new ways for thinking about measures for success.

CHAPTER 4

Girls and the Changing Family

Introduction

Group discussion:
Rachel: I don't want to get married. I want to get my own job and do it all myself, have everything, just for me . . . I want a boyfriend, but I don't want to get married. . . . I want a good job, and maybe one kid. And I want to be able to, like, party once in a while on the weekends.
Diane: But no husband? Is that what you mean? One kid but you don't necessarily need a father?
Rachel: I need a boyfriend who is the father.
Diane: But he doesn't live there?
Rachel: Sometimes, most of the time, but he has his own house.
Diane: So you want control of your own place, no matter what?
Rachel: Control of everything myself.

(Rachel, 13, working-class, Mansfield, USA,
quoted in Brown, 1998, pp. 61–2.)

In this chapter, we explore a social institution that has historically been associated with girls and women, namely the family. The realm of the family has undergone considerable changes in Western societies within the past few decades, in connection with other sweeping social transformations, particularly in working-life, which was explored in the previous chapter. At the same time, understandings of family roles and family members' relations to each other, as well as practices connected to them have also altered considerably (see Silva & Smart (eds), 1999). Many of these changes have been attributed to women's redefined position in society.

A larger proportion of women have jobs outside of the home than ever before. The percentage of full-time home-makers has

decreased considerably (Gerson, 1991). Divorce rates have multiplied compared to the first part of the twentieth century (Beck &
Beck-Gernsheim, 1995), and various types of alternatives to the traditional heterosexual nuclear family have become more common
(Silva & Smart (eds), 1999). Many young people are postponing
marriage, while many couples are also choosing to cohabit without
marrying. The proportion of single people has increased considerably, particularly within urban areas (Gordon, 1994, pp. 21–2).
There are also more single parents, and many of them are young
women. Global migration has also had its effect in the diversification of family models within Western societies. It has even been
claimed that there is no longer a single culturally dominant family
pattern (Stacey, 1991, p. 19). Even popular cultural representations
of families have become more diverse in the past decades, showing
a wider range of family types as well as altered relations between
family members (see Kaplan, 1992; MacDonald, 1995).

Conceptions of childhood, youth and adulthood as life-phases
have also been renegotiated during recent decades, and people's
life-courses have become more individualized (Buchmann, 1989;
Wyn & White, 1997). Children's position within the family has
gradually been altered, as families consist of fewer children than
before, and the cultural ideals and practices concerning their
upbringing have generally become more liberal and child-centred
(see Hays, 1996). Children's and young people's everyday lives
have also gradually become more structured and supervised by
adults to a growing extent, with the increasing professionalization
of children's daycare and education, and even their freetime activities (see Fine & Mechling, 1991).

In today's late modern societies the public and private spheres
are in constant interaction with one another, each feeding into
and affecting the other. Families are no exception: they are deeply
affected by various social institutions and changes within them,
such as the gender system, educational institutions, social policies
and work life, to name only a few examples. Families have to adapt
to outside influences to a considerable degree; for example, they
often have to negotiate their timetables in relation to those of educational institutions, as well as those of work. The state has certain
demands and responsibilities it expects families to fulfill in relation
to the upbringing of their young. And families have a crucial role
in translating society's demands for their children.

While there has been a great deal of worry and conflict regarding the future of the family, as a result of these many changes, the

situation can also be approached from the viewpoint of new possibilities and alternative ways of understanding the family. We shall
concentrate particularly on the shifting positions of girls and young
women as daughters growing up within (or without) their families
of origin, and their possibilities of negotiating new kinds of family
futures for themselves.

Families in Crisis?

The public discourses surrounding the family have mainly focused
on the problematic aspects of the above-mentioned changes in the
family sphere. In many countries there has been a heated discussion about the 'erosion (or crisis) of the family' and its causes (see
Silva & Smart (eds), 1999). The problems of the family have been
attributed to, among other things, the changing position of women
in society. Women are no longer as likely to stay in unsatisfactory
marriages, as their economic independence has increased with
their growing engagement in the paid labour force (Beck & Beck-
Gernsheim, 1995; Silva & Smart (eds), 1999; Stacey, 1991).

Also, it has been claimed in countries where services, such as
children's daycare services and care for the elderly and disabled
are provided by the state, that there has been a blurring of the
public and the private. Many functions which were previously
the responsibility of the family, and particularly the women of the
family, were gradually moved outside of the family, to social
institutions funded publicly by the state, in the 1970s and 1980s.
However, since the 1990s, new economic policies have undermined
this development. As a result, many public services have been pri-
vatized or discontinued, and considerable monetary cuts have been
made in various social programs. Families with small children have
often been affected the most (Julkunen, 2001).

Simultaneously, there has been a strong international outcry for
the 'revival of lost parenthood', as educational experts have
claimed that parents have abandoned their children for the sake of
their careers (see Jallinoja, 2004). While this is a gross exaggeration,
it can be confirmed that working life has globally undergone huge
changes, many of which place considerable pressures on the family
(see Chapter 3). More and more people are routinely required to
work overtime, at the same time as many, particularly professionals in prestigious positions, are also finding their work life a more
satisfactory part of their life than their family life, and therefore

investing more of their time and energy in their work careers than in their families (see Hochschild, 1997).

The criticism towards parents is strongly gendered and concerns mothers more than fathers: it is precisely career mothers who are blamed most severely for forsaking their children for their careers. Even women who are not yet mothers, are sometimes blamed for being too career-oriented. Ambitious middle-class young women are reportedly postponing motherhood until well into their late twenties and thirties, and a growing number of them are also choosing never to have children. For many women, it has become difficult, if not impossible, to combine family with a working career, and having to choose between the two – although emotionally difficult – is becoming increasingly prevalent for today's young women (Hays, 1996).

Further, the crisis discourse of girlhood, analysed more extensively in Chapter 2, has emphasized the negative consequences of the changing family sphere particularly on girls. Pipher claims that today's 'families are under siege', and that 'parents are more likely to be overworked, overcommitted, tired and poor', and 'less likely to have outside support' than before (Pipher, 1994, p. 80). As a result, she says, girls of today 'navigate a more dangerous world but are less protected' than previous generations of girls, which makes them more vulnerable to trauma (Pipher, 1994, p. 22).

Pipher's laments, although influential, are only one voice in a choir that has expressed serious concerns about the state of the family in recent years. In Britain, for example, policy makers have feared that the growing diversity within the family sphere is a sign of the demise of the family, and there has been a push for 'restrengthening the family' (see Silva & Smart (eds), 1999). However, as Silva and Smart (1999, p. 6) argue, despite changes in family forms, the role of families as agents of emotional support and transmitters of cultural capital has increased, not decreased. They claim that holding on to monolithic views of 'the family' may actually cause further social problems rather than help solve them. Instead, they vouch for more openness towards family diversity in the society, and for the recognition that families are a context of fluid relationships rather than stable entities (Silva & Smart, 1999, pp. 5–7). Indeed, there is considerable false nostalgia for a past when the ideal heterosexual nuclear family is imagined to have dominated. Family diversity has been longstanding, if unacknowledged. For example, Barron (1997, p. 235) points out that young women with disabilities are often raised by large numbers of adults, experiencing a type of extended family through various caregivers, role models and service providers beyond their parents. Many cultures hold that child rearing is a responsibility that ought to be shared, and in some indigenous communities, for example, adults have formal duties in the bringing up of children who are their 'family' even if they have no biological connection to them.

Interestingly, although social policies have lagged behind the actual diversification of family forms, at least the popular representations of the family have become, according to many researchers, more diverse. Recent media narratives – both documentary and fictional – include images – even if still rare – of single and divorced mothers having and raising children alone, gay and lesbian partnerships, divorcees forming new families with both parents' children from previous marriages, and so on (see Silbergleid, 2002; MacDonald, 1995; Kaplan, 1992). Feminism has had some influence on the representations of women, particularly those of mothers, in the popular culture, while there is still no shortage of more traditional gender representations (MacDonald, 1995; Kaplan, 1992). Some of the new portrayals of nuclear families are clearly intended to be 'read' as ironic, playing with and commenting on the former representations of the rigid patriarchal family, where both gender relations and generational relations remained unchallenged.

Such representations, for example, the internationally popular TV family comedy series portraying a 'typical American family', (albeit in an animated version) 'The Simpsons', revealingly depict the far-from-harmonious life of suburban families. Similar themes can be discerned in the widely acclaimed movies focusing on families and family members' relations with each other such as 'American Beauty' (1999) and 'The Ice Storm' (1997). A contemporary family show may include a mixture of characters such as an unemployed father whose greatest desire is to have sex with his daughter's friend, a daughter with a drug habit, a gay activist son, as well as a sexually frustrated mother with a lover. There are other, even more challenging symbolic reworkings on such family-related themes as mothering, as in the Aliens-movies (see MacDonald, 1995, pp. 152–4). However, while these new family representations have drawn some research interest, as indicated above, the changing role of the movie/TV-daughters in them has not received much attention.

Renegotiating Generational and Gender Positions within the Family

The realm of the family as the context for young people's growing up process has been a neglected area within youth research. Liza Catan suggests that this is partly because there has been a 'cultural predilection' in Western societies that emphasizes young people's early independence and their 'existence as free-standing individuals in the areas of work, training and leisure activities' (Catan, 2001). Catan speculates that this representation of youth has been eagerly promoted by the media and the consumer industries, who benefit from portraying the young as independent consumers and free-standing creators of culture and fashion. Young people actually often strive to leave their family home relatively early, but they often continue to be financially dependent on their families long after they leave home (Catan, 2001).

Families continue to be of primary importance in determining the futures of their children, in an interaction with other social institutions shaping youth transitions (see Wyn & White, 1997). As Pat Allatt (1996) has pointed out, youth transitions are based on a cumulation of earlier, childhood transitions. The material, cultural and social resources that have or have not been available within a particular family environment, have a huge impact on a young person's access to choices. Without such resources, even young people with ambition have great difficulties in negotiating their way towards adulthood (see for example Thomson *et al.*, 2003).

To explore the relationship of the family and young people's lives further, it can be argued that changes in the family sphere have actually had a strong impact in the current cultural understandings and formulations of youth as a life-phase in itself. Similarly, the changing position of young people in society has deeply affected family relations, generational roles and practices within families. However, there are considerable national as well as social differences in cultural practices and attitudes concerning young people's relation with their families.

The period of youth has been extended from both ends particularly after the Second World War, resulting in the creation of a long in-between period between childhood and adulthood, during which young people's social status is unclear. They remain strongly dependent on their families of origin economically, regardless of whether they live in their childhood home or elsewhere, while continuing their studies and trying to get established in unstable labour markets (Buchmann, 1989). This is in stark contrast with young people's position as a special target group within the capitalist consumer market, where particular clothing styles, sports equipment and other consumer goods are designed and marketed especially for young people with independent lifestyles and disposable income (see Quart, 2003).

As a result of changing parenting ideologies and declining family sizes, the meanings of generational positions within families have been redefined. Parents in the twenty-first century Western societies are more likely to negotiate with their children over decisions that affect them, than dictate unequivocally what they can or cannot do (Hoikkala, 1993; Hays, 1996). These changes have been seen as typical to late modernity: there are increasing pressures on individuals to make continuous decisions about various aspects of their lives even at a relatively young age (Furlong & Cartmel, 1997). Therefore, in many families parents try to encourage their children's individual agency: they are to grow up as autonomous subjects, ready to take responsibility over constructing their lives in an increasingly confusing web of choices (Wyn & White, 1997). However, even within a particular society, families may have widely differing attitudes and practices regarding their children's upbringing, depending on their social, cultural, ethnic and religious backgrounds.

While the more liberal and less authoritarian styles of parenting have been widely accepted, they have also raised suspicion. Mary Pipher, for example, (1994), in the US context, posits that daughters with loving but strict parents usually have an easier time in adolescence than middle-class daughters of less controlling parents. She claims that daughters from more controlling families do not have an equal burden in making choices in a confusing world, as their parents have already chosen for them. Many other girls feel they do not get enough support in making difficult decisions, according to Pipher (1994). Nevertheless, in Pipher's view the stricter style of parenting daughters is not unequivocally the 'best style'. Pipher argues that even other kinds of parenting may also result in a successful adulthood, although perhaps with more problems during the daughter's growing up process. (Pipher, 1994, pp. 99–100).

Interestingly, the neo-liberal discourse of 'making individual choices' is portrayed as particularly problematic to girls in adolescence by Pipher (1994). A curious omission is the importance of social differences; the varying extent to which daughters from families from differing social backgrounds can draw on material and social resources in making their choices, is probably even more important than the kind of parenting style their parents exercise (see Allatt, 1996; Walkerdine *et al.*, 2001).

> He's [my father] always saying: 'Oh, you'll never do that'. He wants to push me to do better so he thinks if he says that, I'll try and prove him wrong, and I try to do my best. But he's never encouraged me, never. (Maria, 19, Greek-Cypriot, quoted in Sharpe, 1994, p. 41.)

Many aspects of the late modern experience of youth create tensions within families: there are constant negotiations about young people's rights and responsibilities, freedoms and obligations for as long as they stay in their parental homes, and sometimes even after they move away. These negotiations regarding generational relations within the family are deeply gendered. For girls and young women there are increasing tensions between their simultaneous but contradictory positions within the family as 'dutiful daughters' and 'autonomous young adults'. Girls have to balance the gender-neutralizing neo-liberal ideas of individualization and of exercising independent rights in society with the recognition of the continuing importance of the family as a community, and the multilayered gendered interdependencies between family members that require constant renegotiation. For example, girls are still often expected to baby-sit for younger siblings, prepare food and clean at home more than boys (see Niemi & Pääkkönen, 1995, p. 44), while most parents also consider it important for girls to acquire an education for themselves. However, there are important differences between families from different ethnic, social and cultural backgrounds and what they expect from their young, and these expectations are further complicated by the prevailing social and economic contexts.

In a study focusing on Mexican American families who had recently migrated to the United States, it was found that their daughters were caught between two forms of gendered social control; one that was related to their family experiences, and another, related to their schooling experiences in the US (Williams *et al.*, 2002). At home, these girls were expected to help their families by assuming caretaker duties, such as childcare, previously held by their mothers. Now their mothers were working outside of the home, and in the changed situation, the daughters were expected to take on more household chores than they would have been expected to in their homeland, where the extended family shielded young girls from such demands. Their brothers, on the other hand, were expected to take jobs outside of the home. One of the girls interviewed in the study said that nowadays she had to take care of her younger siblings, but that she preferred it to work outside of the home, which she had tried for a while. However, her family rather has her stay at home (Williams *et al.*, 2002, p. 572).

However, even if the girls had to, out of obligation to their families, help at home, they resisted the historically conventional idea of a 'domesticated Latina'. They aspired to become professionals through education, even if it was not easy for them in the US school system, where they were seen as headed for a domestic career and/or the lower service sector labour market (Williams *et al.*, 2002, pp. 572–3).

Diverse Families, Diverse Futures for Daughters?

As seen above, the regulation of femininity varies between various ethnic groups, as well as according to social background. Middle-class and working-class girls are both socially regulated, but in different ways. Walkerdine and her colleagues claim in their study that middle-class girls become gradually trained in self-regulation and learn to pursue their educational and career goals in a rational and determined manner. This process is described by the research group as the 'conveyor belt' (Walkerdine *et al.*, 2001). (Upper)middle-class daughters are not 'allowed to fail', according to Walkerdine and her research group: both the girls' parents and their teachers demand from them dedication both to school-work and even to valuable extra-curricular hobbies, and the girls gradually learnt to demand them from themselves.

> I had musicianship classes, orchestra, I actually had more orchestra, choir, quartet, quintet, piano lessons, violin lessons . . . if you do something and you don't do it well . . . I didn't do it well, you didn't want people to think that I couldn't do something well. If I can't – if I couldn't do it well I wouldn't do it at all. (Hannah, white, middle-class, quoted in Walkerdine *et al.*, 2001, p. 179.)

At the same time, working-class young women are subjected to a more external surveillance by the various educational, social and medical experts they encounter, and they receive much less unequivocal support in their educational path. The working-class women who succeeded best in the educational system, had parents with some experience with further studies. However, even when the young women from working-class backgrounds went on to higher education, they had to tackle difficult issues regarding their social identities and new social positions, fearing alienation from their families of origin on the one hand, while not fully belonging to the social group achieved through education (Walkerdine *et al.*, 2001, pp. 187–210).

Ethnic background is another important axis of social difference. Most of the young women in Walkerdine's and her colleagues' study were white, but Heidi Safia Mirza's study focused on the varying educational experiences and attitudes of young women-of-colour and their parents in Britain (Mirza, 1992). According to her, black families are often treated as an homogeneous group, although their class positions vary in the same way as their white counterparts, even if their experiences are always marked by their disadvantaged position in a racially prejudiced British society (Mirza, 1992). Mirza found that her informants, young women of West Indian background had, at the threshold of a school-to-work transition, regardless of their parents' occupational status, relatively high, although realistic, career aspirations. The parents of the young women often offered strong moral support, and when possible, also financial support, but generally had to rely heavily on the school to provide the academic help their daughters required. The interviewees' parents – most of them first-generation settlers from the Caribbean – saw education as an important asset in the social struggle to secure a better life for their children. The young women, similarly, did not aspire to similar occupations as their mothers: they wanted to do better, even if they admired their mothers, as one of them argued:

> I don't want to rely on anyone. What I want is a good job as I would like my life to be as comfortable as possible, and have a nice environment to live in so my children can grow up with everything they require. (Laurie, 16, West Indian descent, Britain, quoted in Mirza 1992, p. 154.)

Mirza (1992) compared the young women-of-colour to another group of young women with a migrant background, white young women of Irish descent. They, in turn, expressed little ambition in careers, and instead expected not to work outside the home after getting married. As both of these groups went to similar schools and lived in the same neighbourhoods, Mirza interpreted the different future occupational visions of these two groups of young women as resulting from a different cultural gender system. In Irish society, women have traditionally been home-makers, and men have been responsible for providing the income for the family. In contrast, in the West Indian community, men and women have held more equal positions, as two incomes have usually been necessary for sustaining the family. Many women also strive for economic independence, as single parenthood has often been a part of the Caribbean women's life-course (Mirza, 1992).

Parents from different backgrounds have a range of ways of supporting their children (see Thomson *et al.*, 2003). All kinds of families try to enhance their children's prospects, but with varying strategies. Some families actively choose between schools, trying to secure their children a good education, while others try to promote in their children a gradual transition to reduced parental monitoring and increased responsibility over their own homework, and still others try to direct their children to hobbies that they hope will increase their options into desirable occupations (Allatt, 1996).

> They really want their daughters to do well like them so they sort of plan it for their kids, so if their kids like it (job), well sure; or else they'll pick something else that's in their parents' class, sort of ... (Mona, working class, Pacific Islander, New Zealand, quoted in Jones, 1991, p. 168.)

However, it is particularly educated, professional upper- and middle-class parents who have the most cultural, economic and social resources to invest in their children's education and well-being (see Vanttaja, 2002). Today middle-class parents usually expect both their daughters and sons to have professional careers, while in the past daughters were not necessarily encouraged to do so. As Walkerdine and her colleagues argue, while middle-class young women have successfully entered many of the previously male-dominated occupational fields, they have done so to a considerable emotional price. They have had to abandon ideas of early motherhood, and often ignore the emotional sides of themselves in order to succeed in the rational world of education and work (Walkerdine *et al.*, 2001).

In late capitalism, the social divisions between the well-to-do and the socially marginalized are growing, not diminishing

(Furlong & Cartmel, 1997). Social disadvantages such as unemployment and substance abuse tend to get passed on from one generation to the next within the family, creating a continuum of social marginalization, if there are no efficient social policies to counteract this process. Gill Jones and Robert Bell (2000) have argued that in the United Kingdom, the social policies since the 1980s have created an uncertain situation, where there is no legislation about the actual extended responsibilities of parents of young people over the age of 18 but below 25. The social policies that have been augmented simply assume that parents are willing and able to provide sufficient support for their young (Jones & Bell, 2000, cited in Catan, 2001). Similar kinds of social policies have been applied in other countries as well. As a result, young people under the age of 25 have been denied many social benefits they were able to claim before, thus making them more dependent on the financial help from their parents and other sources of income.

The amount of parental support to their young is, however, not necessarily directly dependent on the parents' income. The majority of parents increasingly provide at least partial support for their adult children, but this depends on the family resources as well as on the personal relationships within the family, and it is essentially a private agreement, requiring a lot of intricate negotiation (see Catan, 2001). As Andy Furlong and Fred Cartmel (1997) suggest, these changes in social policy have postponed many young people's transition to adulthood and forced them into a prolonged period of semi-dependence on their families. Their citizenship has thus become more questionable (Jones & Wallace, 1992; Wyn & White, 1997).

Daughters, Parents and Control

My ma don't let me do nothin'! I like to go places. She won't let me go to a party jus' out kickin' it with my friends. She wants me home at 6 pm, before dark! I ditched the whole six weeks of summer school. We went to 'ditching parties'. I need more freedom to just do what I got to do! (Denise, 15, USA, quoted in Schaffner, 1998, p. 276.)

While youth research has not had much to say about family relations, that has not been the case with feminist and gender studies. For decades, feminist critiques have attacked the traditional patriarchal family model, and problematized the monolithic family ideology as disadvantageous for women. For example, the unequal gender division of housework and the invisibility of domestic violence against women and its dire consequences have been criticized heavily (see for example Thorne, 1982; Gittins, 1985; Abbott & Wallace, 1990; Gordon, 1990).

Although the family has been constructed as the best option for raising children and young people, not all families work. In the worst case, family relationships can be abusive and violent, and some families simply fail to provide the amount of emotional care and support, or even the basic material resources that children and young people require (Pallotta-Chiarolli, 1998, pp. 120–1). In many countries, there is a growing number of homeless young people, whose parents have not been able to provide for them for various reasons, or who have been thrown out of their homes for being gay or have escaped other forms of abusive family relationships. These young people often receive no education, and they are vulnerable to further violence, sexual exploitation and substance abuse (see Jones & Wallace, 1992).

The patriarchal family model, idealized in images of the 1950s in the United States, was based on the male breadwinner and the female housewife and their dependent children who formed a family. Home was seen as primarily a site for leisure and consumption, where the mother provided for other family members' emotional and material needs (Silva & Smart, 1999, p. 6). This model still has a strong effect on family practices, although society and gender roles have changed considerably since then. It has been pointed out by feminist critiques that mothers, even when they have full-time jobs outside of the home, continue to bear the brunt of domestic responsibilities, with most fathers only 'helping out' with the household chores. Statistics also indicate that the gender division applies even to the family's children: girls spend more time on housework duties at home than boys (for example Niemi & Pääkkönen, 1995, p. 44). While there are trends indicating changes in the gendered distribution of housework and childcare, towards a more egalitarian model, the process is relatively slow.

The composition of family relationships has been central even in defining young people's development. In traditional psychological theories on adolescent development, girls have been seen as more dependent on other people, particularly their families, than boys (see for example Erikson, 1968). It has also been believed that in adolescence it is necessary for a young person to 'rebel' against adult authorities, including parents. If a young person does not

demonstrate a sufficient level of independence in relation to
his/her parents, s/he is labelled as having a problematic transition
to adulthood. The emphasis on young people's independence has
been quite influential in creating an image of youth where families
appear marginal in relation to peer culture, education and leisure
activities. This image is, however, highly problematic, as it does not
take into account differences between various types of families and
different cultures.

Feminist critiques have questioned the whole presupposition
about the necessity of rebellion for reaching a successful adulthood.
They point to serious problems within traditional developmental
theories: they are heavily biased and actually refer mainly to white,
male, middle-class young people: girls and young women,
working-class youth have been shown as curious exceptions in the
male-centred model, and cultural differences have not usually been
taken into account (see, however, Erikson, 1968, p. 93). The developmental theories have thus emphasized the autonomous individual at the expense of relationships, neglecting the centrality of the
family in young women's lives (see Jordan *et al.*, 1991; Taylor *et al.*,
1995). This is a highly problematic omission.

For example, in her study on Finnish teenaged girls who played
in amateur rock bands, Jarna Knuuttila (1997) showed that while
the girls in her study scored highly on levels of independence, they
nevertheless emphasized the importance and warmth of their
relationships with their families, particularly with their mothers.
Their independence had not been gained by rebelling against their
parents. Other researchers have come to similar conclusions. In a
British study, ethnic background made a difference in young
women's attitudes towards their own autonomy: girls from Asian
backgrounds reported that they took their whole family community more into consideration when making decisions, and did not
only emphasize their own individualistic goals (Woollett &
Marshall, 1996, p. 210).

Rebellion against or separation from one's parents are not necessary precursors in young people's development into adulthood,
even if the individualist ideology places a strong emphasis on a
young person's growing independence over decisions affecting
his/her life, as well as his/her gradual separation from the family.
In many cultures the parent-child-relations are seen differently.
In a US-based study, the daughters of Vietnamese American
parents spoke about a strong value set upon family relationships,

as well as the effects it had on their lives (Zhou & Bankston, 1998).

> This may sound very silly, but a youngster who is becoming too American is the one who is having too much fun, too much fun in doing non-typical Vietnamese things such as enjoying yourself, unwilling to do hard work, and not obligating yourself to your family's best interests. To be an American, you may be able to do whatever you want. But to be a Vietnamese, you must think of your family first. (College student, Vietnamese, quoted in Zhou & Bankston, 1998, pp. 165–6.)

Another constant claim regarding family relations is that girls are restricted by their parents more than boys (see Katz, 1993). While the current parental attitudes may favour a less controlling approach to the upbringing of children, it still seems that the daughters' movements and timetables are often controlled more tightly than the sons', in order to protect them. Daughters may even be controlled more strictly as they get older (Katz *et al.*, 1993, pp. 88–106). Young women with disabilities are often 'protected' by families and caregivers in ways that are particularly delimiting. The National Information Center for Children and Youth with Disabilities (NICHCY) (1990, p. 2) quotes a parent thus: 'I try not to think about Sarah having an apartment, being independent'. The NICHCY (1990, p. 1) argues that 'while issues of independence and self-determination obviously apply to sons with disabilities as well as daughters, the degree to which daughters with a disability are encouraged to strive for an independent life may be critically less'. In times that are felt to be risky and unpredictable, young women with disabilities are perceived as even more vulnerable and frequently subject to greater, if well-meaning, control.

There are also stereotypical notions concerning families of different ethnic backgrounds; it is thought that many immigrant families, particularly Muslim and those of Asian origins, restrict their daughters more severely than white families (see for example Pyke & Johnson, 2003; Zhou & Bankston, 1998). According to the observations of Karen Pyke and Denise Johnson in the United States, even daughters of Asian immigrants themselves upheld bipolar views, constructing the white American culture as a prototype of gender equality, and their own Asian American cultural world as quintessentially patriarchal, even if they themselves reported varying experiences from both cultural contexts (Pyke & Johnson, 2003, p. 33 and 48; see Zhou & Bankston, 1998).

These dichotomic stereotypes concerning gender relations are problematic, as they do not take into account the variation that exists within every culture, and the shifting situational contexts of gender displays. They also help to 'naturalize' and 'normalize' the white family as the 'normal' family form, and all other models as inferior to it. Furthermore, immigrant cultures and their gender arrangements are likely to experience fundamental changes as a result of the family members' altered status in their new environment (Pyke & Johnson, 2003, p. 38 and 47; Williams *et al.*, 2002).

The signifiers and meanings of ethnicity in a migrant context undergo rapid change in globalizing and hybridizing environments, and these forces are often driven by youth cultures. In long-established migrant communities, first and second generations are sometimes bemused by, but often proud of, the third generation's capacity to re-invent and reclaim ethnicity. For example, Longo's study of families of Italian-Australian women found that mothers were excited that their daughters were not ashamed of being Italian (as they themselves had been), and daughters often spoke of ethnicity as 'trendy' and 'hip' (Longo, forthcoming). At the same time, however, young immigrant women in Western countries are still often presented with what appear to be two different sets of expectations; those of their family, trying to keep alive at least some aspects of the culture of their country of origin, as well as those of the surrounding society, both of which are important for them for various reasons. Often, they are in a double bind, trying to please both their teachers as well as peers in the new environment, and their family at the same time, which is hard to achieve. The young Asian American women, mentioned above, tried to solve this problem by shifting their gender displays according to the cultural context: among their relatives, at least in public, they tended to remain passive, obedient and quiet, but in mixed settings and at home with a boyfriend they could be more assertive and vocal (Pyke & Johnson, 2003, pp. 44–8). Similarly, research into Lebanese-Australian youth by Noble, Poynting and Tabar (1998) has found that young people can draw on ethnicity strategically and creatively for their own uses, for example, by being very 'Lebanese' in relation to Anglos at school (for example, in order to claim moral rights) and very 'Australian' in relation to parents (to win more freedoms). The strategic use of both cultural and gender performances depending on the context is a way in which they actively negotiate these conflicting expectations to their own benefit.

In a Finnish study (Aapola, 1999a and 2002), most girls routinely negotiated with their parents about housework, and even about such contested behaviours as the use of alcohol and smoking of cigarettes, as well as about going out and dating (see Paglia & Room, 1998). In these negotiations, both parents and their daughters frequently referred to the girls' age. The state has in most countries established legal age-limits concerning sexual relationships and the purchase of alcohol and cigarettes, and in some countries there are even curfews determining what time young people should be at home in the evening. While these legal age-limits are important in regulating young people's sexual and drinking behaviour, parents may sometimes knowingly allow their children to violate these official age-limits. For example, some of the 15 to 16 year old girls reported, in a happy tone, that their parents sometimes bought them alcoholic drinks. This indicates that many parents in Finland accept (moderate) use of alcohol as a part of their daughters' youth, even if it has formerly been more accepted for young men (Aapola, 2002). Similarly the results from a Dutch-Italian study concerning intra-familial problems and conflicts resulting from parent-child disagreements about various behaviours in adolescence confirm that differences between girls and boys were not significant (Bosma *et al.*, 1996).

However, there are often discrepancies between the way that young people see their own abilities and freedoms and how their parents regard them. In Aapola's study (1999a), girls often positioned themselves as good daughters, who wanted to please their parents, be trustworthy and simultaneously show them that they were reliable and sensible, autonomous individuals, who could make informed decisions about the kinds of activities they engaged in. They expressed their satisfaction when their parents appeared to trust them in various situations, and often proudly announced that they had not betrayed this trust (Aapola, 2002). It seems that girls tend to internalize their control, and try to take into account the feelings of others in estimating the consequences of their actions (Näre, 1992).

Negotiating Teenage Sexuality within the Family

Even if the late modern notions of youth emphasize independence in many areas of life, sexuality continues to be one of the most contested subjects between parents and daughters. This is the case although the cultural customs and attitudes related to young people's sexuality have changed considerably since the 1950s. Young people mature physically earlier, and many of them lead active sex-lives from a relatively early age. It has also generally become more acceptable for youth to engage in heterosexual pre-marital and gay sex. For example, in a 1992 survey, approximately 87 per cent of all under 55 year olds in Finland accepted sexual intercourse in young people's regular relationships, and a small percentage even in their more transient relationships (Kontula & Haavio-Mannila, 1993, pp. 59–62).

> I came out to my mom by leaving a poem on the kitchen table about a girl I liked. My mom said, 'I guess you are bisexual or something.' I said, 'Yeah, I don't think about it too much', which wasn't totally true. 'Don't you think it would be easier if you picked gay or straight?' I told her, 'Mom, I can't change the way I am.' (Angie, 17, quoted in Gray and Phillips, 1998.)

The change in the general morality regarding young people's premarital sexual experimenting has been explained by growing secularization. religious ideologies have tended to outlaw prema-rital sexual relationships, but in sex education the religious content has gradually been replaced with medical views, thus shifting the emphasis from trying to restrict young people's sexual experiments to preventing unwanted pregnancies and sexually transmitted diseases (Kontula & Haavio-Mannila, 1993, pp. 88–90). These issues will be explored further in Chapter 6.

Even if the general attitude towards girls' sexual relationships has become more tolerant, within families their relationships have to be negotiated with parents or other guardians. There may be bitter discrepancies between young people's wishes and their parents' views (Schalett, 2000). As Sari Näre has remarked, the social control of girls within families often actually means sexual control: parents want to prevent their daughters from having early sexual experiences (Näre, 1992). Even if parents are most concerned about protecting girls from being exposed to sexual harassment and violence, they often try to stop girls from engaging even in the kind of sexual activities that girls themselves would want to experiment with (Thompson, 1995). Gay, lesbian and bisexual young people face even more difficult situations regarding parental attitudes towards their sexual relationships (Valentine, 2001; Thompson, 1995).

There are significant cultural differences in the ways parents define young people's sexuality and also in their strategies in trying to control it (Schalett, 2000). For example, Schalett (2000) has found that parents from the United States tended to 'dramatize' and problematize their teenage children's sexuality and attribute it to the 'raging hormones'. As a result, they wanted to exclude their sons' and daughters' sexuality from the family context as harmful. In contrast, Dutch parents saw young people's heterosexual relationships as a normal part of their social life-phase, and often allowed their teenage children to bring their girl- and boyfriends home even for sleep-overs, thus including their children's sexual relationships in the family circle (Schalett, 2000, p. 76).

Other researchers have confirmed that attitudes towards young people's sexuality in the United States have become more strict during the 1990s, and the percentages of teenage sexual activity have been somewhat reduced (Risman & Schwartz, 2002). Abstinence education has become more and more wide-spread within the United States, and as a result, many young women have acquired what Sharon Thompson (1995) calls 'sexual fear'; she claims that it may actually lead these girls to become more easily sexually victimized than those girls who have come to accept sex as a part of their growing-up process (Thompson, 1995). In interviews with sexually active girls Thompson found that often parents did not know what their daughters were doing, as the girls were quite resourceful in hiding their sexual activities. Even in the cases where parents were physically trying to prevent their daughters from going out, they were often less than successful (Thompson, 1995, pp. 170–80).

While negotiations about teenage dating and sexuality may cause disputes in any family, this issue is often particularly heated within immigrant families. Western liberal attitudes concerning sexuality are viewed with suspicion in many cultures. In a study on Vietnamese American families, many young women spoke about their difficult task of having to balance the expectations of the American youth culture with their parents' strict views concerning dating at a young age (Zhou & Bankston, 1998, pp. 167–70). Often, they felt they were caught in between two cultures, as one of the young women testifies:

> When I was in high school, my parents did not allow me to go out on dates because they were afraid that I might get hooked up with bad guys, that I might be taken advantage of, and that I might get distracted

from my study. They worked all the time and never seemed to know there was such a thing as popularity. When they finally agreed that I could go out, they set a time when I should be at home. If I was a little late, they would get really upset. They always told me that they worried, and that I was a girl, and that girls shouldn't be out late. I had always hoped that my parents would someday open up just a little to realize that we were living in America and not in Vietnam. (College student, 19, Vietnamese American, USA, quoted in Zhou & Bankston, 1998, p. 169.)

In Aapola's study (2002), the parental attitudes reported by the girls seemed more in line with the permissive Dutch parents in Schalett's study (2000). In some cases the parents would even have allowed their daughters to have sex before the legal age-limit. However, more often than not, the young women reported that their parents tried to control their heterosexual behaviours in various ways. They would, for example, set curfews for their daughters, tell them not to start dating at a young age, and refuse to let their boyfriends stay over if they were dating, reprimand them for getting too close with boys at the disco, and so on (Aapola, 2002). Similar, often highly tense negotiations have been reported in other studies as well (Thomson, 1995). There is a constant negotiation about what is considered appropriate, as one of the girls in Aapola's study explains in her narrative:

When my boyfriend, whom I have been with for eight months, stays overnight at our place my mother thinks it is outrageous to think that my boyfriend could sleep in the same room with me but in a different bed. Sleeping in the same bed is of course out of the question. This matter is talked about every now and then and I always get the same answer. Somehow my mother just cannot speak sensibly about this, she keeps repeating her view. Of course she is afraid that I will get pregnant, but there won't be any babies if we sleep in different beds! (Girl, 15, Helsinki region, Finland, quoted in Aapola, 2002, pp. 139–40; translation from Finnish by Sinikka Aapola.)

Often, young people who choose to 'come out' to their parents risk considerably more than just getting into a fight. Some of them are actually disowned by their families, others face difficult emotional processes and are sometimes blamed for other family members' distress. Some parents may fear public shame that could result from having a non-heterosexual family member, which is why they may find it hard to accept their daughter's or son's sexual orientation (Valentine 2001; Thompson, 1995, pp. 176–83).

> Many times it seems that – on the basis of what I have talked with [gay and lesbian] people – that many experience like . . . that there is a delay in a way.. In their own – like – that you actually dare to think that you are interested in someone [of your own sex]. If it is directed at someone of the opposite sex then it is easier in a way. Then you get to practise it in your teenage years, you know, falling in love and all that. But if you cannot do that because you think 'I cannot be interested in him/her, as that is not appropriate', then you have to . . . maybe hide your whole sexuality. For a long time. And quite a few people have told me that. I don't know how it is with young people nowadays but it feels like many times gay people start to date later and everything. I don't know if it is such a bad thing, always. (Mira, 22, university student, lesbian, Finland, personal interview, translation from Finnish by Sinikka Aapola.)

However, not 'coming out' is a tough choice for the young people as well, because it may result in feeling emotionally alienated from the rest of the family, and having to hide central elements of one's life (Valentine, 2001). As Gill Valentine points out, it is important to realize that young people and their identities are always embedded in wider family relationships, and their 'individual' decisions sometimes have wide-ranging effects for the whole family and vice versa (Valentine, 2001). One of the related topics that remains relatively uncharted, is an exploration of the kinds of family relationships young lesbian women form when they find partners and start families themselves. According to Dunne (1999), lesbian couples are often actively trying to avoid the heterosexual family model and find more egalitarian ways of partnership and childraising.

Moving Out – and Back Home Again?

Young people are often expected to leave their childhood families and establish their independent households relatively early, even if their economic independence has been postponed (Pickvance & Pickvance, 1994). The process of moving out of the parental home into various types of housing arrangements for young people varies for youth with differing social backgrounds, and there are also gender differences within this process. Disability is another

factor that affects young people's possibilities of living independently (see Barron, 1997):

> I want an accessible kitchen and they tend to think that since I need a
> great deal of assistance that 'why should you have that?'. But I think
> that it would be rather nice to be able to look inside my own kitchen
> cupboards and being able to look in the pots and that. It's difficult
> to tell an assistant what to do when I can't even see what's happening
> on the stove. And plus the little I can do myself even if it's only to
> get a glass of water myself. It would be rather nice to do it myself.
> (Britta, wheelchair user, Sweden, quoted in Barron, 1997, pp. 236–7.)

Young people's transitions into adulthood are culture-specific,
and the culturally appropriate timing of moving into one's own
apartment varies considerably (see Chisholm & Hurrelmann, 1995).
Generally, Southern European cultures tend to prioritize close
family ties at the expense of individual interests as opposed to
Northern European cultures where the importance of early
independence for young people is emphasized (Chisholm &
Hurrelmann, 1995). In line with these value-sets, within Southern
European cultures, such as Italy and Spain, young people tend to
live at home well into their late twenties and thirties, moving out
only in association with getting married. By contrast, in Northern
European societies, young people tend to move out of their childhood home in their late teens/early twenties in order to study or
work, even if it requires considerable financial investments (see
Pickvance & Pickvance, 1994 and 1995).

While moving out of the parental home is seen as an important
marker in a young person's process to adulthood, it has become
increasingly difficult to define the milestones of adulthood in the
late modern society. Many of the markers that were previously significant in the growing up process, have become less significant
(see Chisholm & Hurrelmann, 1995). Also, some of the transitions
that were previously thought of as permanent, have become more
or less transient for many young people. Even if many young
people are trying to make planned transitions to their preferred
type of housing, some of them have to resort to chaotic emergency
strategies in dealing with unexpected family crises and financial
difficulties, and many experience periods of homelessness (Ford
et al., 2002). For many, meeting the financial demands of independent housing is difficult (Pickvance & Pickvance, 1995).

Economic independence has become increasingly difficult for young people to reach, as a result of the ever more temporary jobs that are on offer in the youth labour market. Thus, to secure a stable sufficient income for oneself is a dream that remains out of reach for many young people. Independent accommodation, especially from the private sector, is therefore not secure for young people: they may lose their accommodation at the same time as they lose their jobs. Moving back to the parental home is therefore a step that increasing numbers of young people are forced to take even after years of living independently.

Young women are even more vulnerable to labour-market fluctuations than young men: more young women than men only hold temporary jobs. Nevertheless, even though it appears even more difficult for young women to ensure a sufficient income during their early work careers, they are even more eager than young men to move out of the parental home and into their own accommodation. They are also more reluctant to move back to their childhood homes even when they face financial difficulties living alone. This has been attributed, among other things, to the often stricter parental control young women are exposed to in their childhood families (see Furlong & Cartmel, 1997).

Young Women's Decisions about Motherhood

Increasingly, young women are finding that they have to choose between either having a career or having children; having both at the same time is a very difficult task, and often, simply not possible for many young women. The average age for young women to have children in many Western societies has been postponed well into their late twenties (for example, in Finland the average age of the mother at the birth of her first child is 27 years (Kartovaara, 1995, p. 14)), and in Australia the median age is 30 (Australian Bureau of Statistics, 2002). Although more and more young women are postponing having children for various reasons, often trying to establish a stronger foothold in the labour market, there is also a substantial number of young women who give birth while they are still in their teens. This has alarmed some educational and developmental experts and social policy-makers (see for example Phoenix, 1991; Bullen et al., 2000). The birth rate for 15–19 year old women has been rather stable in the US since the mid-1970s (about

27–29 births per thousand, amounting to about 12–18 per cent of all births) (Nathanson, 1991, pp. 25–30).

In Northern Europe the numbers of teenage mothers have started to increase only recently. This tendency has been attributed to insufficient or lacking sex education, but also to other factors such as economic deprivation. According to Ann Phoenix, there is less reason for young women who do not have high hopes about brilliant careers or even about a decent income to defer mother-hood until later: this may be one of the reasons why less affluent young women are more likely to have children earlier than the more well-to-do women (Phoenix 1991, p. 26). Similarly, Saxton, Fidducia, Chang and Montañez (1999, p. 8) point out that in the US at least, 'girls with disabilities are at twice the risk for pregnancy and dropping out of school than their non-disabled peers, a symptom of low self-esteem, low academic achievement and a per-ceived lack of life options'. There may be other reasons behind early pregnancies, such as lacking information on avoiding pregnancy, and inadequate access to contraception or abortions.

> Abortion is the woman's choice, I think. But according to Islam – which is my religion – a woman can only have an abortion if it [the pregnancy] risks her health. I think that a woman should be able to decide for herself, even if I would not have an abortion myself. (Samira, 18, Sweden, quoted in Thulin & Östergren, 1997, p. 87, translation from Swedish by Sinikka Aapola.)

There are ethnic and social differences among young women in relation to early motherhood. Both in Britain and the USA statistics indicate that young women of colour more likely to have children early than their white peers, and also that more of them are single mothers than their white peers (Phoenix, 1991; Nathanson, 1991). However, as Ann Phoenix (1991) argues, teenage pregnancy is hardly a black phenomenon in the United States nor in Britain: white women's proportion of teenage pregnancies has grown sys-tematically, and now black teenage motherhood is only a part of a more general trend (Phoenix, 1991; Nathanson, 1991). According to a study concerning the educational and vocational decisions of young women of colour, they were more likely to combine full-time work and childcare than their white counterparts, and this was often possible because of the support of their male partners (Mirza, 1992).

Young mothers have been subjected to a set of problem discourses that tend to define them either in terms of disturbed development or even opportunistic welfare dependency: having children just in order to be able to claim social benefits (Bullen *et al.*, 2000; Phoenix, 1991; Nathanson, 1991; Griffin 1993; Hirvonen, 2002). Many young mothers are also unmarried. Out-of-wedlock pregnancies have often been seen as morally highly problematic, and unwed mothers have sometimes been severely punished for breaching the moral code of the community. This is still the case in many parts of the world, particularly in highly religious communities. Although attitudes towards young and/or single mothers have become more tolerant, they are still often seen as bad or suspect mothers, who cannot provide for their children economically or emotionally (see Nathanson, 1991, for a more thorough discussion about US policies towards young women's pregnancies).

According to Phoenix (1991), however, it is ill-advised to believe that teenage motherhood 'causes' social problems; rather, young women who have already been structurally disadvantaged are more likely to become young mothers. They would have had low social status even if they had postponed having children. As Phoenix strongly argues, teenage mother's problems are not individual pathologies, they are large-scale structural social problems that cannot be solved by blaming the young women who choose early motherhood. (Phoenix, 1991).

> They're all, this generation. Children raising children. I'll say, 'Well, you know, . . . that's your opinion . . . but you never know, I might be a better mother than you'. (Ana, Chicana, USA, quoted in Thompson 1995, p. 115.)

The young mothers themselves, even if admitting that bringing up a child as a teenage mother is not easy, are determined to make it work. Many young mothers consider their youth an asset in childrearing. In a number of recent studies, it has been suggested that once having overcome the initial surprise of the unplanned pregnancy, young women saw their motherhood as natural and unproblematic, and felt that their main problem were the prejudiced social attitudes they encountered (Hirvonen, 2002; Niemelä, 2003).

Young motherhood seriously questions the current conception of a normal life-course: it is expected that a young person will have an education, acquire a vocation and enjoy one's youth before s/he starts a family. Having children is not part of this model of youth.

Despite this, young mothers often see motherhood as an integral part of their growing up as women.

> When I was even a little younger than now, those were really good times, but it is not a problem for me to have had a child early. So now I have a more peaceful youth, I enjoy this too. This is nice, but it is different, yes. (Heidi, young mother, Finland, quoted in Niemelä, 2003, p.174, translation from Finnish by Sinikka Aapola.)

Many young mothers have mothers, even grandmothers, and sisters who have also become mothers at a young age (Hirvonen, 2002). This has been seen as a strong predictor of early motherhood (Nathanson, 1991). Teenage motherhood has been the target of many policies and campaigns, aiming at reducing early pregnancy for girls, as it is seen harmful for their futures. However, while these campaigns often draw heavily on the concept of risk of social exclusion and welfare dependency, they fail to address the gendered situations and life contexts of girls and young women making choices about sexuality, contraception and reproduction at a young age (Bullen *et al.*, 2000).

In their critique of British sex education campaigns, Bullen and her colleagues point out that these campaigns are mainly based on traditional, masculinist, moralist and rational ideologies concerning the family and transitions to adulthood, and hence they are not going to be successful in preventing teenage motherhood. Instead, there is a need to consider the standpoint of young women, and their understandings of their own choice and risk biographies. This means that young women's desires concerning sexual relationships and motherhood need to be taken into account, not suppressed, in any family policy oriented at young women (Bullen *et al.*, 2000). These campaigns do not usually include young men to the same degree. In sex education, young women have been allocated responsibility in heterosexual relationships, for preventing unwanted pregnancies and disease; young men are seen as 'having uncontrollable sexual urges' which is why they are not expected to share the responsibility (see Harris *et al.*, 2000).

There is a marked social difference between the attitudes regarding young motherhood in middle-class families versus working-class families, as is suggested by Valerie Walkerdine and her colleagues in their study on young British women's differential paths from school into the world of further education and work (Walkerdine *et al.*, 2001). Whereas middle-class girls thought that their becoming pregnant before having finished their higher education and moved on to working careers would 'kill their mothers', as they said, working-class parents were much more tolerant towards their daughters' pregnancies even in their teen years. They were usually willing to include the newcomer to the family as well as to provide various forms of material help for their daughter and her child. The attitude of the working-class parents towards their daughters' vocational and family future was condensed by Walkerdine and her colleagues into a phrase: 'as long as she's happy' (Walkerdine *et al.*, 2001).

As the above research results indicate, young women's family relations are viewed differently, but usually critically, depending on the onlooker's point of view; whether they are medical experts, social policy makers, social workers, educators, parents or other young people. It appears that it is difficult for young women to make the 'right' reproductive choices; if they become pregnant early, they are easily seen as educational failures and 'welfare cheats', but again, if they postpone motherhood, they are seen as 'selfish' and too career-oriented. In this climate, young women are struggling to plan their own family lives in ways that make sense to them.

> No sacrifice
> Too young to be a mother
> Yet too old to know better
> Condemned by society
> Shunned an outcast
> Conceived unknowingly
> But a saviour to me
> Deserted and forgotten
> . . .
> No longer carefree with unknown goals and wild dreams
> But a tiny person to love and care for
> Surrounded by society's judgements
> Their accusations and harsh realities
> Yet in my eyes an overwhelming unconditional love
> Who has given me more goals and
> Higher, wilder, dreams
> My other life, no sacrifice
> For all the love she brings.
>
> (Sine Kincaid, Australia,
> quoted in Pallotta-Chiarolli, 1998, p. 125.)

The family is not a gender-neutral arena: generational roles are intertwined with gender roles in various ways. Even with the huge increase in women's participation in the paid labour force, they continue to be those who bear the most responsibility for children's upbringing and housework. This imbalance is reflected in the attitudes of today's young women towards starting their own families: they are more hesitant than previous generations of women about having children. It is particularly young women who are affected by and forced to take temporary forms of employment, as shown in the previous chapter. In this situation, many young women have chosen to postpone starting families, as they want to first secure a more stable financial situation before having children. They are considering the personal costs that having children would mean for them, particularly in a situation where divorce is ever more common. Because of this, young women are often labelled as selfish: they are seen as placing their own needs first, and wanting to be freed from caring responsibilities. However, their decisions should be interpreted as life-strategies in the context of growing uncertainty in the labour market.

There is a substantial number of young women who have children early in their lives, even if they too are generally viewed with suspicion. In their case, it is suspected that they aim opportunistically for welfare dependence by having babies at an early age. In addition to that, they are often seen as inadequate mothers both emotionally and materially. However, it is rarely acknowledged that for these young women, early motherhood may seem a lucrative choice for many reasons beyond that of welfare subsidies. For them, early motherhood is connected to a value system where heterosexual relationships, parenting and adulthood interlink (Bullen *et al.*, 2000). Although their financial situations are often precarious, young mothers refuse to be treated as 'problem' mothers, and emphasize the positive aspects of early motherhood to the mother-child relationship. For these young women, raising a child is seen as an integral part of their growing up process.

Conclusion

While it is clear that there have been tremendous changes both in social institutions affecting the family as well as in ideologies concerning gender roles, parenting, childhood and youth as life-phases, and that adapting to these changes has created tensions within families, these difficulties should not be seen as indicating a major demise of the family. Rather, they indicate a qualitative change in family ideologies and cultural practices concerning the family. Views and practices concerning children's upbringing, gender and generational roles and family formation are becoming more and more negotiable, which may involve more choices and positive possibilities for girls growing up in their families of origin, as well as for young women making their own family-related decisions. The changes within the family sphere are neither exclusively positive and empowering, nor negative and damaging for today's girls and young women; they can be either or, depending on the social context and the resources they have at their disposal.

Girls' futures are strongly affected by the types of support they get from their childhood families. However, girls are also actively taking part in their own growing up process, and creating various strategies concerning their own futures, sometimes with the help of their parents, sometimes more autonomously, drawing on support from a wider network of friends and mentors. We argue this may be a necessary development in a world that requires that individuals make their own life choices and bear the responsibility for them from an early age. Girls and young women constantly have to balance the demands of individualist ideologies with those emphasizing the value of the close relationships of the family. Their choices are not easy, and they require constant reflexivity in the rapidly changing social climates of late modern societies.

CHAPTER 5

Re/sisters: Girls' Cultures and Friendships

Introduction

Girls' cultures and friendships are active social formulations, in a constant process of change, and warrant exploration against the background of the changing cultural and social realities. For young people, social relationships that are formed independently of their families and often also beyond their immediate local environments, are increasingly important, despite and perhaps because of the individualizing tendencies of society. Girls' friendships and their cultural practices also indicate a great deal about the changing gender system. Discourses of individualization affect girls' friendships and social relationships in particular ways, as do the cultural forces of globalization and some of their practical manifestations, such as new communication technologies.

In this chapter we shall explore the changing meanings of friendships for girls, as well as their connection to the predominant discourses surrounding girlhood, those of 'girlpower' and 'crisis'. We analyse how relationships between girls mediate their identity formation in an era marked by an emphasized attention to 'relationship narratives' and 'self-understanding', and how gendered meaning making is accomplished through friendships and girls' cultures; in short, what are friends for in the lives of girls and young women?

Conceptions of Girls' Friendships Revisited

Sometimes we have unbelievable fun, you know, sometimes we're numb with laughter in the dining room, when we remember some stupid thing. (Ida, Helsinki, Finland, quoted in Gordon *et al.*, 2000a, p. 22.)

Growing up as a girl has traditionally been defined first and fore-most via the ability to create close and lasting personal relation-ships. Historically, women and girls have been aligned with the affective, and juxtaposed to the properly human and rational (Walkerdine, 1990). These views have been constantly repeated in developmental models of girlhood and adolescence, ever since G.S. Hall, the 'father of adolescence' (Hall, 1904; Erikson, 1968). Successful development for a girl has meant increasing social skills in close friendships with other girls, followed by a long-term romantic heterosexual relationship which culminates in the forma-tion of a family. Adulthood for women has not meant autonomy, but relatedness, while for men, independence has been the key indicator of mature adulthood (see for example Erikson, 1968). Youth has been defined in masculine terms of independence and growing autonomy from previous close relationships such as the family. It is obvious that balancing these two opposing trends is a challenge for girls: how can individuality and independence be achieved without risking one's close relationships as well as one's femininity? Whatever girls do, they run the risk of being inter-preted either as failed in terms of femininity, or as not capable of fulfilling the 'normal' developmental pattern of adolescence (Hudson, 1987).

In the early literature girls' friendships were theorized as a kind of a prelude to heterosexual relationships, which is why they have sometimes been seen as less valuable. Young women are sometimes expected to drop their female friendships if and when they start dating boys, or at least consider their same-sex friendships as sec-ondary. This view has been challenged in recent ethnographic research. Not only are girls seen to highly value their friendships, and try to maintain them at all costs (see for example Griffiths, 1995; Kleven, 1993), but more complex understandings of girls friend-ships have been offered as well. Friendship is seen as a part of the web of social practices that mediate and constitute gender identi-ties. Valerie Hey (1997, p. 30) argues that, 'the so-called private, marginal realm of schoolgirl friendships is a significant place where the "social" is indexed. It is between and amongst girls as friends that identities are variously practised, appropriated, resisted and negotiated'. A similar argument is developed by Barrie Thorne in her study of interactions among primary school students and 'the fluctuating significance of gender in the ongoing scenes of social life' (Thorne 1993, p. 61). Numerous other ethnographic and qualitative studies of young people and friendship, often drawing on critical traditions within Cultural Studies, have elaborated the political and sub-cultural significance of friendship practices (Eder *et al.*, 1995; Gonick, 2003; Griffiths, 1995; Aapola, 1992).

There has also been a recent surge in popular books about girls' friendships (Lamb, 2002; Wiseman, 2003). In these books girls' friendships are often represented as full of intricate inner conflicts, power struggles and exclusions demanding endless amounts of energy and time, and which can cause considerable social and psychological damage. However, while girls' disputes are easily pathologized or ridiculed, it is usually not recognized that these frictions and tensions between girls are partly caused exactly because more direct expressions of aggression are not considered acceptable for ideal femininity (see Hey, 1997). We shall pursue this question further below.

Some of this literature focuses on the school environment as an important site for the development and enactment of friendship. This is often also the site where some of the more problematic features of young people's relationships with each other occur: bullying, teasing, and ostracizing. Often girls' associations with one another are treated suspiciously by adult authorities, as they are believed to interfere with school-work. Rarely are they seen as a positive resource that could be utilized for educational ends (see Hey, 1997). Gordon *et al.* (2000a) point out, however, that girls offer each other many forms of social support in various contexts. This support makes it easier for them to make spaces for themselves and express their voices within the school environment, to stand their ground against boys' teasing and express their opinions in the classroom (Gordon *et al.*, 2000a; see also Brown, 1998).

Another common focus of treatments of girls' friendships is the institution of the 'best friend'. The exclusive and intense liaisons between girls are variously presented as a normative aspect of growing up female, and as a pathological feature illustrative of girls' irrationality. Other types of friendships have not received much attention. However, girls create a multitude of different types of friendships, alternating between various kinds of social ties. The 'best friend' is only one form of girls' friendships, although an important one (Aapola, 1992; Hey, 1997; Tolonen, 2001; Wulff, 1995; Lesko, 1988).

Girls' friendships are more than an important, albeit complicated sphere of life for girls, where they can get support for themselves and have fun. They are a powerful cultural force, representing sites of collective meaning-making, and a necessary requirement in the multilayered process of making gendered identities. Often, girls' friendships are approached as a phenomenon that remains the same throughout time, but we argue for a more historical analysis that is sensitive to changes within girls' social worlds. Girls' cultures and friendships are also deeply affected by the geographical, social and cultural aspects of their environments, and girls from different class and ethnic backgrounds may demonstrate widely differing forms of friendships as well as cultural practices (see Hey, 1997; Brown, 1998).

Friendships, Individuality, Sociality and Gender

Although individualization has been formerly reserved for male adulthood, young women's struggle towards individuality has demonstrated itself in various ways: postponing and/or rejecting marriage and having children, leading single lives in unprecedented numbers, and heavy investments in education and professional careers, as well as an increasing involvement in public spheres such as politics and the media (Bjerrum Nielsen & Rudberg, 1994). (These issues are discussed more thoroughly elsewhere in the book.) Individualizing processes can be seen in girls' friendships and social relationships. Friendships for girls are important sites for identity-creation as well as for trying out various forms of femininity. For young single women in early adulthood, friendships with other women often form an important social sphere that allows them to feel connected to other people, while still remaining relatively independent and autonomous agents in their own right, able to explore other social spheres. A growing number of Western young women (and men) are choosing to lead single life-styles well into their late twenties and early thirties, and a large proportion of them never marry. In this situation, friendships take on a new meaning as one's 'adopted families'. This is reflected in the many popular TV comedies, such as 'Friends', portraying groups of mainly single young adults who spend most of their spare time with their friends, live together as well as fall in and out of love with each other. For many girls and young women, networks of friends have a more central role in their lives than ever before.

However, for young women the connection/autonomy tension must also be understood as a feature of the ways in which femininity has been constructed. According to Carol Gilligan, the juggling of the desire for personal freedom and success with a compelling sense of emotional responsibility poses problems for young women. She says, 'for girls to remain responsible to themselves they must resist the conventions of feminine goodness; to remain responsible to others, they must resist the values placed on self-sufficiency and independence' (Gilligan *et al.*, 1990, pp. 9–10). While Gilligan's work has been critiqued by many feminist scholars for the way in which it universalizes and essentializes girls' experiences, it has had an incredible popular appeal. Others have pointed out that the tension between autonomy and connection should be seen not merely as the result of feminine psycho-sexual development, as Gilligan does, nor as the lack of self-esteem or of ambition. Rather, it is an effect of a culture that incites us to remake ourselves (McLeod, 2002). McLeod (2002) points out that feminist reform may be heightening the connection/autonomy dilemma for young women. On the one hand, feminists have argued for more public valuing of girls' and women's capacity for friendship and affective relations. On the other, feminism expects and rewards success at school and in the world beyond. These twin imperatives produce new dimensions to the autonomy/connection conflict for girls.

In late modern societies, there are strong pressures on young people to engage in constant identity work, to produce themselves as particular kinds of individuals in various social contexts. This identity work cannot happen in a vacuum; it is a thoroughly social and interpersonal process, which requires a constant, engaged, friendly yet critical audience, as current social theorists such as Stuart Hall (1996) and Valerie Hey (2002) have pointed out. They suggest that the processes of individualization should not be seen as opposed to forms of sociality, but as actually achieved through sociality (Gonick, 2003; Hall, 1996; Hey, 2002). For young people, friendships formed with peers in a similar social situation are therefore of central importance, as they try to negotiate their pathways in the quickly shifting social territory. Social relationships are important sites of collective meaning-making (Harrington & Fine, 2000). And friendship for young people can also be seen as an ideal practice of the reflexive self.

We're individuals who stick together. It's like a track team. You do individual events, but yet you score as a team. (Lydia, 12, white, middle class, Acadia, USA, quoted in Brown, 1998, p. 84.)

Friendship in itself should be regarded as an activity, one that requires constant reworking and reconfirming, in order to keep it going (Hey, 2002). Friendship as a particular kind of cultural activity is also gender-specific; girls and boys do different kinds of 'friendship work', as has been suggested by many researchers (see for example Hey, 2002). Within their friendships, young people experiment with ways of making sense of and applying the varying discourses and rapidly changing social and cultural practices surrounding central life areas such as gender relations and sexuality.

It seems that for girls and young women, the connection side of the connection/autonomy tension produces a strong focus on jointly agreed rules as well as discussions. For example, Kehily *et al.* (2002) discuss a group of British school girls who met during breaks at the school yard, and agreed on a topic to discuss jointly. Very often the talk focused on issues such as puberty, infatuations with boys and male teachers as well as other relationship issues. In this group, girls who expressed views that were deemed 'out-of-line' with the general understanding concerning proper behavior for a girl, were reprimanded by the rest of the group, and they were expected to mend their ways if they wanted to be part of the group (Kehily *et al.*, 2002). Kehily argues that friendship talk enables certain femininities to emerge and be sustained, while others are discouraged. As such, friendship talk can be seen as part of a medium of social relations that is productive of complex, conflicting emotional and psychic investments and identifications.

Changing Friendships

Valerie Hey suggests that girls' friendships constitute a gendered, collective cultural code (Hey, 1997, p. 84). There are many intricate rules about interactions, and particular discourses that are utilized. However, these rules vary according to social and ethnic backgrounds (see for example Hey, 1997; Wulff, 1988; Amit-Talai & Wulff, 1995). There are also some national differences. Girls' friendships, as well as the cultural practices connected to them, have varied even historically and changed along with general social changes affecting women's and young people's position in society.

In the early twentieth century, most Western middle-class girls prepared for a domestic career. Their youth was usually short and tightly controlled. They received some education, but often had extensive family responsibilities, and thus had relatively little time to spare for their own interests. For working-class young women during this time, friendship was a luxury they had little time for, as a result of long working hours. In rural areas, children participated in household duties as early as possible, and young girls were often expected to mind their younger siblings, help with cooking and so on. They left home at an early age, often for work in other people's households, to earn their living (see for example Markkola, 2003). In urban areas, girls helped their mothers who sewed or washed clothes for wealthier people, and frequently they took jobs as maids. Despite the limits set by the community, friendships have offered girls welcome possibilities to escape their domestic responsibilities for a while, and freely discuss issues. Many girls and women cherished the friends of their youth as life-long companionships, even if they could not meet very often (Aromaa, 1990, p. 136; Cott, 1977).

As schooling provided by the church or the state became more common, it was easier for children and young people to create contacts with each other. In many Western countries there have been local traditions that have helped young people create associations with their peers, such as community dances, festivities, and sports events. Usually the friendship groups of young people have been gender-segregated (Schlegel & Barry, 1991), although mixed groups have become more common and culturally accepted.

Young people's lives started to change with the onset of mass education in the early twentieth century, as they became less involved with paid labour. Particularly from the 1950s onwards, the modern phase of youth was formed, with an increase in young people's spare time and their consumer power. Popular culture has become more and more influential in young people's lives, and they have gained more visibility in society (Wyn & White, 1997). Their social relationships have also been transformed in the process, as peer cultures have become increasingly important both within and outside of the school environment. Various kinds of social groupings of youth have been formed on the basis of popular cultural preferences, ideological stances and other common denominators. The flourishing peer cultures of young people have also often been seen as a social problem. The image of young people's social groupings has been predominantly masculine, and girls' relationships have not received as much attention. However, in the last decades of the twentieth century, young people's peer cultures received more and more attention in youth studies, and girls' social groupings became more visible from the 1970s onwards (McRobbie & Garber, 1975/1991; Hey, 1997).

Currently, in urbanized societies, many children's and young people's leisure time has become more and more structured and organized around activities led by adults. Upper and middle-class young people especially have less time to spend freely, as they balance various time-consuming hobbies and interests, school-work and family commitments (see Amit-Talai, 1995; Walkerdine *et al.*, 2001). This reflects changes in attitudes towards children's upbringing; it is considered socially disadvantageous for a child or young person to spend time alone in the afternoons, before their parents come home from work. As the percentage of family house-holds where both parents work has increased in the past decades, children and young people are often enrolled in various types of after-school activities, such as clubs and sports, in order to keep them under adult supervision (Hoikkala, 1993). Children represent an emotional and economic investment for their parents (see Fine & Mechling, 1991; Beck & Beck-Gernsheim, 1995), and middle-class parents particularly spend growing amounts of time and money to provide their children with the best life-chances. Often, children are encouraged to take up hobbies and interests that will provide them with useful social networks as well as skills that help propel them forward at school and later, when they are seeking jobs (Ziehe, 1991).

Leisure time has become more structured both because extra-curricular activities are perceived to enhance young people's opportunities, and because roaming freely is constructed as dangerous. People in urban areas, particularly big cities, have also started to feel more and more insecure about the safety of their neighbourhoods. As a result, children's and young people's time has become more and more structured, and they have less time to spend with friends outside of adult supervision. For example, car pooling has replaced unsupervised travel to and from school and after-school hobbies. This has consequences for social relationships; it is possible that as time spent in adult-led activities grows, the meaning of spontaneous friendships is diminished for many young people. Girls' leisure time is often even more pro-tected and controlled than boys' (Schlegel & Barry, 1991). Although young people today have more spare time to use at their own leisure than ever before, many of them balance various responsibilities and commitments at home, at school and at work, and cannot invest much time and energy in their peer relationships (Amit-Talai, 1995).

In times that are marked by both risk and a new public presence of youth, and young women in particular, girls' social relationships tend to be located in a borderland between the public and the private life spheres; they create private, even exclusive, social spaces within such public spaces as the classroom, school yard or the youth club (see for example Kehily et al., 2002; Tolonen, 2001; Wulff, 1988). At the same time, from within their private social spaces, girls may venture out together to explore such public spaces they would not risk entering alone.

Mobile phones and other information and communication technologies have disrupted previous understandings of the relationship between the public and the private spheres (Henderson et al., 2001). Young people in particular have embraced the new communication technologies and used them to facilitate new forms of sociality. Often, this has involved flexible movement between public and private arenas as well as between formal and moral economies. ICT technologies have made it possible to create private spheres within public spaces (for example, talking to a friend on the phone in a bus) or vice versa (for example, opening one's bedroom to global publicity through the Internet) (Silverstone et al., 1992; Reimer, 1995, cited in Henderson et al., 2001; Harris, 2001a; Leonard, 1998). Thus, the meaning of the public/private divide is transformed (Fahey, 1995, cited in Henderson et al., 2001), as are the notions of masculinity and femininity that were formally attached to it (see Ganetz, 1995).

Henderson and her colleagues conclude in their study (2001) of young people's use of the mobile phone: '[t]he social forms that the mobile phones gave rise to generally appeared to be experimental, emergent and transitory'; they 'breed change in young people's social forms.' However, the practices connected to ICTs are embedded in local cultures, and shaped by class, geography and temporality. For young women, the mobile phone offers some new possibilities to claim greater personal and sexual freedom, away from the confinement of the domestic sphere, into the more public spheres and becoming more independent (Henderson et al., 2001). At the same time, it makes them more accountable and increasingly surveilled by parents and other authorities (Harris, 2004).

Rules and Negotiations – Girls' Friendship Cultures

Girls' friendships are often organized around what Valerie Hey calls the 'ethical rules' of female friendship – reliability, reciprocity, commitment, confidentiality, trust and sharing (Hey, 1997, p. 65). She sees these social rules as 'the exact opposite of undisciplined individualism. However, friendship is also a vehicle for access to social power. Thus, the workings of social power through friendship must be reconciled with its ethical rules.' This combination is a difficult balancing act compounded by the ways in which feminine friendships are also constituted through the socially coercive presence of the male gaze, which regulates expressions of femininity. The result is that girl's relationships with each other are often highly charged. As Hey phrases it, 'girls' divorces are messy' (Hey, 1997, p. 65).

> I can't believe that Isabella would behave in this way when someone new comes into the school. I can't believe that she would ignore us all and act as if she didn't even know us. (Francesca, high school student, Quebec, Canada, quoted in Amit-Talai, 1995, p. 155.)

The requirement to juggle the desire for social power through friendship with the ethical of rules of friendship also helps to explain how girls friendships often take the form of tight, exclusive cliques and why tensions between friends are difficult to resolve. As Amit-Talai (1995) argues, girls' friendships are based on the ideal of mutual intimacy and reciprocal commitment. As a result, it is not easy to include new friends. New friendships are more likely to replace rather than complement previous ones (Amit-Talai, 1995, pp. 155–6).

It is important to note the different ways in which the negotiation of social power and ethical rules of relations between girls shifts somewhat depending on their social background. These differing friendship ideals are not arbitrary; they are linked to different versions of raced, classed and sexed femininities that are being worked out within girls' friendship formations (see Brown, 1998; Hey, 1997).

Middle-class forms of femininity tend to emphasize being 'nice'; at home, at school as well as in friendships (see Brown, 1998). (Although of course sometimes girls who invest a lot to 'blend in', 'follow the rules' and 'get along with everyone' within the school

environment may experiment with other types of behaviour
outside of the school; see Lesko, 1988, p. 133). 'Niceness' means
controlling one's emotions and first and foremost one's aggressive
feelings, being sweet and friendly, succeeding at school and
obeying one's parents (see Hey, 1997, pp. 55–65; Brown, 1998;
Lesko, 1988, pp. 131–3). However, for working-class femininities
'niceness' is also conflated with academic achievement. A strong
investment in educational success may be interpreted as 'kissing
up' to authority and trying to 'better oneself' in relation to one's
peers and family. There is a lot involved in working-class social
relations in not being defined a 'snob' (see also Eder *et al.*, 1995;
McRobbie, 1991a). At the same time, the losses may be greater than
the rewards, as changing labour markets mean that high educational achievement does not necessarily guarantee better jobs (see
Walkerdine *et al.*, 2001; Brown, 1998).

'Being nice' does not seem to operate for working-class girls in
the ways that it does for middle-class girls. Nancy Lesko's (1988)
observations of a small group of non-conformist girls in a Catholic
high school in the USA found that these girls did not try to please
everyone, not even the school staff, and their behaviour was often
interpreted as 'hard' as opposed to the 'nice girls' who tried to get
along with everyone (Lesko, 1988, pp. 132–5). In another US-based
study focusing on white working-class girls living in a rural setting,
Lyn Mikel Brown (1998) found that the girls were not afraid to
express their differing opinions and resentments to their friends
nor other people around them, and that they strongly valued
women's emotional and physical toughness and resistance to
passivity. This was linked to the harsh realities of their everyday
lives, where they often encountered economic hardship and even
physical abuse (Brown, 1998, p. 22–6 and 40–58).

In Valerie Hey's ethnographic study (1997), the central aims of
friendships for the working-class girls were pleasing themselves,
'having fun', reconfirming heterosexual attractiveness and gaining
knowledge about sexuality. They managed their conflicts more
openly than the middle-class girls, as solidarities seemed to be
more shifting and emotional investments were not as huge as in
middle-class girls' friendships (Hey, 1997, pp. 68–84). The friendship group was relatively volatile, and their rules and ideas about
power relations and loyalties differed from those of the middle-
class girls (Hey, 1997). Particular, self-reliant girls would sometimes
assume a 'motherly' and protective role towards other girls; they
would 'take care' of a 'lonely' girl when her 'best friend' was away,

and this was generally accepted within the group. Conflicts followed, however, if a girl revealed her friend's rule-breaking behaviour to school authorities, or questioned someone's reputation publicly (Hey, 1997, pp. 68–84).

There is a 'problem' or 'crisis' discourse of female friendship which tends to emphasize conflicts and problems within relationships between girls. This discourse can be found in several recent studies which have focused on the negative social consequences of indirect forms of aggression (Lagerspetz, 1998; Wiseman, 2003). Psychologist Kirsti Lagerspetz (1998) has suggested that girls' expectations regarding friendships – high levels of intimacy, loyalty and dependence – make their friendships more vulnerable and more prone to indirect aggression, which is particularly effective in close relationships (Lagerspetz, 1998, pp. 95–6). In a peer review, girls mentioned several behaviours that other girls used against persons they were angry with, and which can be classified as indirect aggression: excluding a person from social interactions, sulking, talking behind someone's back and seeking other friends as revenge. This type of behaviour was found to be a particular problem for girls from age eleven onwards, but became less a feature of friendship as they got older (Lagerspetz, 1998). Often this pattern is interpreted as a sign of increasing maturity as girls move into adulthood. Lyn Mikel Brown (1998), however, suggests that girls' increased anger and aggression at that age reflects their newly emerging comprehension of the culture they are about to enter and a vision of their subordinated place as young women in it. Brown continues: 'That their reaction to this awakening would be shock, sadness, anger and a sense of betrayal is not surprising. Moreover, since these strong feelings emerge just as girls move into the dominant culture, at the very moment when their anger is most disruptive to the social order, proponents of the status quo have much invested in covering or pushing these feelings out of public view' (Brown, 1998, pp. 15–6). The later decline in young women's aggression thus presents itself more as a result of resignation than maturation.

Indirect forms of aggression ought to be put in their gender-specific context. It is still culturally more unacceptable for girls and women to express any type of aggression, particularly in public arenas, than for men. For example, Valerie Hey (1997) describes how the middle-class girls in her study tried to keep their conflicts secret, as they wanted to appear compliant and 'nice'. Otherwise they risked their relationships being treated as disciplinary

problems within the official school (Hey, 1997, pp. 55–65). Hey recognized that in conflict situations, girls tended to 'other' each other;
for example by defining their opponent as not attractive enough or
by questioning her reputation. 'Bitching' about other girls was also
a central way for the working-class girls in her study to present
themselves as popular, normal and respectable: they sometimes
accused other girls of being sexually 'loose' and 'cheap' (Hey, 1997,
pp. 74–5). As Nancy Lesko and other feminist researchers have
demonstrated, young women who break the norms of traditional
feminine behaviour in some way, run the risk of being labelled as
sexually promiscuous, even if they are not (Lesko, 1988; Lees, 1993).

Similarly, popular girls can be labelled negatively solely because
they are popular, regardless of their actual behaviour (Eder *et al.*,
1995; see also Brown, 1998). In a US study, Donna Eder and her colleagues (Eder *et al.*, 1995, pp. 36–40) found that within the middle-
school student culture, being part of the high-status girls' group
was strongly associated with friendship with the 'top girls', in this
case, cheerleaders. This led to a lot of ill feeling among the girls
who were not welcomed in the elite group, although they felt equal
to them in many ways. The popular girls were thus often targets
of jealousy and resentment, and they were gossiped about negatively among the other girls.

Very often the issues that cause problems within girls' groups
are similar to those that cause tensions within the wider society,
such as social and economic inequalities and ethnic relations.
However, while girls and young women are often very aware of
social differences within the social contexts they grow up in, difference does not always mean tension or conflict, as will be shown
below.

The Difference Difference Makes

Friends often share a similar background socioeconomically,
religion-wise and ethnically. Also, friends are usually of a similar
age; as a result of the age grading system in schools students from
the same form tend to spend time together (see Akers *et al.*, 1998,
cited in Tyyskä, 2001, p. 161; Amit-Talai, 1995). Young people may
consider even minor age differences such as less than a year as
socially meaningful, and possibly problematic, within friendships
(Aapola, 1999b). Younger members in a group see their position as
problematic, as they can end up feeling marginal, if they cannot

participate in the same activities as their older friends. This applies particularly to those friends who have already reached the age of majority.

Ethnic, cultural, sexual practice and class differences between girls and the associated tensions may often actively hinder the formation of friendships over these socially invested borders, and cause tensions if formed nevertheless (Wulff, 1988; Eder *et al.*, 1995).

> Different to the others
> They all stare at her
> As she enters the school yard,
> Keeping a far distance
> As if she carried an infectious disease.
> Nobody will talk to her
> But will talk about her,
> Spreading rumours that
> Spread like a wild bushfire
> On a hot summer's day. . . .
>   (Qing Ling Lu Tran, 14, Australia,
> quoted in Pallotta-Chiarolli, 1998, p. 149.)

Young people's friendships and groups are often formed in opposition to another group, and identities formed in opposition to other identities, such as 'nerds' versus 'toughies', 'skinheads' versus 'hiphop' and so on (Lesko, 1988, p. 127; Eder *et al.*, 1995; Brown, 1998; Allard, 2002). These categories are often also coded for race, class, and ethnicity. Valerie Hey reports in her study (1997), how some white working-class girls in a friendship group disassociated themselves from their former close alliances to Pakistani or black girls and in this way produced themselves as 'proper' girls within the dominant group of white girls. In the process they labelled the girls of colour 'slags' (Hey, 1997, pp. 68–71).

Social class was one of the most important factors that differentiated students within the US middle-school studied by Donna Eder and her colleagues (Eder *et al.*, 1995). There was a clear social hierarchy at work within the school, where visibility and popularity were the main factors allocating students within the hierarchy. Higher status – visible and popular – students such as those belonging to the school sports-team, clearly differentiated themselves from lower-status students, and avoided contact with them. Lower-status students, on the other hand, often regarded high-status students as snobbish, and did not seek their company either.

Their resentment became all the more obvious while they pro-
ceeded through middle school. Although working-class and rural
students were often put down and ridiculed by the more elite high
status students, outright elitism was not regarded as proper behaviour within the school's student culture, even among high status
students (Eder *et al.*, 1995). Eder and her colleagues argue that the
social inequalities of the outside society were further enhanced in
the middle school student culture they studied; if not directly, then
indirectly. For example, participation in some of the social activities that were most highly visible and strongly linked with being
'popular' required considerable economic investments that many
students, coming from less affluent families, could not afford (Eder
et al., 1995). As a result, many working-class and rural students
were excluded from these activities and ended up ranking lower
in the school's social hierarchy. Lyn Mikel Brown (1998) has
made similar observations among a group of middle-class girls in
a Maine junior high school: they were bitterly aware of their
particular gendered and classed position within the three-tiered
social and material hierarchy of their school.

> Kirstin: We're in the middle class.
> Lydia: I mean, you have some friends that –
> Lyn: What does that mean, middle class?
> Kirstin: I'm cast out.
> Lydia: Us, you know, like –
> Elizabeth: Regular people.
> Lydia: Yeah, regular people. You're not popular, like the talk of the
> school or anything, and you're not like cast out, spit upon . . .
> . . .
> Jane: Because we're too smart.
> Kirstin: 'Cause we're girls –
> Jane: And we're too smart.
> Elizabeth: And we don't play all the sports.
> Lydia: We're smart and we're different. . . . We don't wear GAP jeans all
> the time, we wear homemade clothes.
> Others (laughing): We do?
>
> > (Junior high school students, white, middle class,
> > Acadia, USA, quoted in Brown, 1998, pp. 72–3.)

Educational performance, dress and other shared cultural codes
were all part of the social process whereby different groups were

formed and recognized within the school environment (Brown, 1998, p. 73; Allard, 2002).

Sometimes physical development can be used in a girls' group to create differentiations or as a common denominator. Girls who are physically at a similar level of development tend to be drawn together. For example, girls whose periods have already started, sometimes form a special group or gain special status in a group (Aapola, 1999a; see also Kehily *et al.*, 2002). Ideals about physical development, beauty and femininity can also draw together friendship groups of young women with disabilities in particular ways. As Barron (1997, p. 231) argues, because 'the images portrayed of the ideal woman via media are not those of wheelchair users', young women with disabilities may be idealized by non-disabled peers for 'coping' with not meeting the normative ideal of physical beauty. Friendship groups of others with disabilities are important networks for sharing knowledge and complex experiences of being both marginalized and idealized for being outside the norm.

> With disabled friends, you don't have to prove anything. They know how it is. (Alice, second year university student, Sweden, quoted in Barron, 1997, p. 231.)

Finnish sociologist Tarja Tolonen (2001) has used the concept of 'gender style' to describe not only the appearance of a girl, but also other issues regarding her embodiment, attitudes towards school and its rules, her sexuality and male-female relations and so on. She found in her ethnographic study in two Finnish secondary schools with a middle- to working-class student body, that even within the same friendship group, different gender styles could be present. However, a similar style could enhance girls' friendships (Tolonen, 2001). Girls within the same study group saw clear distinctions within their group of girls regarding differences in relation to smoking, attitude towards school-work, dating, make-up and so on. In their final year of the school, the girls whom Tarja Tolonen observed saw their relationships with each other as affected by many things, but most importantly, by their appearance and style, attitude towards school-work, and affiliations to local gangs (Tolonen, 2001). These had some connections to the girls' family background, but the differences were mediated in a complicated way. The girls' group in the school environment was

divided into smaller groups and twosomes, along these dimensions
of difference, even if the atmosphere among the girls was generally
neutral during their final year of school (Tolonen, 2001).

Girls frequently differentiate between an 'us' who are defined
as 'ordinary' or 'normal' and 'them'; other girls whose style is seen
as outrageous or strange (Tolonen, 2001). For example, in Margaret
J. Finders' (1997) US study of two very different groups of girls
in junior high school (one whose parents were affluent and
upper middle-class, and another whose parents were working-
class or unskilled and had a meager income) both presented themselves as the 'real' or 'normal' girls, while the other group was seen
as either lacking or 'overdoing' some important features, that had
to do with dress style, conduct and academic performance (Finders,
1997).

Although style can differentiate between groups of girls as well
as individuals, it can also tie people together who would otherwise
easily see each other as different. In Helena Wulff's study, ethnic
styles functioned as common denominators for white and black
girls within the social networks formed around a mixed youth club
in South London (Wulff, 1988 and 1995; see also Tolonen, 2001).

> There's no difference really between black and white girls. There's a
> difference because of their parents . . . People used to live in poor coun-
> tries. Their food's different. Sometimes their clothing's different. . . .
> There are black people who are English inside. (Vicky, white, London,
> Great Britain, quoted in Wulff, 1995, p. 67.)

There are several areas of girls' friendships that have yet to be
studied in depth. For example, few studies exist of friendships
between young lesbians, or between groups of friends whose
members are both gay and straight. Similarly, there is a dearth of
literature about friendships between girls of colour (for exceptions
see Mirza 1992 and Kehily *et al.*, 2002), nor do many studies exist
that focus on groups of friendship whose members are from a
diverse range of raced backgrounds (for exceptions see Gonick,
2003 and Wulff, 1995). In Helena Wulff's study of a group of
girls of varied ethnic backgrounds in South London, girls formed
various networks of friendship, sometimes transgressing ethnic
and cultural borders (Wulff, 1988 and 1995). She has suggested
that girls in general may be more open towards identity experimentation and mixing culturally with girls from other ethnic
backgrounds in their friendships than boys (Wulff, 1988, p. 64).

Of course, this openness does not apply to all girls, some of whom subscribe to racist ideologies (see for example Perho, 2002).

Heavenly Creatures: Representations of Girls' Friendship in Popular Culture

In a famous and widely acclaimed film, directed by New Zealander Peter Jackson, 'Heavenly Creatures' (1994), two teenage girls from different social backgrounds form an intense and exclusive friendship and possibly a lesbian relationship. They create their own secret fantasy world together, full of drama, imagination and excitement. At the same time, their relationship to reality starts to blur. When their parents finally threaten to separate the two, they set out to murder the mother of one of the girls in order to prevent this from happening. They are punished and separated as a result, losing their friendship. The film, although released several years ago, remains one of the most powerful and fascinating movie portrayals of young female friendship ever. The film, which was based on a 'real' incident, albeit interpreted artistically, represents a cultural fascination with girls' close friendships as powerful, dark and dangerous. With the question of their sexuality left open, the film also draws on a notion that continues to fascinate, intrigue and confuse Western societies: the mysterious power of girls' sexuality.

Girls' friendships have rarely been portrayed from this angle in popular culture. In most movies they have either been absent, or at best a marginal reference in the main storyline. If they have been a more central part of the plot, they have usually been depicted as amusing at their best, and annoying at their worst. Positive depictions of girls' friendships have been infrequent. An early twenty-first century US film, 'Ghost World' (2001), however, focuses on a close twosome of girls on the verge of adulthood, fresh out of high school, from the angle of a dissolving friendship. The film is very interesting for the way in which it uses the image of the girl to depict the alienated world of youth and the society which has abandoned them as a result of neo-liberal policies and the dissolving of the welfare state. It provides an opportunity to understand the crisis of youth as part of a broader crisis of labour, political agency, democracy, and the future (Giroux, 2002). 'Coming-of-age' stories and coming out stories focusing on young women's friendships and love affairs are now slowly gaining more ground: recent years have seen the release of 'Set It Off' (USA, 1996), 'The Incredibly True Story of Two Girls in Love' (USA, 1995), 'Crossroads' (USA, 2001), 'Show Me Love' (Sweden, 1998) and 'Thirteen' (USA, 2003). However, portrayals of young women in films who are not positioned in relation to a man, and not in relative isolation from (positive) female relationships remain rare.

Other presentations of girls' friendships within popular culture have also been problematic. Angela McRobbie's classic study (1991a) of the photo-story genre that was eminent in British girls' magazines in the 1970s suggested that girls' relationships were often presented in the light of disloyalty, competence and conflict. Girls frequently faced a dilemma: whether to be a 'good girl' and 'loyal friend', dedicated to promoting the common good and caring for others, or to resort to immoral and cunning strategies in promoting one's individual, selfish interests, which were often related to success at school or within heterosexual relationships (McRobbie, 1991a). However, by the 1980s, these types of images of girls' mutual competition had been replaced by images of girls as friends having fun together. Also, the earlier obsession with securing a romantic relationship to a boy had become less pronounced and the idea of having friends of both sexes was promoted instead (McRobbie, 1991b).

As can be seen from the above examples, popular presentations of girls' friendships have tended to be rather unidimensional in the past, with an emphasis on problems. However, towards the end of the twentieth century, this image was challenged, as girlhood in itself became 'fashionable' within popular culture (see Chapter 1). More recently, there has been a proliferation of imagery of girls' associations with each other, particularly in the entertainment sector. At the end of the twentieth century and in the beginning of the twenty-first century, all-girl-bands such as the Spice Girls were often marketed as friendship groups who had sought their fortune together, through hardship. All the band members were presented as having their individualized personal styles, but performing, having fun and promoting their professional interests together. These images have been culturally powerful. For example, the image the Spice Girls has inspired thousands of girls to form their own groups and practice performing amongst themselves and even to an audience (see for example Fritzsche, 2001). At the same time, there has been a remarkable increase in the number of girls' magazines, clubs and Internet sites which frequently bring up the issue of girls' friendships in a popular form.

Friend test: Life is full of surprises – and so is a good friendship! Sometimes you can be like two of a kind. Sometimes you can notice completely new features in your best friend. Also you can do a fun friend-test together with your friend. All you need is some paper, a pen and a playful mindset!

A good friend does not:

- get into fights
- make fun of you
- talk badly of you
- lie
- embarrass you
- try to own you
- get angry over little things
- get jealous
- care about your appearance
- care about your things.

(Kaisamatti, 2000, pp. 8–10; translation from Finnish by Sinikka Aapola)

In the Internet there are hundreds of girl-only-sites worldwide where girls can find information about and discuss topics such as relationships, health and hobbies, but also buy commercial products such as magazines and various 'cute' paraphernalia symbolizing friendship. That girls are expected to give each other gifts of various sorts is an interesting phenomenon, and one that renders a financial importance to girls' friendships. It can thus be said that girls' friendships in late modern societies have been commodified commercially to an extent, which is analogous to the commodification of heterosexual romance (see Illouz, 1997). Eva Illouz has convincingly showed how various types of consumer items and commodified social practices, including flowers, chocolates and restaurant dinners, have become linked to romance. Similarly, girls' alliances are often symbolized by particular types of items, such as cuddly toys and glitzy cosmetic products. These kinds of gifts can be exchanged within girls' one-to-one friendships, but they are also given out in a more collective fashion, for example, at girls' birthday parties (to guests!), as well as exchanged between all-girl-teams in sports competitions. These presents symbolize the value girls place on their friendships, as well as pass on positive feelings to the recipients. However, a failure to produce these gifts in situations where they are deemed appropriate, can even be interpreted as a failure to comply with the 'rules' of girls' friendship culture. In addition, various types of gendered commercial choices regarding, for example, styles of dress can be used as signifiers of social differentiation among young people (see for example Quart, 2003; Allard, 2002; Tolonen, 2001).

While there has been a proliferation of positive images of girls' friendships provided by the entertainment sector, the media has also provided other, less positive images of girls' groupings. In recent years, there have also been heated media discussions – even moral 'panics' – over 'tough girls' and girl gangs. These exemplify the discourse of girlhood in 'crisis', as we pointed out in Chapter 2. While the media debates over problematic or 'tough' girls in different countries have varied, they have had some common themes, such as girls' increased use of alcohol and drugs, their violence and changes in their sexual behaviour (see Honkatukia & Aaltonen, 2001). The 'tough' girls have usually been labelled as potential delinquents and as 'abnormal' and unfeminine by the general public and the authorities, and they have been regarded with fear and resentment. At the same time, they have also been psychologized and pitied as young people who have been either physically or emotionally neglected by their parents, and who are causing most harm to themselves. Their control can thus be justified as 'protection' (see Lesko, 2001; Griffin, 1997).

Girls' supposedly strong emphasis on relationships has even been seen as a potential problem in relation to delinquency: it is often believed that girls' join 'gangs' and engage in potentially criminal or risky activities as they are more susceptible to peer pressures. However, the relationship is not that simple; girls' membership in gangs does not necessarily mean that they engage in criminal activities (Campbell, 1991). Most importantly, girls join gangs because they receive social support from their gang in their otherwise difficult life-situations in impoverished neighbourhoods with inadequate social policies, and in the midst of abusive family and other relationships (Campbell, 1991). However, there are often even other kinds of social and material rewards in joining a gang, as a female gang member explains:

> They just (were) having fun, going to parties, kickin' it, staying out all night, new clothes, new shoes, selling drugs and all that. I wanted to be like that too. I wanted to wear name brand shoes, name brand clothes, I wanted my hair done and everything like that so that's what I done. (Pam, 18, African American, St. Louis, USA, quoted in Miller, 2001, p. 43.)

Anne Campbell has pointed out that many of the girls who get involved with gang activity, share a similar type of background: they have had unstable family relationships, frequent geographical relocations, inadequate schooling and other factors that have led them to a socially difficult situation, where they fear for their safety and feel socially isolated (Campbell, 1991, pp. 253–5). She also notes that other sources of support outside of the gang seem to have become even more scarce for many of these young women, thus making the gang even more vital for them (Campbell, 1991, p. 268).

Some of the worries expressed in relation to 'tough girls' are linked with the consequences of marked social changes in gender relations and the mixed emotions they have raised in many directions. This can be defined as a kind of 'backlash'; a desire to re-emphasize gender divisions and traditional forms of masculinity and femininity. Uneasiness with 'tough girls' is obviously also related to class-based suspicions: it is particularly middle-class fears that generate a need to control young people in public spaces, and it is particularly working-class forms of youth culture which are objected to. As the traditional view of girls positions them in their private and invisible 'bedroom cultures' with their friends, their active and collective use of public space and joint expressions of their voice in public arenas can be seen as a serious challenge to the traditional gender order, especially, if they are considered 'tough' girls 'running wild'.

In public imagery, it is obvious that the 'sweet' or 'girlpower' versions of girls friendships are far more popular than the controversial representations of 'tough girls'. However, there are similarities in these seemingly different versions of girlhood. Both phenomena concern girls finding their spaces and voices, although in very different ways. Images of 'sweet and fashionable' friendship groups are not threatening, as it seems that they do not plan to 'take over' public space, nor do they instigate fear in their surroundings; rather, they are represented as taking others into account (see Näre & Lähteenmaa, 1992) and aiming to please others (especially a male audience). In contrast, the representations of 'tough girls' show them as claiming their space no matter what other people think, and aiming to please themselves first and foremost, even if by ridiculing or aggravating others (see Honkatukia & Aaltonen, 2001).

However, in the end, both these groups of girls are positioned as 'vulnerable', and in both cases it seems the girls themselves are to blame for their potential problems. In the traditional view of female friendship girls are thought to be vulnerable to internal conflicts and indirect aggression, which are hard to handle and may have serious social consequences for girls on a personal level. In the new imagery 'tough girls' are seen as jeopardizing first and foremost themselves by exposing themselves to risky behaviours, even if they may also seem to be a threat to others in some cases.

In both cases, then, girls' relationships are presented as a risk factor in their lives. This is in stark contrast to recent popular representations of girls' friendships as empowering. That girls' friendships can at the same time be seen as 'empowering', 'too empowering' or 'not empowering enough' and 'risky' suggests that new analytical tools need to be developed in studies on girls' social relationships, in order to analyse how these constructions work in girls' lives.

Conclusion

In recent years, groups consisting of girls and/or young women have become more visible in the media – albeit in a sometimes controversial manner. Discourses of girl power and crisis have been used in relation to girls' relationships with each other. Girls' friendships are today also more tightly connected with commercial interests than before: representations of girls' friendships are used to sell various types of products to girls, from magazines to cosmetics and toys as well as hygiene products. Commercial cultures are even significant in producing differentiations within and among young people's groupings through the choice of hairstyles, branded clothing and sporting equipment, to name a few examples.

The contradictory public images of girls' friendships provide an important site for discussion, panic, and admiration. The proliferation of images stand in contrast to previous times when girls' friendships were not seen as a viable topic in its own right. The interest in and public visibility of girls' friendships and associations is a novelty, and linked to the heightened visibility of girls and young women in many other areas of life, as we show throughout this book.

Friendships and social groups form an important cultural space for girls and young women to explore different types of activities and subjectivities. However, girls' friendships can either support traditional ideas of femininity, or help girls in resisting and rene-gotiating them within their local environments. Girls can collec-tively challenge the patriarchal gender order, and look for ways of self-expression. However, not all types of activities girls engage in within their social networks are necessarily 'empowering'.

To return to our original question posed at the beginning of this chapter: what are friends for in the lives of girls and young women? As shown above, the answers are multiple, depending on the different social and cultural contexts where girls' social worlds are negotiated, as well as depending on the various ethnic, classed and educational backgrounds of the girls involved. According to the earlier mentioned 'girl power' discourse, girls' and young women's friendships are first and foremost for having fun, empow-erment and discovering their full potential together with other girls. The 'crisis' discourse, on the other hand, while recognizing the central importance of friendships to girls, depicts them as an emotional minefield where popular girls exercise their power over others, and where teary dramas are everyday occurrences. Neither of these simplifications catches the constantly shifting and renego-tiable, polymorphous social processes that girls and young women are involved in and that can be highly rewarding at the same time as they can be deeply problematic. Most importantly, it can be said that friends are important for girls in today's individualized soci-eties as a site for identity creation, which is an ever more demand-ing and difficult process requiring constant attention to emerging choices.

CHAPTER 6

Sexuality and the Body: Old Binaries and New Possibilities

Introduction

In this chapter, the focus is on the various ways girls construct their embodied subjectivities and create sexual relationships amidst contradictory discourses of femininity, sexuality and agency. The key 'tasks' of adolescence – achieving sexual, physical and emotional maturity – are shown as deeply gendered and gendering experiences. These tasks are delineated in psychological, developmental and sociological terms, the effect of which is to establish normative understandings of what it means to be a girl. Young women who cannot meet, or who reject these norms are often excluded from prevailing definitions of femininity on the basis of their race, class, ethnicity, ability, and sexuality. Often these norms set up binaries setting girls and women apart: good/bad, virgin/slut, straight/gay, popular/nerd. While the coercion of these norms can be seen to differently affect the lives of girls depending on how they are positioned in relation to race, class, ability and sexuality, the rise in eating disorders and body image problems are indicative of a widespread anxiety and stress focused on girls' bodies and sexualities.

Questions regarding embodiment are also at the centre of the current ideology of individuality, as several social and feminist theorists have shown. Today, the control of the body is regarded highly, and girls and young women constantly struggle to contain their bodies in acceptable ways. This requires a lot of energy and time, as well as participation in a gendered consumer culture. At the same time, the body is also a source of enjoyment and pleasure,

132

and girls and young women seek different ways of expressing themselves, for example, through body-art, dance and movement. These agentic interpretations of the female body are strongly present in the 'girl power' discourse. Some of the appropriations of this discourse emphasize girls' equal participation in sports, even in the kind that have formerly been defined as masculine, such as football.

Here we look at the ways girls in their diversity draw on and challenge the prevailing discourses and cultural practices surrounding sexuality and embodiment and how they make meaning of their bodies. We ask, how do young women negotiate their agency in the sexual sphere: what kind of practices are seen as 'good/bad', 'risky/safe' and for whom? And, to what extent is the range of sexual expression and embodiment expanding for young women? What kind of strategies do they employ in order to feel good about themselves and their bodies?

Young Women, Sexuality and the Body

Embodiment and sexuality are among the most contested spheres in young women's lives. It is difficult to find any other issue where young women are bombarded with more contradictory messages. On the one hand, traditional discourses of female chastity and sexual vulnerability, even danger, are still very powerful in discussions of young women's sexuality, but on the other, there are also new and conflicting discourses in circulation. These new discourses emphasize the centrality and positivity of sexuality and a range of possible ways in which sexuality might be expressed for both (young) women and men.

There are equally contradictory images and discourses in circulation in relation to female embodiment. Feminist discourses since the 1960s have emphasized the rights of women to have control over issues that are related to their embodiment, such as sexual relationships including those that are non-heterosexual, as well as contraception, abortion, pregnancy and childbirth (see for example Oakley, 1981 and 1984). While there are strong feminist critiques of the way in which women's bodies are objectified, commodified and sexualized in the media and advertisements, and of the distorted images of female embodiment that have been produced in these contexts (see for example Bordo, 1993; Gill, 2001), there are also 'sex positive' feminists who seek to reclaim sex, sexiness, and expressions of sexuality. Repeated claims that the manipulated media images of thin, perfect female bodies contribute to young women's problems with self-esteem, severe psychological problems, and eating disorders (Bordo, 1993; Frost, 2001) seem to have had few successes in limiting the circulation of standardized images of feminine beauty. Media images of women tend to reify dominant cultural standards of beauty, rather than support the diversification of images of femininity (Lloyd, 1996).

Young women – but only certain kinds of young women, who are slim and beautiful – can reap the economic and other benefits of the ever-increasing demand of the visual media for appealing images. At the same time, girls and young women also face growing pressures to modify their appearance in order to fulfil ever-changing feminine beauty ideals, which are practically impossible to attain (see Frost, 2001). These ideals are highly problematic also because they are still deeply affected by, and continue to reproduce Eurocentric, imperialist notions of beauty, portraying predominantly only white women as attractive. Girls and women of colour are thus marginalized to the place of 'the other' in the process of defining hegemonic notions of female beauty (Mirza, 1992).

> Marnina: So, how about people who come from Vietnam or China. Do you see pictures of models like that?
> Laleen: No.
> Marnina: Why do you think that is?
> Lin: It's like – only English people? They think that if you're not English – you're ugly or something. English people are the best. They're pretty.
> Tammy: It's like Chinese people are ugly.
> Trinh: Asian people.
> (Elementary school students, 11–12 years of age,
> Asian Canadian, quoted in Gonick, 1997.)

As Rosalind Gill (2001) has pointed out, while contemporary advertising has responded to feminism by starting to represent (attractive) young women less as passive sex objects and more as desiring sexual subjects who make their own choices, one of the effects has been a neoliberal promotion of 'commodity feminism'. Some of feminism's goals for women – such as independence and control over their own lives – are presented as things that the individual woman can achieve by purchasing certain products or services that help her please herself, instead of through a collective struggle for social and political change in society. (Gill, 2001.) In these instances, the critical content of feminism has been neutralized and made more or less into a mere visual style in advertisements. However, some of the products advertised in this way have become very popular with girls and young women, who seem to welcome them as signifiers of their independence as individuals in the consumer society (Gill, 2001). This topic is developed further in the next chapter.

Young women are at the epicentre of the sexual/embodiment debates: their bodies, in varying degrees of (semi-)nudity, are repeatedly and routinely depicted, not only in media specialized in sexual content, but even in other contexts, such as in music videos and advertisements of various types of products and services. Attractive young women who expose their bodies daringly in the media are often rewarded with large sums of money and plenty of contradictory publicity: they are celebrated as courageous and 'daring' on one hand, while on the other, they may be presented in negative contexts, such as causing sex scandals. In recent years, even men's bodies have become more important as visual effects in advertisements and the media, but it is still obvious that women and men, even when portrayed similarly, convey different kinds of cultural images. Traditional perceptions of femininity and masculinity are constantly reproduced in cultural products (Sankari, 1995, p. 32). While young women are among the avid consumers of magazines that concentrate on beauty, fashion and celebrities, there are also those who are eager critics of these images.

> I am not a size 8, but I am happy. I never really believed that was possible. I'm not always completely comfortable in my body, but most of the time I'm fine. . . . I'm much healthier as a larger person than I was as a very thin person. I have a life – not just an obsession about food. . . . To all young women, I'd like to say:
>
> - Don't let anyone define your sense of beauty for you.
> - You have a right to be angry with a society which tells you that beauty only belongs to a few people.
> - You also have a right to change that definition.
>
> (Amanda, Australian, quoted in Pallotta-Chiarolli, 1998, p. 36.)

It is also possible to read magazine images of woman queerly and to thereby produce a range of other meanings and effects of these images. For example, Anna Mills (2001) suggests that there is something intriguing about the sexualized images of women found in magazines whose audience is also women. She argues that there may be more going on than feminist analyses of the male gaze makes room for. She asks: 'how can the sensual, the erotic, and the sexual not be woven into those complex and intense emotions that women feel when they compare themselves to each other? How can women's intense interest in other women be totally divorced from sexuality?' (Mills, 2001, p. 35). These magazines might also, therefore be considered a pedagogical site for the recognition and expression of non-heterosexual desire.

Whichever reading of media images of women one uses, it is recognized widely that the body and appearance have become more and more central for Western people's identity during the past decades. Culture in late modernity has become ever more visual and aesthetisized, and this development has placed new pressures on individuals regarding the presentation of their bodies. The body both expresses and produces individual identity (Ziehe, 1991; Sankari, 1995); Goffman has defined this as the creation of a 'suitable surface presentation' of identity (Bordo, 1989, p. 17; Goffman, 1969, cited in Lloyd, 1996). There is an increased aware-ness of the importance of personal attractiveness in people's rela-tions to each other. Particularly for women and girls, it has been argued, there has been a shift away from codes of behaviour to a concern with the appearance, and visual aspects in the production of femininity (see Brumberg, 1993; Goffman, 1969; cited in Lloyd, 1996). Urban space in itself has become a site where various per-formances, based on commercialized fashion as well as lifestyles, compete with one another (Turner, 1984, pp. 110–12). Urban public space has been reorganized into arenas of public display, such as discos and malls. Young women and girls have ventured in growing numbers into these public spaces, experimenting with ways to make these spaces their own (Nykyri, 1996; Ganetz, 1995).

The Objectified Female Body Revisited

Young women are encouraged to relate to their bodies as objects that exist for the use and aesthetic pleasure of others, and to work on the improvement of their appearance. The body is to be held away from oneself, considered critically and judged by its attrac-tiveness or unattractiveness. Girls are told from a very early age to pay attention to their appearance. Thus a young woman '... becomes for herself the object who is being worked up to correspond to the textually defined image. She becomes the object of her project' (Smith, 1988, p. 49). Girls are encouraged to create an objectified relationship with their body. For example, magazines for girls are full of detailed beauty tips, such as these, telling the readers how to prepare for a dance:

> A dark and dramatic Cinderella. If you are dark, you get the best result by choosing a pure colour, for example red, black or violet. Because of the strong colours you will get attention, perhaps because you otherwise avoid these colours. . . . If your eyes are dark, it is best if you choose a light violet make-up, which is opposite to the brown of your eyes. Combine this with a light rose lip gloss, so your eyes will draw attention. . . . (Kurki, 2000, pp. 4–5; translation from Finnish by Sinikka Aapola.)

The 'discovery' of young women as a consumer group has brought particular contemporary manifestations to this phenomenon. Due to elusive, shifting and limited notions of beauty perpetuated by the profit motives of the beauty industries, and the hazy representation of men's desires, women's bodies can never be quite right, and can always be improved. This improvement becomes an imperative of identity and happiness for young women due to the complex relationship between self and body (see for example Brumberg, 1997). For example, although cosmetic surgery has been primarily targeted at older women, increasing numbers of young women (and their families) are willing to invest large sums of money for breast enlargements, in order to meet the beauty ideals of the day, sometimes at the cost of their health ('Health warnings call for cosmetic surgery', 2001). It has also been suggested that sometimes young immigrant women living in the West undergo cosmetic surgery in order to better conform to the prevailing beauty ideals (Ellburg, 1996, cited in Bengs, 2000, p. 120). However, while many studies report that young women do consider having some form of cosmetic surgery, fewer actually have the means to do so, as surgery is expensive (see Bengs, 2000, p. 120).

In traditional Western thinking, women are their bodies, and yet they are expected to use their minds to control their bodies' excesses, inadequacies and unruliness. Western culture has, since the Enlightenment, constructed the body as something apart from the self, but only offers real rewards for this separation when these selves are men. The fact that women also have minds means that their very selves must be harnessed in the reproduction of their bodily value. Satisfaction with the body becomes integral to a sense of happiness with one's self. Crawford *et al.* (1992) suggest that happiness in youth is often associated with mastery and knowledge, but that '. . . girls gain this competence with regard to the body, boys with regard to material things' (Crawford *et al.*, 1992, p. 88). A sexually mature young woman must learn to competently manage her unruly body to receive the appropriate amount of heterosexual approval. In the early twenty-first century, the Western ideals of embodiment emphasize not only thinness, but rather control of the body, fitness, and firm muscularity, particularly for young women and men. The current Western idea of success is linked with control within all areas of life, including the body, and this applies particularly to women.

The hetero-normative culture means that women are constantly being viewed and reviewed in terms of attractiveness (to men), but this surveillance is particularly heightened in such public spaces as discos and restaurants (Nykyri, 1996). However, this surveillance is not only perceived as a negative phenomenon; sometimes women want to be seen and receive attention from other people, and they willingly go to places where such attention is forthcoming (Nykyri, 1996). The idea of these spaces is to present one's body to the gaze of the others, to see and to be seen simultaneously, and to create contacts across the gender divide. Young women who frequent discos talk about the amount of maintenance work that goes into achieving an attractive appearance. However, this is not necessarily perceived as laborious and anxiety-provoking, but can be a joint, enjoyed activity of friends, who act as stylists and hairdressers for each other (Nykyri, 1996). In this way, girls' collective culture has integrated in itself the 'beauty projects' that are required of individual girls and young women (Brumberg, 1997). There is pleasure to be derived from the knowledge that one fulfils the feminine beauty ideals, while there is also pain associated in the awareness that one does not.

> I don't exactly have the most beautiful body in the world. My back is crocked [sic] and sticks out. But there's nothing I can do about that. (Tora, 21, Swedish, quoted in Barron, 1997, p. 229.)

Some girls worry about, and spend a great deal of their money and energy on, their appearance, clothes and adornment (for example Frost, 2001). For many young women, relationships to their bodies are in terms of sites of various 'beauty projects', and they are inclined to view their own bodies critically, as always lacking and in need of improvement. Failure to fulfil the dominant beauty ideals may lead young women to develop serious body image problems and even body-hatred (see Frost 2001; Brumberg, 1997). The female body has come to be seen as always 'under construction', a 'working site', whose maintenance and improvement requires a lot of time and attention; time spent on doing fitness or planning a low-fat diet, as well as acquiring trendy clothing, applying make-up, adorning one's hair and so on. Traditionally, this maintenance work is required to remain hidden from view (with the exception of working out), with only its final product – a good-looking appearance – to be displayed (Nykyri, 1996). There may be increasing exceptions to this rule, however, as when girls use their 'beauty projects' such as doing each other's hair or applying make-up to bond with each other in school (see, for example, Gordon *et al.*, 2000b, p. 169; Hey, 1997). Further, the popularity of reality TV 'makeover' programmes suggest that increasingly, the work one does on oneself is suitable material for public scrutiny.

> I am not a pretty girl
> That is not what I do. . . .
> I am not a pretty girl
> I don't really want to be a pretty girl
> I want to be more than a pretty girl.
> (Ani Difranco, singer-songwriter,
> USA, 1995.)

Young women's work on their appearance may sometimes take on playful and experimental meanings. Girls often try out various styles of dress, hair-do and make-up before defining their 'own style', and while this process can be anxiety-provoking, it may also have some liberating and unifying dimensions.

TT: Do you think there has ever been friction between the groups (of girls)?
Ronja: Well . . . it's just that Helmi and they . . . dress a little differently than other people usually do. . . . I do admit myself that I was a bit astonished to see Ansa with her red hair at school. . . . Why do they do such things, whatever has struck them all of a sudden . . . before some of them were ordinary. I cannot explain, it's as if they change all of a sudden . . . whatever has struck them? But then you think that the people have not changed at all. If they dress differently, so, well let them.

(Ronja, secondary school student, Helsinki, Finland, quoted in Tolonen, 2001, p. 112, translation from Finnish by Tarja Tolonen.)

Tolonen notes that the differences in the dress styles of the girls in her study symbolize their differences in relation to embodiment in general, with some girls choosing to remain more subdued in the school community, while others seek agency, voice and visibility (Tolonen, 2001, pp. 106–15).

A Difficult Balancing Act

It has been argued that women are expected to always 'submit themselves to the male gaze', and present their bodies in such ways which aim to please men. However, young women are also expected to exhibit responsibility in avoiding unwanted male interest. Responsibility thus extends to unsolicited as well as desired heterosexual contact. For example, through heterosexualizing discourses of adolescence, many female body parts become associated with sexuality even if they serve no innate sexual function (see Haug, 1987). The consequence of this is that young women must monitor and control what can and cannot be seen, and be responsible for the effects of the sexual meaning of their body parts in social relations. Girls themselves keep a close eye on each other and create distinctions between those girls who get it 'right' and those who are 'wrong'.

> I think of a slag as someone who's ... just ... there's a lot of them around this school. They walk around sort of clicking their heels, sort of their bums swaying from side to side and they're caked in makeup. And it's so obvious that they are out to 'get the boys' really. That's it! That's what I'd say a slag is. (Suzy, Britain, quoted in Hey, 1997, p. 117.)

However, as Sue Lees has testified, girls get labelled as slags for many reasons, many of which have nothing to do with their actual sexual conduct (Lees, 1993). It is also important to acknowledge that within the traditional Eurocentric discourses of sexuality, young women of colour have been labelled as stereotypically more sexually active and morally 'loose' than their white counterparts (see for example Mirza, 1992). These stereotypes are still visible within media representations of women of colour as 'exotic', erotic temptresses.

German researcher Frigga Haug and her research collective write that for women, 'innocent' parts of the body become 'guilty'; that is, they are utilized for the production of sexuality (Haug, 1987, p. 153). In particular, 'innocent' body parts such as legs, hair and stomachs are drawn into the representation of female sexuality as passive and display-oriented; valuable and meaningful for '. . . being touched and looked at . . .' (Gilbert and Taylor, 1991, p. 13). The sexual connotations of areas such as shoulders, thighs, backs and the like ensure that young women are preoccupied with the accidental or intended messages their flesh may display. As a result, they learn to restrict their movements so as to preserve 'modesty' and to attempt to display their bodies as 'neutral' in order to allow them to do everyday activities without the ascription of sexual meaning. Wex's classic study of male and female body postures establishes that after the age of ten or so, girls stop sitting with their legs apart in school photos. That is, once they learn the sexual meaning of their bodies, they must take extra measures to maintain its neutrality (Wex, 1979, p. 16). Even the school photograph, which is designed to represent the membership of the school as students (not gendered, not sexual), presents as a site of the struggle over the production of female bodies as sexual.

Nancy Lesko argues also that girls' school dress codes that emphasize modesty and restraint perpetuate the image of '. . . girls' bodies as dangerous and needing to be controlled' (Lesko, 1988, p. 130). 'Covering up' is thus a strategy to defend against sexual meaning even whilst reproducing that meaning. For girls, the transition from youth to adulthood is marked by learning to read the female body as sexual and then taking responsibility for this meaning. The need for containment is a consequence of the attribution of sexual meaning. Becoming sexually mature, then, means becoming responsible for the sexual meanings attributed to the female body; sometimes gaining the sexual attention of men, but at the same time being responsible for exercising caution within sexual relationships (see Harris *et al.*, 2000).

Contested Sexual Knowledges and Sex Education

The growing commercialization of sex and spreading of sexual images across more and more spheres effects young women in their everyday lives. Popular magazines directed at girls and young women continue to give them beauty and weight-loss tips, but in the late twentieth century, they also publish sex tips in a similar fashion: young women are advised on erotics, seduction and sexual technique, various positions and other ways to increase sexual enjoyment for both (heterosexual) partners, but particularly the man. While it can be argued that it is in a sense positive development that sexuality is no longer a taboo in materials directed at young women, and that they are seen as active, desiring sexual beings, a straight reading of the main discourse of sexuality within the women's magazines seems nevertheless to reproduce traditional gender ideals, where the woman is responsible for pleasing the man. However, as previously mentioned, a queer reading can produce other meanings: one in which shots of 'half-dressed models are a secret, perhaps unconscious way for women to desire women' (Mills, 2001, p. 37).

Other unofficial sites of sex education include the porn industry and 'adult entertainment' (euphemism for the sex industry), the effects of which on young people, particularly girls are an issue of concern. For example, the director of the women's crisis centre for victims of rape and sexual violence in Helsinki, Finland, has voiced her concerns about young women who think they are supposed to engage in such sexual acts that are depicted in pornographic materials. Kristiina Valkama argues that this kind of submissive and even violent sexual acts and techniques are seen as 'normal' and even routine in heterosexual relationships by many young people who consume products produced by the porn industry. She reports that many girls – some as young as thirteen – had consented to various kinds of sex acts suggested by their boyfriends, such as sadomasochistic sex acts and group-sex, but had later regretted their involvement, and sought help from the women's crisis centre (Saarilahti, 2002).

It seems that girls' and young women's attempts to position themselves as active and knowledgeable sexual beings may also be exploited, if they are not aware of the possibly problematic power relations within sexual relationships, and particularly within such sexual acts that are portrayed in porn videos and magazines. The question, then, is not only about the unequal power relations between men and women in heterosexual relationships, but also about the type of sexual knowledges that are available to girls and young women.

The discussion surrounding the vulnerability of young women and girls in heterosexual relationships can be seen as related not only to the issue of sexual violence against women, but also to

Loan Receipt
Liverpool John Moores University
Library Services

Borrower Name: Hardman-Singleton,Megan
Borrower ID: ******

Ecology for beginners /
31111002200275
Due Date: 02/02/2017 23:59

Young femininity :
31111013485949
Due Date: 02/02/2017 23:59

Total Items: 2
26/01/2017 14:49

Please keep your receipt in case of
dispute.

another old debate regarding the kind of sexual knowledge girls and young women should have. In the Victorian era, unmarried women and girls were to be protected from any knowledge of sexuality, and anything that was seen as related to reproduction or embodiment, even subtle references to undergarments, was seen as shameful (Brumberg, 1993).

Ideas emphasizing the female virtues of chastity and sexual innocence started to change at the turn of the twentieth century. Particularly doctors and other medical experts started to promote a hygiene-based discourse of reproduction, and in relation to this they required that mothers teach their daughters the basic facts of reproduction, and particularly menstruation (Brumberg, 1993). As the topic was seen as difficult to take up in mother-daughter relations, doctors started to produce leaflets that explained the 'facts of life' and instructed girls and young women on the hygienic management of menstruation. The medicalization of women's bodies is a central development of the twentieth century: many phases of women's life cycle and embodied phenomena not formerly thought of as medical problems have in recent times been redefined as requiring medical advice, drugs and treatments (Martin, 1989).

Sex education has caused a lot of controversy from different viewpoints, ever since it was introduced to schools. Religious conservatives in many countries have tended to consider even the most basic sex education for children and young people as morally damaging, while more liberal voices have criticized it for heterosexism, for excluding gay sexual practices, as well as for being too focused on reproduction (see Measor *et al.*, 2000). Feminist critiques, ours included, have pointed out that it would be important for sex education to critique the unbalanced power structures inherent in traditional discourses of heterosexuality and their problematic consequences for young women (Harris, 2001b; Kehily, 2002). Young women's and men's sexual behaviour are evaluated differently, and deeds that are seen as 'heroic' for young men can still be seen as deeply morally questionable when performed by young women. This 'double morality' has been recognized and challenged by girls themselves.

> I tend to think I'm an exception to the female role in terms of sexuality. I view sex as a notch on my belt and don't have a problem picking up a guy. Sex is an experience for me, and I don't have to be in love. The TV and the media never show women as that outgoing, unless they're evil characters. I find that when I initiate sex, it can scare guys. But if

the guy's not ready, then I can take on the role of 'Hey, that's cool' and pick up whatever we were doing and not go any further. (Mariah, 17, USA, quoted in Gray & Philips, 1998.)

Usually sex education materials address the topic of adolescent boys' sexual desires, but fail to recognize girls' and young women's sexual feelings. This has been described by Michelle Fine (1988) as the 'missing discourse of (female) desire'. One way to bring these issues up in sex education materials would be to draw upon the experiences of young women themselves, and use their cultural productions, as a starting point for discussions. The importance of same-sex friendship groups as sites of social learning about sexual relationships should also be recognized (Kehily, 2002, p. 208). These approaches could perhaps help pave way to enable young women to become protagonists of their stories about sex, and ultimately result in positive, agentic experiences for them across the spectrum of sexualities (Harris *et al.*, 2000; see also Thomson, 1995). This is particularly significant for young women whose sexual agency has been rigorously controlled or denied. For example, disability rights activist Harilyn Rousso (1988, p. 2), writes about her own adolescence, only a generation ago, that sexuality was considered irrelevant to her. She says,

> One of the myths in our society about disabled women is that we are asexual, incapable of leading socially and sexually fulfilling lives. When I was growing up, my parents and I accepted this myth without question. We simply assumed that because I had a disability, I could not date, find a partner, or have children. As a teenager and young adult, I put aside any hope of a social life and concentrated on my studies. It never occurred to me that I had any alternative, that I could have both a career and a romantic life. Betty's lifestyle (another woman with a disability), her successful marriage to an interesting, dynamic man made me question for the first time the negative assumptions I had about my social potential. She planted the seeds of positive possibilities. (Rousso, 1988, p. 2.)

For young women both with and without disabilities, medical and hygienic discourses have dominated in the types of sexual information given out within schools as well as by public health organizations (Measor *et al.*, 2000), although this kind of information is still not provided in all societies. However, in the early twenty-first century there are also other discourses around sexuality at play.

Comments on sex education at school:
'I wish we could do some work on other ways with relationships and
how you feel in certain situations, like that idea of role play on dealing
with pressure from boyfriends. That would be a good one.'
'I wish they would talk more about peer pressure and confidence – how
to stand up for how you feel, to have sex when you are ready for it.'
One of the girls expressed a wish to get information about oral sex:
'Well, you are much more likely to give someone a blow job than to
have full-scale sex with them. It is something which has changed since
your generation.'

> (Female secondary school students, Ferryfield and Streamham,
> Britain, quoted in Measor *et al.*, 2000, pp. 131 and 135.)

Some young feminists have worked towards circulating other
forms of sexual knowledges through the production of feminist
erotica. They use explicit language and images to create a feminist,
pro-sex response to the heteropatriachal norm. According to Hanne
Blank, sex positivity has at its core a substantial, multi-levelled, and
radical sexual politics:

> By creating politically alive smut, we create alternatives to the erotics
> and sexual politics on which we have been weaned. We give ourselves
> the chance to decolonize our brains and our cunts. The common denom-
> inator of politicised smut is that it goes deeper, thinks harder, and
> demands more of itself and of us, opening us to progress without sac-
> rificing heat. (Blank, 2002, p. 91.)

Previously we have discussed the proliferation of sexual content in
the media, and this includes magazines for young women. These
often provide various types of sexual information to their readers,
namely advice on sexual technique, stories about erotic encounters,
and expert opinions on sexual problems. The various discourses
they draw on in their discussions of sexuality range from romance
to feminism, spirituality to legal discourse. It remains to be seen
how these affect the types of sexual knowledge that girls and young
women have access to, let alone how they apply the information
they have received in their own life situations. It is nevertheless still
often the case that in most materials on sexuality, young women
are the passive object rather than the active subject. However, it is
clear from research that these kind of magazines and their portrayals of sexual matters are attractive to girls and young women,
and that they eagerly discuss issues brought up in magazines in

their friendship circles, and make sense of them together (see Kehily, 2002; Finders, 1997).

> Group discussion after a sex education class at school:
> Joanne: The boys were dying of embarrassment!
> (all laugh)
> Ruth: Yeah, I know, maybe 'cos we read the magazines, they don't read them. Like for us there is a problem page in every magazine, girls' magazine, but they don't have them in boys' magazines, like football magazines and that – you don't see a problem page – so that's probably why.
> (Female students, 14–15, East Midlands, Britain, quoted in Kehily, 2002, p. 123.)

Many feminist-oriented youth workers have explored ways to approach issues such as sexuality in a different way, in an interaction with girls. Sites have been set up on the Internet to provide open information about sexuality for girls (see for example, US-based www.sextec.org, www.siecus.org, www.scarletletters.com). In a girls-only youth centre 'Tyttöjen talo' (Girls' House) in Helsinki, Finland, special evenings are held by female sex educators and youth workers for small groups of girls, and they have been hugely popular. In these gatherings, the group leaders have open discussions with the participants about the mixed messages concerning girls and sexuality, as well as about safe sex. Girls have the chance to discuss their own perceptions of sexuality, and ask sensitive questions they would not express in a larger group. The educators also encourage the girls to explore their own bodies and embodied pleasures in order for them to be more aware of the kinds of erotic contact they are willing to engaged in (www.tyttojentalo.net). Researchers and youth workers are also talking about the importance of including boys in sex education in new ways, in order not to leave the responsibility for changing the terms of sexual relationships solely to girls (Measor *et al.*, 2000, pp. 159–62).

Growing Up, Heterosexuality and Double Standards of Morality

> The focus on boys is hammered into us pretty early through the magazines and through society; the normal situation is to have a boyfriend. And if the girl ever ends up without a man at the end of the stories, we

know that she will soon have one again because she is so attractive. (Annika, 16, middle-class, German, quoted in Herrmann, 1998, p. 240.)

The process of growing up is highly gendered. One of the key social processes that shapes and regulates young women's experience of entering into 'adulthood', is the institution of heterosexuality (Rich, 1984). Discourses of compulsory heterosexuality are part of a network of power relations governing women's lives, and they have traditionally been crucial for girls and young women in positioning themselves as 'properly' female and mature. However, as Rich suggests, the distinctions between heterosexual and homosexual identities are categorized more rigidly than they are necessarily lived. There is much that is fluid about identities, sexual practices and experience. Female subjectivities are collectively formed in, and by, historically changing, social and cultural contexts, structures and practices concerning femininity (Haug, 1987). Body management, as discussed previously, and responsibility in heterosexual relationships are among the most important social regulations structuring young women's experiences within the sphere of heterosexuality.

Adolescence is particularly marked by physical changes that enhance girls' sexualization. Physical/sexual changes are often socially and textually represented as inevitable, universal and natural. The physical changes in puberty are seen to cause movement toward 'sexual maturity', and specifically, heterosexuality. The desire for the 'opposite sex' is constructed as natural and healthy, and youth is isolated as the stage at which such desire, previously dormant, should emerge (see Harris *et al.*, 2000). Adolescent sexuality can be seen as '... a social institution, in which heterosexuality is defined as normal, compulsory and a mark of maturity, resting on the representation of femininity and masculinity as complementary opposites' (Griffin, 1993, p. 160). This view is represented for example in school textbooks throughout Western societies, although the degree of heteronormativity varies (Aapola *et al.*, 2002).

The phase of youth is constructed as a stage in life for the creation of a normatively inscribed mature physical, sexual and emotional identity. These discourses of natural development persist despite more recent theorizing that would suggest young people are increasingly more fluid in their identities (Wyn & White, 1997). However, current notions about individualization of youth biographies do not tackle the persistence of discourses that naturalize and universalize adolescence. This is most evident when we examine the idea of sexual maturity for young women. The achievement of sexual maturity is a key element of successful female adolescence, but the hegemonic definition of sexual maturity is often prescriptive, limiting and oppressive to young women. In particular, to be seen as properly female requires an exclusively heterosexual identity, and the expression of this heterosexuality through complex and at times contradictory practices of relationship responsibility and body management.

Heterosexuality is still too often represented as the only normal and natural sexual expression of healthy growing girls. Heterosexuality is portrayed as natural, biological and inevitable, and in order to be perceived as sexually mature, young women must exhibit heterosexual desire. This hegemony of heterosexuality can be seen in the negative representations or silencing of young lesbians and bisexuals, and in the commonsense view of what constitutes sexual activity. It is a popular understanding that to 'have sex' means to participate in heterosexual penetration, and that youth is the period in which most women will first do this. Participation in the institution of heterosexuality is thus a sign of 'normal' development toward maturity (see Harris, 1996, Aapola, 1997 and 1999a). Young women can 'prove' their normality and maturity by providing evidence of heterosexual orientation in the form of crushes and then boyfriends. Being accepted by young men is represented as an accomplishment, especially if they are the 'right kind' of boy. For example, for young women with disabilities, it may be very important to attract a non-disabled boyfriend in order to feel that one is successfully performing mature, feminine heterosexuality.

> It has been very, very important to have (a boyfriend) who is not disabled. It was almost most important when I had relations exclusively with disabled boys. Then it was like this 'yes, but he has a disability, but it won't be like this later because later when I really meet the right one it will be someone who is not disabled.' I was determined about that. But then well, it changed some years ago. It happened at the time of my first real relationship with a boy who wasn't disabled. Then I realized, I think it was that, kind of, that wasn't the most important thing. That I had proved that I kind of was good enough and didn't have to prove that any more. (Lotta, 22, Sweden, quoted in Barron, 1997, p. 231.)

Not only must young women attract the appropriate kind of boyfriend, but they are obliged to tread very fine lines to emphasize their heterosexual desire, without actually doing too much heterosexual activity, in order to be perceived as mature. Achieving female sexual maturity involves expressing heterosexuality through the sexual hierarchy, wherein women are dependent on men, derive sexual identity through managing their bodies with male desires in mind, but are simultaneously responsible for the sphere of sexual relations (see Harris *et al.*, 2000).

Adolescence is still typically described as a period in which young people shift from reliance on others to autonomy. However, as noted by feminist scholars, the notion of a linear progression from dependence to independence as a passage of separation is a masculine model (Gilligan, 1982). Young women instead continue to learn that to be a female adult is in part to relate successfully to a male partner (Johnson, 1993; Wyn & White, 1997, p. 49). Young women are seen to achieve adult identities through relationship management rather than independence; particularly in their placement in heterosexual relations. Traditionally, this has been depicted as a transference from a father to a husband, with the implications of infantile dependence and subservience that go with such a relationship. While this image is fading in some respects, and singleness is no longer pathologized in the same way it was earlier, parents are often reluctant to perceive their single daughters as independent individuals and may try to interfere in their lives (Gordon, 1994). Further, while today young women are encouraged to express freedom and independence in 'sexual choices', it remains that these choices are structured by the institution of heterosexuality and its rules about femininity. If a girl transgresses these rules, she risks being labelled as a 'bad woman' either by being defined as 'too sexual' or 'not sexual enough'. If she operates outside the heterosexual norm altogether, she risks being excluded from prevailing definitions of girlhood.

> I do think that it is appropriate for girls to ask boys out. This is because the boys should not be expected to have to ask the girl out and the girl should have the same opportunities as the boys do. (Aimee, 15, Australia, quoted in Pallotta-Chiarolli, 1998, p. 66.)

The discourse of female sexual maturity is built around the concept of responsibility. 'Responsibility' is associated with freedoms and choices – it is the 'price' of maturity, but it is also an aspect of true individualization in late twentieth century Western culture. However, the meanings of responsibility for women often under-cut its association with freedom. It is young women alone who are seen to be responsible for the consequences of the development of reproductive capabilities associated with adolescence. They are obliged to take on the issues of pregnancy, as though reproduction is only a female concern. Further, they become the gatekeepers of what is seen as biologically driven, powerful male sexuality and therefore must negotiate the 'slags or drags' phenomenon (Lees, 1986); that is, be available but not too available to men for sexual service, whilst also managing contraception (see Harris *et al.*, 2000). In recent years this responsibility has developed a new twist due to the HIV/AIDS crisis. Australian educational campaigns promoting condom use have been directed specifically at young women, encouraging them to 'tell him if it's not on, it's not on'. However, this kind of campaign only directed at girls and young women fail to address the power relations within heterosexual relationships (see Holland *et al.*, 1992).

Young women are held responsible for ensuring that safe sex is a reality, and for protecting both their own health and their part-ners'. A sexual double standard thus prevails: young women alone are expected to bear the responsibility in heterosexual encounters. They are the ones to act rationally and cautiously, whereas young men's sexual desires are seen to be beyond control. Thus boys are given freedom in the sphere of sexuality, while girls are to bear the responsibility over the various risks that are involved in hetero-sexual contacts (see Harris *et al.*, 2000). For some young women, however, this double standard is further underscored by public and private attempts to deny them even the limited agency offered by this risk management. For example, Saxton, Fiduccia, Chang and Montañez (1999, p. 8) have found that women with disabilities in the US and elsewhere are subject to involuntary sterilization laws, are more likely to use permanent methods of contraception, receive inadequate contraceptive information from health practitioners and report difficulty finding obstetricians to help manage their pregnancies. Even the somewhat problematic responsibility for the risks and consequences of heterosex is denied to many young women in these ways.

Moreover, sexual maturity is not just linked to responsibility within heterosex. Young women are simultaneously expected to manage their bodies but not to experience their sexuality positively and autonomously. This remains the preserve of men. As Sue Lees says, 'Men are involved in sexual acts and conquests; women are the objects of male desire' (Lees, 1986, p. 19). Young women learn to experience male heterosexuality as uncontrollable, forceful and autonomous, and female sexuality as reactive, receptive and inferior. Women are supposed to attract men, and therefore derive sexual value and meaning from their physical attributes, while men are supposed to be the initiators of sexual encounters and the chief beneficiaries of the central heterosexual practice – penetration – especially in youth (see Kinsey *et al.*, 1967; Koedt, 1973; Hite, 1977; Holland *et al.*, 1992). Young women learn that it is their sexual attractiveness to men that gives them legitimacy and value.

Young women are involved every day in complex negotiations over desire and passivity in heterosex that both draw on and conflict with the dominant discourses of sexuality. These have been well documented in a number of studies (see Halson, 1991; Holland *et al.*, 1992; Gavey, 1993; Wyn, 1994). Young women involved in cultural resistance object to sexual objectification in various forums; they want to be seen as people, and as sexual people, rather than objects. This can be witnessed in the various websites created by young women in recent years. In the cybergurlzines, a recurrent theme is a critique of the sexist images of young women presented in the media. There is a strong awareness among many young women of the distorted media presentations of their sexuality, and they have launched various campaigns to ridicule and counteract these images. For example, Nomy Lamm's zine *I'm So Fucking Beautiful*, and her writing, performances and rock opera, all tackle normative beauty ideals through cultural activism on queer, fat and disability pride (Lamm, 1995). These kind of campaigns have a history within the feminist movement, which has tried to act against oppressive media images of women as well as the pornographic industry (see Bordo, 1993).

However, there seems to be a real difficulty in trying to combine a critique of sexual objectification with the idea of female sexual agency and desire. Young women often run into problems in trying to present themselves as sexual beings without being objectified, because the discourses critiquing sexual objectification seem to offer little room for discussing women's desire and agency. A young woman can, in the sexual discourses available, either want sex or love; not both; she is presented as either a good girl or a bad girl; it is difficult to find a position that would not exclude one or the other (see Harris *et al.*, 2000). Girls and their sexual conduct are often monitored closely, not only by their parents and other adults, but by their peers and class-mates as well (see Measor *et al.*, 2000). Tolonen (2001, p. 251) claims that a girl's reputation at school is often very dependent on her (alleged) relationship(s) with boyfriends; she is supposed to be loyal and affectionate to her boyfriend, but not to express her sexuality too strongly, and if she violates these codes, she can end up as an outcast within the school community (see also Lesko, 1988).

However, even though girls are under strict surveillance in many spheres, and not encouraged to choose desire over love, some young women nevertheless choose differently. For example, in the Finnish 'stories' project (Aapola, 1997 and 1999a), several girls told autobiographical stories about their relationships with boys, and not all of them emphasized a long-term relationship with a boyfriend as their ultimate goal, although many did. Some girls described brief but enjoyable erotic encounters with boys, without activating the discourse of romance (see Harris *et al.*, 2000). The emphasis on long-term relationships is not surprising, as the dominant discourse of female sexuality heavily emphasizes the risks for a young woman in becoming sexually active: losing her 'reputation', facing sexual violence and risking unwanted pregnancy or venereal disease (see Aapola, 1999a).

Girls are supposed to only become sexually active within the romantic discourse, which emphasizes the importance of a 'continued', 'safe' relationship (Holland *et al.*, 1992 and 1998.) In many stories written by girls, continuity in relationships was regarded highly (Aapola, 1999a). Several female writers discussed the future of their relationships with their steady boyfriends and expressed their wish to stay together. It seems that particularly girls living in the city areas are more able to express their enjoyment concerning casual encounters with boys, than girls living in the countryside, where there may still prevail a more strict control on girls' sexual behaviour.

> Last summer I got a trip to Turkey as a confirmation present. My friend 'Kaisa' and my father all went on the trip. The sun was shining and life was happy. 'Kaisa' and I got to know the locals. Especially boys. We went to discos and had lots of fun. In the evening or more accurately at night when we came back to the hotel, my father was already asleep. 'Kaisa' and I laughed at all the funny things that had happened that evening and looked slightly amusedly at certain marks on our necks.

'I wonder what father will say?' we wondered and went to bed. In the morning we woke up and father saw the marks on our necks. Nothing but yelling came of it. Father said that I was only a child, 15 years. We were both yelling, and at that moment father was so unfair and unreasonable. That evening we sat in the hotel, offended. We were so annoyed and on top of everything we were ashamed. We were so absurdly ashamed. Father's words 'the whole trip has been ruined' haunted my mind. Thinking about it afterwards maybe I was quite childish. But, when you think again, at 15, it's my own business!! (Girl, 16, Helsinki, Finland, quoted in Aapola, 1999a, pp. 268–9, translation from Finnish by Sinikka Aapola.)

Parental control over young women's expressions of sexuality is a hotly contested issue. Some young women are perceived as particularly vulnerable to sexual exploitation and dangerous situations, and disability is frequently cited as a reason for increased protection of girls as they explore their sexuality. As the National Information Center for Children and Youth with Disabilities (1990, p. 14) notes, 'Many parents react to their adolescent's developing sexuality with alarm, and increase, rather than decrease, their vigilance. This is particularly true when the adolescent is female. Yet, when an adolescent female has a disability, the increased protectiveness of her parents may be accompanied by a tendency to treat her as if she were asexual, still a little girl.' Young women therefore have several discourses about safety, adulthood and sexual expression to negotiate, depending on their personal circumstances and family situations.

It is a powerful position for a young woman to be evaluated as attractive and desirable by men within the heterosexual sphere, but it is also a position potentially linked with dangers. Girls are aware of this, and often they are warned against going out alone at night, in order to avoid sexual violence by strangers. However, girls encounter sexual objectification and harassment in various types of contexts, such as the school, in their own homes, and frequently by boys and men with whom they are already familiar, such as boyfriends, schoolmates and male relatives.

In a large survey conducted in Finland, 41 percent of the 15–16 year old female respondents said that they had been harassed sexually at some point in their lives, and one third reported that they had been harassed during the previous year (Honkatukia, 2000, p. 22). There were no significant differences between girls coming from different kinds of backgrounds, but there were some minor regional differences. Similar results have been derived in other countries. The forms of sexual harassment the girls in this study had encountered ranged from unwanted invitations to sex, to attempts of touching and even sexual violence, physical coercion and rape. Over half of the harassment situations had occurred in (semi)public places such as on the street, at school, in shops, public vehicles or swimming centres. Discos, bars and parties were also frequently mentioned in the girls' answers, but about 10 per cent of the cases they described had happened in private homes, either in the girls' own home or in the homes of their acquaintances. (Honkatukia, 2000, pp. 22–37.)

> A no is a no. I happened to go out with a guy who did not respect that. I said no four times and then I was forced to hit him in self-defence. After that I broke up with him. (Patricia, 16, Sweden, quoted in Thulin & Östergren, 1997, p. 111, translation from Swedish by Sinikka Aapola.)

Women are legally granted sexual autonomy in most countries, and sexual violence is criminalized, but it is still not unusual that in the case of sexual violence, the woman who has been targeted is blamed for having 'asked for it'. Even in the courts, it is still often the case that the woman's behaviour and dress are judged to see whether she had 'sent sexually charged messages' to men and thus provoked the attack (Pohjonen, 1992, p. 196).

As we can see, it is not easy to make 'new' choices regarding sexuality as young women in the early twenty-first century. Some young women have, nevertheless, tried to actively balance the boundaries between being either a good 'nice' girl or a 'bad' girl and move beyond such definitions, as we have seen above. Their strategies include, among others, getting 'accomplices' for their transgressions; that is, other girls to join them in actions that might otherwise be risky for the individual girl. Also, they may seek sexual adventures on their trips to other towns or abroad, where they do not have to fear that their 'forbidden activities' are revealed to their acquaintances, as in the above story. Often, girls hide their sexual activities from their parents, which is an understandable strategy given that many parents try to restrict their daughters from sexual activity, but at the same time, it may make it difficult for a girl to seek help from her parents in the case she has experienced sexual violence or other problems related to sexuality.

Lesbianism and Bisexuality

Within the heteronormative developmental discourses of adolescence, homosexuality is often referred to as a temporary phase in young people's development; a phase they grow out of during their maturation process (Hall, 1904; Erikson, 1968; see Aapola, 1999a). This heterosexist view, while normative in its definition of a 'normal' sexual development, nevertheless opens some possibilities for young people to explore their sexuality outside the mainstream. They are seen as experimental with the expectation that they will end when an individual achieves a more 'mature' i.e. heterosexual identity. Within girls' friendships in general, physical intimacy is not as restricted as in male friendships, and this intimacy may sometimes lead to more consciously sexual contacts between young women. It may also be easier for girls to hide their erotic relationships with other girls, as sleep-overs and physical closeness are traditionally regarded as parts of girls' culture.

For some young lesbians and bisexuals the binary positions defined for women in the heterosexual discourses are not operative. This may be a liberating experience for young women, some of whom feel that as lesbians they do not face the same pressures to fulfil the normative feminine beauty ideals as heterosexual women do. There are also other liberating aspects in the identity of a lesbian for a young woman. However, at the same time the homophobia that continues to prevail produces outright harassment directed at gay people, severely restricts both young lesbian and bisexual women's recognition of their sexual feelings and their expression (see Tolman, 1994; Owens, 1998).

The expression of same-sex desire is not restricted in all societies; attitudes in many Western countries, such as Sweden and Netherlands, have become more and more open in recent years, and sometimes same-sex desires are more or less integrated in the mainstream society. In Canada, for example, same-sex marriage is legally recognized. Other societies, however, remain more homophobic, and polarize lesbian and gay sexuality from heterosexuality very clearly (Herdt & Boxer, 1996, p. 3). For a young lesbian, 'coming out' may thus mean very different things depending on the cultural and social context.

> I moved from Växjö to Stockholm to be able to come out. . . . I have never understood those gay guys and lesbians who stay in little towns like Växjö and Åmål. If I walked hand in hand with [my girlfriend] at

Storgatan in Växjö, people there would stare their eyes out, only to go home later and write letters to the Editor of [local newspaper] about how these women are not in accordance with the Bible nor nature. (Jenny Svenberg, lesbian, journalist, pianist and artist, Stockholm, Sweden (Svenberg, 1999, p. 107) translation from Swedish by Sinikka Aapola.)

In many countries, homosexuality has until quite recently been labelled as a crime or a mental illness, and heterosexist attitudes still prevail strongly. For too many young lesbians, feeling alienated from their peers is still a part of their growing up, and for some, the burden of loneliness is too much to bear and their mental health suffers accordingly (see Thompson, 1995, pp. 202–14). For others, their sexual identities are also an entry into a political identity as they find or help to create a gay community in which they are supported and loved.

> At fourteen, I felt like an outcast because of my bisexual feelings. I decided to be as different as possible. I joined the punk rock scene and became politically active. I went to gay marches, including the gay rights march in Washington, D.C. This helped a lot because most of the time I have had to hold back being bisexual, but there I could just relax. I realized that there a lot more people who are gay than let on. (Angie, 17, USA, quoted in Gray & Phillips, 1998 p. 130.)

The pains, uncertainties, joys and excitement of developing a lesbian identity for a young girl are well represented in the internationally popular Swedish movie 'Fucking Åmål – Show Me Love', by Lukas Moodysson (1998). In the film, young girls in a remote Swedish town are trying to create their sexual identities. One of the girls, Agnes, is a lonely newcomer, who does not find friends, let alone love in the school environment. She is desperately in love with Elin, a popular girl, who is dissatisfied with her life as well, and wants something out of the ordinary to happen. Agnes contemplates suicide and is convinced life has nothing good in store for her. Elin finds a boyfriend and experiments with heterosexuality, but in the end finds herself more and more drawn to Agnes, and leaves her boyfriend. Together the girls daringly face the curious looks of the people in the small town, and start developing a romantic friendship against all odds. It seems these girls have managed to define being 'different' as empowering.

The film demonstrates the gradually shifting discourses of young lesbian sexuality: there are now more positive representations of lesbians than before. At the same time, lesbian and gay communities have become more visible in many countries, and there is more support available for young gays and lesbians. For example, in some areas in the US there is now a tradition, even if limited in scope, of organizing annual all-gay prom dances as an alternative to traditional high school proms which celebrate the institution of heterosexuality (Herdt & Boxer, 1996, pp. 148–51). In the Lesbian and Gay Prom, young people experiment with gender blending and cross-dressing which, according to Gilbert Herdt and Andrew Boxer (1996, p. 150), can be interpreted as a way to rebel against heterosexist norms and to 'poke fun at the moral probity of heterosexual roles'. In this changing climate, lesbian and bisexual young women in Western societies are finding it easier and easier to come out and form positive sexual relationships. New technologies have a particularly important role in the creation of safe spaces and sites for relationship- and community-building.

> I actually met my first girlfriend via the net. I'd accidentally clicked 'reply all' on a long chain letter and, days after, received an e-mail from this girl. After general chit blah blah blah we discovered we were at the same school, met up, built up a friendship and things developed from there. I guess without the net I never would have met her. (Liz, 15, Australia, quoted in Hillier, 2001, p. 126.)

Femininity, Agency, Embodiment and Subjectivity

As severe as the commercial exploitation of young women's bodies in the media is, and as many problems as have been identified in relation to young women's identities and their bodies (see for example Frost, 2001), it is nevertheless important to remember that the body is not necessarily a source of anxiety for girls and young women. It can also be a very positive site of self-expression, identity-creation and enjoyment. However, this topic has not been as popular within research nor in the media; nor has the experientiality of the body received a lot of attention, perhaps with the exception of health-oriented research.

> My body is fucking beautiful, and every time I look in the mirror and acknowledge that, I am contributing to the revolution. (Nomy Lamm, queer, fat and disability activist, USA (Lamm, 1995, p. 40).)

As several researchers have pointed out, today's Western culture is preoccupied with the body: its health, fitness, appearance and many other aspects (see for example Grosz, 1994; Turner, 1984). However, the messages as to how to get it 'right' in relation to the body are contradictory, and even more so in relation to the female body. Women are encouraged to overindulge themselves simultaneously as they are told to restrict themselves; to diet as well as to enjoy consumption; to stop smoking as well as to drink alcohol; to feel good about one's body as it is, as well as to try to modify it through exercise and so on. For a young woman whose body is changing rapidly, it is all the more confusing trying to create a balanced relationship with one's body (Frost, 2001).

Often, to discover what feels best for oneself requires experimentation, and the body is one of the most accessible sites for this experimentation, as Hillevi Ganetz (1995, p. 78) points out. She refers to Kirsten Drotner, according to whom body is essential to the new cultural forms of expression, and who highlights different forms of border-crossings in relation to the body (Drotner, 1991, cited in Ganetz, 1995). For girls and young women, this means that they spend considerable energy on different types of 'beauty projects' that require various forms of body modification and adornment. While for many young women the careful application of cosmetic products such as make-up and hair colours, as well as conscious choices regarding clothing and hairstyles are an essential part of their style experimentation, for some, there are even more enhanced forms of body modification.

In recent years, body piercing, tattooing and other forms of body-art and modification that leave permanent marks on the body have become more and more popular among both young women and men. While these phenomena have previously been typical to the rituals of tribal and Aboriginal societies, they have also been linked with subcultures such as those of drug-users or prison inmates. However, in recent years they have become a more and more mainstream phenomenon, a trendy fashion used by individuals for the aesthetic enhancement of their bodies. This has been received with considerable controversy, especially when young people have been involved; in psychological discourses, body modification has often been associated with self-mutilation performed by mentally disturbed individuals (Pitts, 1999). However, other, more culturally sensitive forms of analyses have been offered as well; tattooing, scarification and piercing have been interpreted as an indication of postmodern neo-tribalism (Maffesoli, 1996, cited in Turner, 1999, p. 41). 'Neo-tribes' are social associations that are voluntary and superficial, and thus the body marking associated with these youth cultures is also optional; as compared to traditional tribalism, where membership was very loaded and highly socially significant for the participants, and thus the marking of the bodies was obligatory. In traditional societies, body marking carried collective meanings, while in today's late modern societies, it is a sign of growing individualization, linked to the consumer culture, and requires an ironic, detached reading (Turner, 1999, pp. 39–49).

The genderedness of this phenomenon has so far not been adequately analysed, but women's body modification projects have often been considered more problematic than men's. It has been claimed, for example, that women use body marking to come to terms with their body dissatisfaction (Pitts, 1999, p. 297). However, as Victoria Pitts argues, these interpretations of women's body modification do not take into account the possibility of young women making political statements with body marking; the discourse of self-empowerment associated with body modification is muted (Pitts, 1999, p. 297). Joan Jacobs Brumberg (1997, pp. 135–6) interprets girls' piercing practices as a statement of sexual liberalism, against conventional sexual norms. She claims that for many girls, piercing and other forms of body marking are a way to differentiate themselves from bourgeois values and mainstream youth culture, and particularly the constricting ideals connected with femininity. However, some heterosexual young women referred to their genital piercing as a 'special secret' shared only with their boyfriend, which made them feel particularly feminine (Brumberg, 1997, pp. 135–6).

Experimentation with the body does not, however, only mean decorative projects for girls and young women; increasingly they do something active and enjoyable with their bodies, for example dance, go to the gym, play football, ride horses and so on. This phenomenon is also related to the increasing amounts of money and leisure time that girls and young women have at their disposal. Forms of physical exercise have traditionally been classified according to gender, and some have been considered more suitable for women, such as dance and gymnastics. However, in recent years young women have challenged gender restrictions even in the area of physical exercise and sports. While girls' bodies may still often be objects of the gaze of others, as discussed above, they are also an increasingly important source of their own pleasure.

Girls and young women find personal enjoyment in their own embodied skills and strength (Ganetz, 1995, p. 78).

Sports and the Limits of Femininity?

The embodied enjoyment girls may get through an involvement in sports in ways that have been traditionally considered masculine, is well exemplified in the popular movie by the female director Gurinder Chadha: 'Bend it like Beckham' (Britain, 2002). In the film a football-crazed teen-age girl of South Asian descent joins an all-girls' football team against the will of her parents, who worry that she will not become a proper Indian woman if she continues to play this sport. For young Jess, however, playing football is the ultimate enjoyment, as she slowly comes to realize her own talent in the game, even if taking part in it means displeasing her family, whose approval is very important to her. The pleasure and energy Jess and her team-members display in their collective effort in a tradition-ally very masculine sport is set against conventional femininity, represented by Jess's mother and sister as well as her team-mate Jules's mother, defined as an aspiration towards an attractive appearance, good home-making skills and ultimately a stable rela-tionship with a man. The latter does not satisfy Jess or her team-members, whose dream is to be recognized as top athletes and to play professional football, although not wanting to sacrifice their close relationships in the process. Interestingly, in this context, the girls' rejection of traditional femininity and bodily adornment for a more active embodiment is interpreted by some of their family members as a rejection of heterosexuality.

As this film demonstrates, it is difficult for girls to balance active embodiment with a more traditional understanding of femininity, and ultimately they may be pressured into choosing one of these, as there seem to be few possibilities for combining the two. Famous female athletes who appear in the media may act as important role-models for girls in relation to embodiment, as an alternative to models and beauty-queens, who are famous only for their appear-ance. However, the borderline between these two categories has been dissolving in the past years, as there is more and more pres-sure on female athletes to make sure their appearance is feminine and attractive. It is no longer enough that women display strength and skills in performing their sport; they are also expected to look attractive (to men) while doing it. For example, Anna Kournikova, an attractive, blond Russian tennis-player at an international level, has been a popular model for various types of products in the early 2000s, and more because of her appearance than her actual tennis-skills. Women do not escape the critical gaze towards their appearance even when they concentrate on their own embodied performance and aim towards perfecting their skills in a particular sport rather than presenting themselves as attractive to the sport audience.

Another interesting, yet remarkably different, sport-related activity which is gaining popularity among young women is working out in a gym. The gym, like a disco, is a semi-public site where people devote their time to maintaining and improving the functionality and appearance of their bodies. In a similar way as dancing in the disco, working out at the gym seems to fulfil many different functions: it can be a space for spending some 'time of one's own' and concentrating on one's own thoughts, while it can also be a place for meeting other people, looking at other people, enjoying other people's company, all in addition to concentrating on one's training (see Sassatelli, 1999). Working out in the gym was originally a very masculine activity, but it has become a more gender-mixed phenomenon in recent decades.

Anne Sankari (1995) has identified two main groups of trainers: the bodybuilders/bodyshapers and the fitness trainers. These two groups have different goals, and consequently also often very different training programmes and even diets. The fitness trainers are the majority at the gym; they are after a more attractive, tighter, curvier, healthier body, while the bodybuilders aim at perfecting their muscles according to a particular bodybuilder aesthetic. Women and men can belong to either of these groups, but the bodybuilders tend to be more men than women, who are usually not encouraged to grow big muscles. However, it has become more and more acceptable for women to aim for a muscular body. At the gym, the body is often seen as fragmented; for example, there are different work-out-machines for each muscle-group, and people may purposely concentrate on shaping particular parts of their bodies, such as the shoulders, the biceps or their buttocks (Sankari, 1995.) Women and men typically use the same machines, but in different ways, with women using lighter weights, and aiming for different goals for their bodies.

CoCo: How do I get beautiful and tight arms?
MoonGirl: By bodybuilding. Use some weights and get some strength!
Diamond: I have the same problem. 'Dips' help for loose arms: you lean on your arms on a shallow table, for example, and then you start

'dipping' yourself. Aagh, I cannot really explain how to do that. But it also helps a lot to do series with light weights. And a diet helps as well. (Excerpt from an Internet chat-forum operated by *Demi*, a Finnish girls' magazine; subgroup 'the body': subject 'loose arms', April 7th, 2003; http://www.demi.fi/keskustelu.php?m=2&f=7&id=202648; translation from Finnish by Sinikka Aapola.)

As these examples of young women's sport-related activity demonstrate, physical activity is always regarded in gender-specific terms. Even the same types of physical activities are interpreted in clearly different ways for men and women, and the limits of acceptable types of embodied activity are different for each gender. In addition, ethnic and cultural differences, as well as social background, affect the scope of these limits, and it often requires considerable determination of individual girls to step beyond these limits; often they need special social support in order to be able to do it. Even within international top-level sports, women's athletic achievements are usually not rewarded with similar amounts of media attention nor monetary prizes as men's achievements.

Dance as Self-Expression

One of the few themes related to young women's bodily self-expression that has received some research interest is their involvement in various forms of dance. Girls have been seen to have a special relationship with dancing as a form of embodied self-expression (see McRobbie, 1987). Dance has been seen as a feminine activity something not for 'real men', unless practised in order to meet women. Some researchers claim that dance for girls in adolescence is a way to come to terms with and in control of their changing bodies and to take over spaces for themselves, as well as a way to relate to other young people, both male and female (Tegner, 1991).

However, there are different styles even within dancing, ranging from androgynous to feminine and to masculine or neutral styles, as Tuija Nykyri argues in her study of Finnish young women who frequent discos (Nykyri, 1996). She noticed that some young women tended to always use the same style of dancing, while others alternated between all the different styles, depending on their mood and the type of music they were dancing to. She also points out that while the young women dancing in the discos appear to perform their femininity first and foremost to male onlookers, they nevertheless sometimes concentrate on their dancing in itself, even when men are actively trying to get into contact with them. It seems that for the young women, dance can serve many purposes: it can be a solitary form of self-expression, or one way to be social, create and maintain contact with other people, to experiment with different forms of femininity, or to get feedback on one's appearance and one's skilfulness at dancing. The new forms of dance music that have become popular in the last decades of the twentieth century, such as hiphop and techno music, have promoted a new kind of club dance culture where the dance floor is more and more a site of individual self-expression and utopian collectivity, and less a heterosexual meeting place (for example Salmi, 1996). At its best, dancing to rhythmical music can offer young women an experience of 'flow' – a feeling of effort-lessness, timelessness, when everything around one disappears and only one's own movement fill one's consciousness (Nykyri, 1996, pp. 68–9).

> . . . often it (my dancing) is very energetic.. I do it with full force so that it is actually like exercise . . . it is the same as if you go to the gym you feel you get your pressures unleashed, perhaps it is the same on the dance floor. (Helena, Finland, quoted in Nykyri, 1996, pp. 68–9; translation from Finnish by Sinikka Aapola.)

Dance has been closely connected with various types of youth subcultures, particularly those that have been based on a particular style of music, such as punk, heavy rock and hiphop. However, girls' participation in the forms of dance connected with a particular subculture is always affected by the ideologies of femininity that prevail within the subcultural scene. This is well demonstrated by Leslie Roman's classic study of young women participating in punk slam dances in the USA (Roman, 1988). She found many gender- and class-related tensions at work at the dance gigs, where the dance space was usually dominated by aggressive male slammers. The women had to negotiate their participation in such ways that they could feel relatively safe from injury. However, young women from middle-class backgrounds as opposed to the young women from working-class backgrounds used slightly differing strategies, and justified their own involvement in different ways.

The middle-class young women defined their slam dancing either in terms of equal opportunity – as their right to participate in the concerts in the same way as the male punks – individual therapeutic release and transcendence from the tensions of their everyday lives, or in the code of bravery – emotional and physical stoicism over the injuries they often got from aggressive male slammers; they wanted to challenge the idea of feminine frailty. The working-class young women, by contrast, were more openly critical of the practices of the symbolic violence of the (often middle-class) aggressive male slammers, and emphasized their camaraderie and collective solidarity with other working-class punk women. For them, dancing to punk music was first and foremost a chance of erotic abandon and rescue, that offered a release from the economically and physically gruelling conditions they often lived in (Roman, 1988).

The meanings of dance as a form of cultural activity and self-expression for young women vary depending on the cultural space, as well as to young women's investments in the context of dance. While dancing can be a very positive experience for girls, it seems that within gender-mixed spaces such as discos and rock concerts they always have to engage in embodied negotiations about their use of space. Within the main-stream disco, outright physically aggressive behaviour is discouraged, and the female dancers have a relatively safe environment to express themselves, even if they are subject to the judging male gaze, but in more subcultural settings, women may be exposed to outright physical violations, even if they just try to enter the dance-floor and create a space for themselves.

Conclusion

In this chapter, we have discussed the relationships between bodies, sexualities and girls' identities. We have shown how the heteronormative demands of femininity produce contradictory positions for girls: to both work at presenting themselves as sexually attractive at the same time as to protect her reputation. Young lesbian and bisexual women experience these dynamics in ways that are different than heterosexual girls, but they can also encounter on-going homophobia, which may put restrictions on the expression of their sexual identities.

Young women try to negotiate ways in which to express their sexuality in such ways that do not compromise their independence and agency. They also look for ways in which to enjoy their bodies regardless of the beauty norms surrounding them. It is a constant struggle for girls to express feminine sexuality in socially accepted ways, while maintaining their agency as individuals and citizens. Various kinds of body projects have become more and more central to them, with the growing importance of the aesthetization of embodiment in Western culture.

Western girls in the early twenty-first century live their lives within confusing, even contradictory historical discourses surrounding maturity, gender and adolescence. They have been exposed both to traditional and feminist discourses of femininity on what it means to be a woman, and at the same time they are also surrounded by the prevailing neo-liberal discourses emphasizing citizenship based on individuality and 'free choice'. In the next chapter, we further explore this new kind of citizenship for young women as they increasingly take their place in the public world.

CHAPTER 7

Politics, Citizenship and Young Women

Introduction

Whereas once young women were simply an absent presence in the making of the 'youth citizen' (see Lesko, 2001), today they have emerged as subjects to be troubled over in their own right. As McRobbie (2000) argues, young women have become increasingly important to civic life and the polity, sometimes even operating as symbols of social change. In the domain of politics and citizenship, we suggest that this is related (but not limited) to a series of contemporary anxieties about the collapse of the nation state, unprecedented waves of migration, crises about new directions for social movements, and globalized economies that have radically altered traditional relations between individual state and citizen and have seen corporate power increasingly able to complicate notions of civic life and participation. This is particularly relevant to young people, as with the collapse of traditional school to work transitions and leisure/labour balances, youth citizenship is increasingly constructed around consumption rather than production.

Citizenship, Lister (2003, p. 13) observes, bestows an array of rights (civil, political and social) and responsibilities on individuals. It also implies a social relationship between individuals and the state, and amongst individuals themselves, in terms of membership of and identification with a national context and culture. While citizenship is traditionally defined in terms of rights or duties negotiated between the state and individuals, it has also been one of the most contested categories of political analysis (Lister, 2003, p. 14).

As Jane Kenway and Diana Langmead (2000, p. 313) have pointed out, there are dozens of problematic questions concerning citizenship, including who can claim ownership to it (and who cannot), on what basis, and for what purposes. The list of questions continues: whose interests does citizenship serve? What kind of consequences are there for exclusions from citizenship? (Kenway & Langmead, 2000, p. 313.)

Feminists have been particularly interested in understanding the gendered dimensions of citizenship. That is, they are interested not only in women's citizenship in relation to men's, but, also in relation to women's affiliation to dominant or subordinate groups, their ethnicity, origin, urban or rural residence, global and transnational positionings. Through tracing the discursive shifts in the meanings of the concepts, rights, needs, justice, dependency, entitlements and responsibility, feminists have exposed the relations of power which configure the terms of inclusion and exclusion in the polity (Kenway & Langmead, 2000, p. 313). The post-war period is generally seen as a time when formal rights were increasingly extended to those who had previously been excluded. It is, however, important to note that there are still groups who continue to be excluded from full citizenship rights, namely, registered alien workers, lesbians and gays, and children. It is also important to note that a series of outstanding issues around citizenship remain unresolved for indigenous minorities in settler societies (Stasuilis & Yuval-Davis, 1995). Taking indigenous land rights seriously entails unsettling claims of national collectivity and legitimacy on the part of what Australian Aboriginals have been calling 'the imposing society'. Often a complex situation arises in which there exist two national sovereign entities over the same territory – one which owns the state and one which attempts to establish a sovereign stateless society within it. The post-war period has also not fully produced equality in social rights which remains a goal that has yet to be achieved. Issues in social citizenship that continue to be goals rather than achievements include cultural, sexual, reproductive rights (Gordon *et al.*, 2000b, p. 187).

Young women face radical changes in their opportunities for livelihood, community affiliations and political engagements from those that existed a generation ago. These opportunities are central to the meanings and practices of citizenship. As we saw in Chapter 3, the shifts in the labour market and the education sector have had a dramatic impact on young women's life chances and outlooks. Here, however, it is important to document the aspects of socioeconomic developments that also affect their relationship to economic autonomy, national identity, community membership, political and cultural engagement. Each of these dimensions of citizenship has been profoundly affected by socio-economic shifts in the de-industrialized world. Young people, but young women in particular, have been at the centre of a re-defining of the meanings and practices of citizenship in accordance with these changes. In this chapter we explore the ways in which definitions and experiences of citizenship have altered for young women, reflecting on the discourses of choice, power, risk and crisis within this process. First, we look at traditional meanings of citizenship, including the set of rights formally associated with the status of citizen, and their relationship to women, youth and de-industrialized societies. We examine current trends in citizenship education as one of the means by which definitions of citizenship are produced. We also analyse the contemporary meanings of a number of dimensions of citizenship: economic independence, national identity, civic engagement, and cultural citizenship, asking how these are experienced today by young women.

Meanings of Citizenship

T.H. Marshall (1950) is considered to be the foundational thinker in the area of citizenship studies. He argues that citizenship encompasses three kinds of rights that are conferred on individuals in society in exchange for their responsibility to that society. These are civil rights (for example, freedom of thought, religion), social rights (economic security), and political rights (voting, standing for office). Marshall's expectation was that the state would be central in guaranteeing people's social rights, and from this strong state support would develop a responsible citizenry engaged fully in their communities. Civil rights and political rights would also be safeguarded by the state, but without a strong grounding in social rights, these would be more precariously achieved. The other important element in traditional theorizing of citizenship has been the balance between rights and responsibilities. Implicit in the contract between citizen and state is mutual obligation. However, what this means in practice has been the subject of considerable debate. This traditional conceptualization of citizenship, that is, social, civil and political rights balanced with responsibilities, has been fundamentally challenged by both feminist and youth theorists. Both point out that the citizen imagined by this framework is an adult male of privilege who is recognized as a rational actor in the public sphere. They suggest that citizenship has always been a more problematic achievement for both women and youth because they have been excluded from the public sphere, their rights have historically been non-existent, granted by proxy or remained subsumed beneath adult men's, and the responsibilities they are required to exhibit are scrutinized more closely and valued less (see for example Lister, 1997). Feminist critiques of this conceptualization of citizenship have included an intense scrutiny of the public/private dichotomy creating these exclusions. What has resulted from the critique is a call to assess gendered power within family, marriage and sexuality, and to provide an alternative to the public/private split (Lees, 2000, p. 259).

Challenges to definitions of citizenship have also taken on a new urgency due to broader socio-economic changes that have undermined both traditional conceptualizations of citizenship and placed new pressure on the critiques made by feminists and youth theorists. De-industrialization, the contraction of the welfare state, border transformations within and between states, the associated growth of multi-ethnic polities, the rise of new social movements for political participation, and the emergence of world transforming technologies of communication and imagination, globalization, and neo-liberal policies, are all forces that have re-shaped citizenship. Perhaps the greatest impact has been felt in the area of social rights. Whereas Marshall and others located economic security as a responsibility of the state, recent times have seen a shift towards privatization and subcontracting of services and withdrawal of welfare programmes. As Nagel and Wallace (1997, p. 52) argue, within de-industrialized states, marketization has replaced social planning. Along with these changes have been shifts in public discourse about entitlements and responsibilities for economic well-being. Marketization, competition and individualization have been significant in devolving responsibility for livelihood onto individuals. As Lister (1997) argues, participation in the formal economy as a paid worker has become an individual's citizenship duty. However, there are clearly gendered, classed and embodied differences in the ways this duty is lived. For example, in the United States there has been an explosion of news stories about highly educated, married, professional women choosing to stay home to raise young children. There is widespread support for women like this to make this choice. At the same time, there is a growing publically expressed resentment of poor and working class women who also want to raise their children at home but who need social assistance to do so. It is this second group of women who live most forcefully the insistence on paid work as a duty of citizenship. On the other hand, it is also important to note how this definition of citizenship may also become a marker of privilege, for the ways in which it might exclude the disabled and others who are not able to work (Yuval-Davis, 1997, p. 21). Economic security is no longer a protected right that is guaranteed by the state. Social rights are thereby re-defined as personal responsibilities, but they are at the same time much more difficult to achieve within conditions of contracted labour markets and global competition.

While the state no longer grants rights without requiring a hefty set of personal responsibilities, the ways it has operated as a symbol of connection and identification is also changing. The market potential of the economies, industries and products and services of states competes with their function as 'imagined communities' (Anderson, 1991). Further, forces such as mass migration, fears of threats to human security, global concerns with risk (see Beck, 1992), and heightened, visible ethnic and religious conflict have made clearer the fictions of a single national community. New world power conglomerations and alliances, disruption to neighbourhoods, the breakdown of old social movements have all affected the civic aspects of citizenship. In the absence of these community-building dimensions to citizenship, discourses of personal responsibility have been used to fill the breach. Fears of declining social connection have also been part of dialogue about the importance of the individual in the making of citizenship. As France (1998, p. 99) argues, the figure of the citizen who takes personal responsibility for their own welfare, but also for the welfare of their family and their community, fills in the space where the nation used to be.

Young People and Citizenship

These shifts towards a more personal, responsibility-based conceptualization of citizenship has had a particular impact on youth. The kinds of conditions that would guarantee citizenship in the past no longer exist for young people today. Their life trajectories no longer ensure that they will make an automatic, one way transition from school to work, from dependent to independent, from child to adult. These transitions also traditionally mark one's entree to adult citizenship. Markers of adulthood, whilst always constructed phenomena, seem even more ambiguous in contemporary times (see Aapola, 1997; Lesko, 2001). Citizenship is not, however, simply about adulthood (although it is often inextricably linked with changeable notions of being 'grown up'). As we have seen, it is associated with formal membership of a community whereby political, social and civil rights are won in return for responsibilities to the state and fellow community members. Whilst children are generally seen to be protected by broader, universalized notions of 'children's rights' (see Ruck *et al.*, 1998), young people are in a transition phase as they are on their way out of the age of minority, and therefore have to 'prove' their entitlement to protections and duties extended to adults. For young people today, demonstrating entitlement has become far more complex than in previous times, for the kinds of proof required are harder to come by. These include economic self-sufficiency demonstrated by an ongoing full time job, independent living away from the family home, non-reliance on welfare, and non-engagement in any aspects of the informal economy (especially the criminal economy). Whilst formal citizenship status does not have to be 'earned' by many young people (excluding large numbers of residents, migrants, refugees and so on), a perception of entitlement to citizenship and the ability to activate it meaningfully does. Citizenship itself has thus become contested territory for youth, with battles largely marked by ideological disputes over emphases on obligations versus rights. The 'transition' model of achieving adulthood is increasingly out of step with young people's lives, yet remains the way in which citizenship is bestowed upon them. Also, it has recently been argued that this view of children and young people as citizens-in-the-making is inadequate. There have been voices – even if still relatively marginal – that children and young people should be seen as citizens and agentic social actors in their own right, and their participation in political decision-making particularly in their local environments should be encouraged (James *et al.*, 1998; Lee, 2001).

Group discussion on young people's participation:
Pauliina: The older you get, when you have some kind of proof, that you can take care of things, then you will be given more possibilities to take responsibility.
Mari: Again, age makes a difference, then when you are older you are listened to more.
Interviewer: What age is that?

Mari: I don't know, when you can like make decisions about your own things and when you can like live alone, decide about your own matters. . . . To take responsibility.

(Female junior high school students, Helsinki, Finland, quoted in Haikkola 2003, p. 84; translation from Finnish by Sinikka Aapola.)

Young people have become central to the shift in the conceptualization of citizenship from state protection of rights to individual responsibility for economic security and social welfare. A new emphasis on responsibility in public definitions of citizenship has put particular requirements on young people. Currently, there is an emphasis on their social debt, and on the importance of establishing youth responsibilities before youth rights. Hall, Coffey and Williamson (1999, p. 503) note a widespread 'shift away from a "passive" rights-based language of citizenship towards a new emphasis on citizenship responsibilities and active participation.' Trouble-making, unemployment, poor school achievement and crime have been identified as key issues associated with young people living in a changing world that can be addressed through citizenship education (see Griffin, 1993). Both punishment and education are seen as solutions to these problems. Young people are thus constructed as a social problem but also a social resource: if they can be taught to be personally accountable for their achievement of citizenship they can be part of the broader re-definition of rights and state responsibilities.

Education for Citizenship

One of the primary functions of education is seen as preparing children to take up their place as future citizens. Schools are expected to confirm the social, political and cultural order of the nation state by regulating ways in which students prepare and are prepared to take their place as future adults. Schools are among the most important everyday sites where young people's conditions for participating in the democratic process are constructed. This occurs through both the official school curriculum as well as through more informal school processes. Activities such as official celebrations, sports days, concerts, and school trips, often provide an arena of training for the skills of the cultural citizen. The body is also schooled in proper comportment. As Gordon, Holland and Lahelma (2000b, p. 197) suggest, the route from unruly child/

adolescent to responsible adult, from pupil to citizen, is predicated on appropriate bodily comportment and control. School is a major site for the collective construction of this conformity. Ritual display in schools is used to point to how one is expected to act in another space, in particular, the social worlds of citizenship and work. However, the patriarchal power relations of schooling, and their connection with the public-private dialectic in society, make the lived curriculum of schools a complex site of both desire and threat for girls. According to Foster (2000), for women and girls, pursuing equal educational and citizenship rights, entails entering a particular space – social, psychological and existential – between and beyond that which is prescribed for women, that is, women's 'place'.

Citizenship education has the potential to assist girls in negotiating the desire/threat of the public-private dialectic by providing a forum for contesting gendered power relations and their differential effect on girls and boys from different class and racial groups. Such a forum might also be used to work through an understanding of the ways in which constructions of masculinity and femininity are both dynamic and intimately related to the private/public sphere. Lees (2000, p. 265) offers a series of other possibilities for what such a curriculum could entail. She suggests for example that one way to link sexuality to citizenship education is through a consideration of bullying and various forms of violence, including domestic violence and social and racial violence. A second way is through a consideration of current debates about the rights of citizenship that are denied lesbians and gay men by excluding them from equal social benefits afforded married couples. Lees argues that if the subject of sexuality is to be addressed effectively, citizenship education needs to include an awareness of gendered power relations which create the constraints on autonomy and choice. Thus, 'citizenship education should begin with a critique of the gender order whereby the social, legal and institutional processes through which citizenship rights are established and maintained can be exposed as gendered' (Lees, 2000, p. 271).

However, the recent interest in Australia and many European countries in developing citizenship curricula does not seem to be taking this route. Foster (1997, cited in Foster, 2000) uses examples from Australia, the Netherlands and Scandinavia, to explore the ways in which the school curriculum mirrors the modern state's valorization of public life and devaluing of the private. In Australia, for example, she finds that curriculum development in citizenship education does not adequately address the public-private dialectic in social life. Private life has not been incorporated into the curriculum. She concludes that despite the revival of interest in citizenship education in Australia, education continues to perpetuate women's and girl's lack of citizenship status. Similarly Lees (2000), finds that the proposed national curriculum in England draws on the conventional political view of citizenship focusing largely on the public sphere at the expense of sexuality and the family. She argues that this narrow focus neglects key issues relating to gender difference. Despite the general tendency of civic education to overlook gender inequalities, there are some encouraging examples where gender issues are integrated in discussions of citizenship. In an international comparison of representations of citizenship in school textbooks, Aapola, Gordon and Lahelma (2002) found that most textbooks represented gender differences as natural, and implicitly equated social citizenship with action in the public arena, which was reserved for men. However, there were exceptions where gendered citizenship was addressed more analytically; for example, in a Swedish book of citizenship education the young readers were urged to discuss the double standards for girls' and boys' sexual behaviour, as well as to look at media representations of women and men critically (Hedengren, 1999, p. 43). This way students were provided with opportunities to reflect on the social constructions of citizenship as gendered and embodied. However, in most cases school textbooks fail to address embodied differences and implicitly construct a white, able-bodied and heterosexual body as a general model (Aapola et al., 2002, pp. 385 and 398). In another study of school materials and practices, Tarja Palmu (2003) argues that in texts that are used in teaching, gender is cumulated: firstly, as a masculine construction which prioritizes male agency and/or masculine language-use, while women's experiences are less valued. Secondly, gender is cumulated in school texts as a clear division in two separate, dichotomic groups, Girls and Boys, Men and Women, which are represented differently. However, the cumulation of gender is sometimes also challenged within particular texts and during lessons when the dichotomic gender divisions were problematized and questioned. According to Palmu, girls were particularly critical of the borders that were constructed between genders (Palmu, 2003, pp. 187–8).

Perhaps not surprisingly, the focus of these curricular materials seems to be mirroring the broader social concern for individualization and differentiation. In Finland, for example, the *Framework Curriculum for the Comprehensive School* (NBE, 1994) states that citizens' 'mutual equality and people's willingness to participate actively in attending to common affairs are some of the characteristics of a functioning society of citizens.' Gordon *et al.* (2000b) find, however, in their analysis of this document that the individualization that is highlighted in the text is more related to celebrating the possibilities of choice and competition than addressing diversity based on gender, ethnicity, and social class (Gordon *et al.*, 2000b, p. 187).

This focus on the individualizing of rights can also be found in other dimensions of citizenship. In the next section we turn to a closer examination of contemporary meanings of economic independence, national affiliation, and civic engagement, and consider how these are experienced today by young women. First, we examine the significance of economic rationalism, self-sufficiency and consumption in understanding the construction of the contemporary young woman citizen as responsible for securing her own social rights.

Young Women, Citizenship and Economic Independence

> I'd hate to be just a housewife. They just stay at home and do nothing. Well, they obviously work, but they don't get paid for it and I don't think it's right. You always have to ask your husband for money. (Fehmida, young Muslim woman, Britain, quoted in Basit, 1996, p. 234.)

In a late modern world, it is economic independence above all that is required of young people as the defining feature of citizenship. To be an active and acceptable member of one's community, it is necessary to be responsible for oneself, particularly in terms of income. As Hall, Coffey and Williamson (1999) argue, new notions of care and responsibility that are associated with active citizenship today actually extend out of the primary idea of self-governance. They say (Hall *et al.*, 1999, p. 503) 'emerging first on the right of the political spectrum in the late 1980s, active citizenship stressed the importance of personal responsibility, and also, working outwards from this, a wider duty of care for one's neighbours and community.' Layered over this is the rhetoric of neo-liberal choice, which is the common accompaniment to economic rationalist state policy. Economic independence is a late modern citizen's right and duty.

Standard Western political, civil and social rights have been radically re-conceptualized around this requirement, so that the individual's responsibility to support themselves must come before the state's duty of care to them. For young women, this has a very specific meaning. Whereas young women already tend to associate growing up with increased responsibilities in the domestic sphere (Aapola, 1997), they are increasingly encouraged to also embrace their rights in the public sphere. However, what this has often translated to in relation to the re-conceptualization of social rights is that they are expected to combine work and domestic responsibilities without 'relying on the state'. Active citizenship for young women frequently means taking responsibility for themselves economically and at the same time taking care of others. What we turn to now is an unpacking of how this version of girls' emancipation and good citizenship negates the problem of family responsibilities. Van Drenth (1998) has conducted a close analysis of the Dutch 'Girls' Memo'; unique in Europe as the only specific social policy aimed at young women. Her work gives us some insight into how this process occurs.

The Girls' Memo focuses on education, labour and stereotyping in politics, sport and leisure. It is concerned with ways to improve young women's career opportunities as well as their life-chances in a range of areas. Barriers to opportunities are represented as girls' own poor choices, sometimes influenced by sex-role stereotyping in broader society. One important issue is therefore how to get young women to make non-traditional choices in order to have greater opportunities later in the work place. The policy emphasizes the importance of individual decisions, options and freedoms; paraphrasing Van Drenth (1998, p. 83), the problem is seen as girls' choices, their upbringing and their education, and therefore the solution is getting girls to make 'better' choices. Broader socioeconomic circumstances are dealt with by individualizing problems, so specific categories of girls are constructed as 'at risk' due to their own personal context. Van Drenth (1998, p. 83) says, '[a] striking characteristic of the Dutch state policy on girls is the tendency to focus on specific categories of girls, that is, those who are considered to be especially vulnerable and therefore needing special attention. These "target groups" consist of girls with little or no schooling, unemployed girls and girls from ethnic minorities.' Further, the 'better' choices that all young women are encouraged to make tend overwhelmingly to be ones that ensure their economic independence without compromising the family unit or traditional heterosexual relations. That is, it is considered to be unproblematic for women to have a full-time job and raise a family, with no special changes required to industrial relations, childcare policy, parental leave, men's attitudes or work place practices as they stand. Van Drenth believes the consequences of this focus on individual choices and personal responsibility is deeply troubling. She says (1998, p. 88) young women are encouraged to:

> regard economic independence as normal for every citizen in the welfare state, including women. They accept a notion of citizenship in which one is responsible for one's own income. It has become self–evident to them that they will participate in the work force, although it is not clear for how long. They tend to hang on the idea of 'individual freedom' that is also given to them in the policy. If their autonomy is stressed by this policy, emancipation can only mean making your own choices as an independent woman. (Van Drenth, 1998, p. 88.)

The perception of young women as a newly liberated demographic group is utilized here to reinforce a neo-liberal agenda of youth citizenship built around economic self-sufficiency. Young women are encouraged to see themselves as the beneficiaries of economic and work place opportunities denied to previous generations of women, and to connect the gains of feminism with taking personal responsibility for their social rights. The thornier issue of how family and work can be satisfactorily combined, as is the plan of most young women today, is put to one side and remains a problem for individuals to work out on their own.

Consumer Citizenship

> I got two pairs of earrings for Christmas – big hoops and shell earrings that hang down? Most of the people in my class wear [Nike]. I don't have the latest ones but I'm getting them – my dad said he'd buy them for me. I like clothes that match and they've [Urban Angels shop] got really nice clothes, and some sort of weird clothes – they're different. I like that girl who does Murder on the Dancefloor – Sophie Ellis Bextor. She's pretty and a good dancer, and her make-up's really sparkly, and I like her film clip. (Olympia, 9, Australia, quoted in Robinson, 2002.)

Economic independence is articulated in at least two new ways for youth. First, as we have seen, social rights have become the individual concerns of young people who must not rely on the state, and instead make 'good choices' in order to achieve economic security. Second, economic viability is no longer linked to one's capacity for production so much as it is evidenced by patterns of consumption. The language of 'clients' and 'consumers' has replaced that of citizenship. With de-regulation, privatization and out-sourcing of many of the state's services, individuals must now engage with private, profit-seeking service-providers with whom they have a 'customer' relationship. Civic rights are to some extent only operationalized if one has the money to enter into this relationship, as Jones and Wallace (1992) suggest. This is particularly problematic for youth, who are most vulnerable in the changing labour market, as we saw previously. As work is diminishing as a meaningful avenue through which to create an identity, young people are increasingly subject to the resources and social capital consumption can afford. However, freedom to make choices in a global marketplace of opportunities does not necessarily coincide with the solid economic foundations on which consumer lifestyles can be sustained, as Miles (2000, p. 125) argues. This new definition of youth citizenship around consumer power rather than productivity is borne out in particular ways for young women.

The opening up of the world of work for young women has to some extent translated into an extended market for youth products. Young women's increased discretionary income is fought over by an ever-growing range of corporations pitching products and services at the 'girl' market. The shift towards the language of consumer rather than citizen can be seen in this construction of young women as powerful players in the marketplace. The gains made by feminism, whereby girls are taking their places in work and public life, are often measured by their power to consume. Their confidence, assertiveness and freedoms are frequently illustrated by way of their purchasing habits. Corporations directly draw on the language of girl power to sell their products (see Lucas, 2000), and market research companies describe young women as the new spenders, courtesy of the confidence and economic opportunities now before them (Bagnall, 2002; Cox, 2000). In this way, economic security is equated with the power to consume, which is then the way young women's citizenship is ascertained. McRobbie (2000, p. 21) argues that for young women, female empowerment is linked exclusively with money. Women's attempts to gain the power and status of citizens in terms of achieving social rights have been drawn into a neo-liberal programme of self-generated wealth and standing and leverage within one's society being based on consumption. Young women themselves are often concerned that opportunities for assertiveness and the political impact of a new emphasis on girls' power have become reduced to empty marketing slogans (see Harris, 2001a). Whilst consumption is an important element of identity and self-expression, the depiction of young women as most effective citizens when they are consuming also tends to exclude those who do not have the means to participate in this form of citizenship.

National Identities: Young Women as Multicultural and Global Citizens

> I think my first realization that I was actually different or perceived as different was when at eight I was told to stand in front of the class and my teacher said to the class 'this is what a Muslim girl looks like'. I was not wearing a hijaab (a head scarf) and was in school uniform. So I looked just like everybody else. That day changed my life as I realised that even though I might look like everybody else, and feel like everybody else, this did not mean that everybody else saw me as the same. (Karima Moraby, young Muslim woman, Australia. (Moraby, 1998, p. 209).)

A second dimension of citizenship is related to national identity, community identifications and a sense of belonging to a nation state. Anthias *et al.* (1993) have argued that it is difficult to delineate between 'race', ethnicity and nationality because migration, colonization and conquest have developed such a heterogeneous body of historical cases. They argue that boundaries which exclude and include are constructed variously on the basis of tribe, nation, linguistic or cultural background and have in common the understanding that the individual is born into or placed naturally into such collectivities. Additionally they make the point that a national group makes a claim for separate political and territorial representation and that in English, the word 'nationality' tends to be synonymous with citizenship and in this way defines one's relationship with a particular state. However, the radical re-shaping of the world order, mass migration, ethnic and religious conflicts, globalization, humanitarian crises and threats to human security have all had a significant impact on national identity and national borders. The dramatic increase in migrant and refugee populations moving into developed countries challenge fictitious although strongly held ideas of homogeneous nationalities. New economic and political organizations require new forms of citizenship, for example, the European Union attempts to develop commitments to 'Europeanness', and the growing transnational non-government bodies to the concept of an 'international community'. Globalized economies and sophisticated communications systems lend weight to the idea that identities are no longer bound by geography, and that nation-specific features, products and characteristics can be taken up, distributed, shared and sold across the world. This situation provokes both a sense of opportunity and fears of the loss of the familiar. Fears of social disconnection, civil unrest and loss of national identity within this context of flux have placed pressure on young people, and young women especially. Youth have traditionally been perceived as the most adaptable and flexible demographic group in times of change. Much is expected of them, as a cultural resource, to show ways forward for new formations of global citizenship that are appropriate to these changes (see for example De Almeida, 2001). At the same time, they are often the ones with the least social and economic capital to make these new global identifications operationalizable.

As Gonick (2000, p. 98) writes, national identities are not simply legal or geographical classifications, but are implicitly structured by categories of racial and ethnic privilege. Inclusion to or exclusion from the nation is constructed through these implicit categorizations. Globalized and multicultural identities have emerged to seriously challenge the national, and citizenship has now become a site of struggle over race, ethnicity, culture, and the local versus the global. This shift has had certain effects on young women, who are sometimes utilized as symbols of international, transcultural citizenship whilst at the same time experiencing the worst effects of racism, anti-immigration policies and abuses of refugee and migrant labour. As Espin (1995) and Yuval-Davis (1992) have argued, young women have always been responsible for managing multicultural citizenship. It is generally young women who are charged with the responsibility to effectively blend 'old' and 'new' cultures, both within migrant and refugee families and communities, and for the benefit of their 'host' nations. They are constructed as symbols of 'acculturation', whereby the benign aspects of their cultures of origin are mixed in with a 'new way of life' in an unproblematic fashion. The common images of multiculturalism which are used to celebrate an unthreatening form of contemporary citizenship are generally associated with the feminine and the domestic realm, for example, cuisine and costume. During periods of unrest, such as which exist in the risk societies of late modernity, the requirements on young women to uphold these images take on a higher order of importance. For example, Johnson (1993) has written about the importance of the young woman as 'ambassa-dress' during times of uncertainty and nation-making. She suggests that Australian society of the 1950s dealt with the perceived threats to identity and social order posed by the increasing migrant population through the image of the compliant, feminine migrant. Beauty contests and pageants, competitions and media stories all constructed young female migrants as the ideal citizens who were happy, hard-working, and keen to simply fit in to their new countries. Could we again be in one of these moments of the utilization of young women to present an image of unthreatening transition to change?

Fears about globalization and migration in particular can be allayed through the construction of young women as the new ideal 'blended' citizen. This occurs through the association of sport, entertainment and glamour with femininity and non-threatening multiculturalism. Feminine multicultural citizenship has become an entertaining performance, enacted literally through events such as the Eurovision Song Contest and the Olympic Games. In such events, mixed cultural identities come to the fore through the physical displays of many young women who perform patrioti-cally for their 'adopted' countries. As McRobbie (2001) and Hopkins (2002) have argued, celebrity, wealth and ambition have emerged as key markers of successful contemporary young femi-ninity. We would suggest that this image is also drawn on to per-petuate discourses of benign multiculturalism during times of change. The hybrid or 'outsider' cultural identities of young women who achieve celebrity and role model status are utilized to demonstrate the non-threatening nature of challenges to cultural and national homogeneity. For example, the marketing of celebrity Latinas such as the pop star Jennifer Lopez and actor Salma Hayek positions their cultural identities as adding an element of the exotic to their personas.

This is not to suggest that these women do not also provide important role models for those who tire of the homogeneous image of feminine beauty promoted by the media and advertisers. However, their political impact is limited when they are used in a discourse of good youth citizenship that contains their radicalism and neutralizes their politics, especially if these politics engage racism, poverty and classicism. In recent times, when young people of cultural minorities and young indigenous people have been vociferously contesting ideas about citizenship and nation across the West, there have been renewed efforts to de-politicize these efforts through appropriation and the construction of the good and compliant girl migrant or indigenous girl who seeks to serve all (not just her community), who is committed to her nation, and who refuses a political stance that would make anyone uncomfortable, instead focusing on inclusive politics and language of 'multicul-turalism', 'reconciliation', or 'unity'. In these ways, young women of cultural minorities are re-worked as a de-politicized, entertain-ing Other. However, assumptions about national identity, assimi-lation and homogeneity are continually being challenged by youth who espouse 'hybrid identities'.

At the same time, the serious consequences of racism and xeno-phobia and the material uses to which many young migrant and refugee women are put are often concealed. For example, Gonick (2000) and Matthews (2002) both demonstrate how young women of South East Asian origin living in Canada and Australia respec-tively learn that the discourse of multiculturalism silences their experiential knowledge of a privileged, Anglo, white national iden-tity. Räthzel (2000) discusses how emerging concerns with national identity and cultural belonging are managed by young women in their use of public space in Germany. She demonstrates how the mismatch between Germany's dependence on immigration and its self-image as a state of homogeneous ethnic Germans is played out amongst young women of different cultures in their occupation of neighbourhoods, thus significantly shaping issues of public safety, community identity and local social resources. It has been well-documented that in the wake of globalized economies, deregulation and multi-national corporatization, young migrant women make up a large part of the vulnerable labour forces in the growth industries of outsourced clothing and footwear manufac-turing (see Nutter, 1997). Similarly, Ige (1998) discusses the plight of seasonal farm workers in the US, the majority of whom are young migrant women, who harvest and pack crops for large US corpora-tions. These young women form the hidden migrant labour force upon whom both multi-nationals and national economies depend.

Young women are forging new identities that promise exciting ways to imagine global citizenship. The old 'torn between two cultures' model of understanding diversity in cultural identity is being dismantled by young people who refuse to choose or be torn. However, this new development in cultural and transnational citizenship is not always supported, either economically in terms of the ways culture separates young women in the labour market, or socially, in terms of perceived threats and risks of multiculturalism. The need for young female migrant labour and the construction of the girl as ideal multicultural citizen is occurring simultaneously. Young women are used both to support globalized economies and allay fears about threats to national identity.

Political Engagements

> Most people, upon finding out that I am female and a minority, usually laugh when I tell them what I want to be (President of the United States). If they don't laugh, they tell me how unhonest politicians are. I want to change all of that. Usually the ones who laugh or discourage me are the ones who I always hear complaining about how the government does everything wrong. These are also the people who do nothing but complain and never do anything to change what they deem wrong. I cannot justify complaining about anything I am not willing to change. (Tammy Sue Lowe, high school senior, Native American (Cherokee), USA, quoted in Carlip, 1995, p. 160.)

A third dimension of citizenship relates to political engagements, that is, the ways one participates in the polity and in civic life. Youth participation has become an increasingly important issue, as the shifting nature of citizenship has fundamentally altered modes of engagement available to them. Participation can be measured both by traditional means, such as voting, and by involvement in 'protest' politics through demonstrations, petitions, and activist campaigns. Both types of youth participation have come under scrutiny, as young people are increasingly depicted as less and less involved in either form of political life. The resurgence of 'civics' education and other curricular programmes to improve youth participation indicates the extent to which this problem has become central to mainstream analyses of youth citizenship. These debates tend to concentrate on the personal qualities of youth that lead them away from engagement. In these ways, this political dimension of citizenship is made an individual problem of commitment and interest. We would suggest, however, that there are fewer real opportunities for young people to participate, and that engagement with the state has become a much more problematic experience for youth than in the past. As we have already seen, the corporatization of many of the state's functions, combined with the commodification of many aspects of social movement politics, have transformed the public sphere into somewhat of a marketplace. Diminishing opportunities for political agency has been the result for youth.

> I'm political, of course putting out a bunch of 'zines, of course putting up with anarchist networks. I'm really not sure of what my political stance is. My favorite form of intangible never-happen government is all the anarchists move out to a damn island, call themselves anarcho-communists and reap the benefits of the free world, but *Lord of the Flies* happens and they start dying off. But that'll never happen. And so, I think democratic socialism like they have in Sweden is really cool. But I haven't really been involved in that much. I've written my 'zines here and there, put out newspapers. I've been to [an] anarchist conference in Atlanta, actually. All sorts of stuff. I'm starting to really get burned out on it, so I just argue with local fascists. Help start up an antifascist group this year. (Sue, 15, punk, USA, quoted in Leblanc, 1999, p. 72.)

Currently, when young people are discussed or thought about in relation to politics it is generally their lack of interest that is highlighted. Problems such as low voter registration or low voter turn out (for those of voting age), lack of knowledge of political systems and history, and boredom with current events are frequently associated with youth. As Furlong and Cartmel (1997) point out, research indicates that young people's involvement in formal politics is diminishing. For example, Buckingham (2000, p. 2) has found a decline in the proportion of young people registering to vote, turning out to vote and being politically active in the US, the UK, France and Germany. Rimmerman (1997) supports this finding in his US-based study; as do Cartmel and Furlong in the UK. More evidence can be found for this phenomenon in the research by Lagos and Rose (1999), which draws on nation-wide sample surveys of political participation and values in 41 countries from European Union Europe, post communist Europe and Latin America. This information suggests that young people's involvement in politics is directly related to specific conditions of contemporary life for youth that were not in place for the previous generation. It points to the problem that political involvement on the part of youth is related to the extent to which they can find a place for participation and the extent to which politicians are perceived to be interested in their needs and views.

> Young people want action, clear answers and honesty. Of course, nobody expects changes to happen overnight. It takes time to make decisions and to implement them, but they have to happen at some point anyway. I don't think it is too difficult to get young people to the voting booths. We only have to be given a good reason to go there. (Woman, 24, Finland, quoted in Lundbom, 2003, p. 93, translation from Finnish by Sinikka Aapola.)

As Päivi Harinen (2000) suggests, if young people feel that the society is 'ready-built' by their parents' and grandparents' generations, and that their citizenship is offered to them 'downwards', from 'up there', it is difficult for them to see their citizenship as anything else than a duty that only 'liberates' them to maintain the already created social order. They see citizenship as something that connects them to the honoured national past, and something they should be content with, rather than as a set of social contracts that can be actively renegotiated. In this situation, young people will see their links to the democratic process as thin, and their voice as citizens will be weak (Harinen, 2000, pp. 213–4).

With the marketization of the state and the outsourcing of many of its services, the political claims of youthful active citizens no longer have a clear forum for expression or accountability. Some young people choose not to vote as a form of protest against the political system that they find untrustworthy, while for others, not voting indicates that they do not find the political campaigns as addressed to them (Hellsten, 2003, pp. 75–6). Further, closer investigation of many common indicators of youth apathy reveals how changing socio-economic conditions constrain participation. For example, Lagos and Rose (1999, p. 16) note that evidence about voter registration suggests that non-registration is attributable to what they call 'lifestyle' rather than apathy. It is commonly assumed that young people do not register to vote because they do not care about politics. However, they have found that 'lifestyle' factors, in particular, moving around for work, are more likely to cause non-registration than lack of interest. In times that require young people to be flexible in their living arrangements if they are to obtain or maintain employment, practical concerns such as registering to vote upon every change of address and potentially electorate may not be prioritized. Rimmerman (1997) also suggests that new economic pressures on youth have meant that they are more concerned with career goals than previous generations, and that it is the time and energy required to deal with these pressures, rather than lack of interest, that generates low registration or turn out. Even interest itself is not necessarily enough, if one has not been able to acquire enough information about political parties and associations, as can be the case with immigrant young people, particularly those who lack knowledge in the dominant language. National political citizenship often requires specific information capital that can only be accumulated locally and nationally.

> I have to admit that I have not bothered to find out terribly much, I do know something about the internal matters in Finland but not as much as I maybe should. Like, where do I suddenly out of nowhere find out what is CP and what is a democrat when you do not know at all? Then it is difficult to read in the newspapers, then you try to look for stuff like why does it not say what is TU, then you are quite out of it in certain matters. Finns do not necessarily notice it but newspaper articles are like a serial story, it is quite rare to find stories where they sum up what has happened in the last year or in the past ten years . . . you should know them. (Nora, 23, Taiwanese-Finnish, Finland, quoted in Harinen, 2000, p. 184; translation from Finnish by Sinikka Aapola.)

For youth who may be less affected by these major economic shifts, political trust remains an issue. In her study of students in England, Denmark, Germany, Netherlands and the USA, Hahn (1998, p. 31) has found cynicism to be rampant. Buckingham (2000) supports this finding in his research in the US and UK. However, he notes that it is politicians rather than politics itself who are seen to be deserving of cynicism. He suggests that young people's alienation from the domain of politics is not simply apathy or ignorance but a response to disenfranchisement. He writes (Buckingham, 2000, p. 219):

> This reflects the fact that, by and large, young people are not defined in our society as political subjects, let alone as political agents. Even in areas of social life that affect and concern them to a much greater extent than adults – most notably education – political debate is conducted almost entirely 'over their heads'.

This supports the argument of Bhavnani (1991), who claims that the ways politics and cynicism are defined determines whether or not youth can be described as politically engaged. Rimmerman (1997, p. 8) suggests that young people are turning away from formal politics as it is not seen as being the forum in which their problems will be heard or solved, but that this does not mean they are rejecting politics in all its forms. Furlong and Cartmel (1997, p. 98) concur, saying:

> We argue that although young people may lack an involvement in formal politics, they do have a concern with broader issues which may be construed as political and, in particular, are sometimes involved in single issue political campaigns on issues which are perceived as having a relevance to their lives. Despite these claims, we are skeptical of the tendency to regard the political priorities of youth as indicative of the ascendancy of 'post materialist' values [Inglehart 1977, 1990, cited in Furlong & Cartmel, 1997, p. 98] or as signalling the demise of emancipatory politics. Indeed, there is very little evidence to suggest that the politics of the younger generation are very different from those of the previous generation.

On this latter point, however, others disagree, and believe that young people are at the vanguard of new social movements (for example, Lash & Urry, 1994) which may at first glance appear as cynicism or even apathy, but on closer reflection suggests radically different modes of political engagement. They argue that new modes of communication and organization have emerged through technological change, and these in turn have led to new alliances and the development of global and amorphous activism (see Melucci, 1996; Siurala, 2000). For example, Klein (2001) notes the importance of the Internet as a tool of information sharing and organising in campaigns against corporate globalization. The internet provides direct access and direct publicity, rather than relying on media channels that are controlled by publishers, editors, shareholders and market forces. In the case of the anti-globalization movement, it has allowed for coordinated, simultaneous global actions without many resources. For young people, who often are the ones who lack resources and media connections, the internet has proved to be a very useful tool in creating a decentralized system of organizing global resistance and protest. Further, the changing nature of the world power blocs, and the importance of challenging multinational corporations and economic globalization have shifted styles of protest. Finally, the absorption of social justice politics into the market has required ever more creative approaches to political agitation, which must remain one step ahead of the advertisers (see for example, Klein, 2001). The fear of youth politics being misused by not only 'big business' but by 'authority' in general has generated cultural forms of politics that can not be so easily appropriated (see Guidikova & Suirala, 2001). This shift may benefit young women's participation in politics, as we shall see later.

Young Women in Politics

> There is very little representation of teenage girls and women in general though. There are still old-fashioned views and politicians aren't willing to change. I'm not particularly interested in politics at the moment. I don't feel they're out to make the world better. They're money-oriented. If you feel someone out there is representing you and you could get what you want, you'll think 'oh well, they understand, I'll give it a go then and vote'. (Girl, 13, Britain, quoted in Katz, 1997, p. 43.)

Regardless of the view taken on whether or not young people's contemporary politics is different from the previous generation, young women's circumstances and perspectives are rarely analysed separately from 'youth' in general. Very little has been said about young women's own political participation or interest. Unquestioned assumptions about youth apathy are often redoubled in the case of young women. This is generally in relation to voting patterns, which is one of the most common (but limited) ways in which engagement in politics is assessed. They are to some extent caught between contradictory assumptions about the two significant 'categories' to which they belong, that is, as women, they are considered to be more conservative, but as youth, are believed to have more changeable views. Whichever category they are subsumed into, the other is minimized as a variable. Either way they are represented as motivated primarily by either habit or whim; they do not emerge as politically committed, engaged or even knowledgeable. These assumptions do not sit easily with high profile activism on the part of young women to register voters or encourage youth to become politically aware and involved. For example, the Third Wave Foundation in the US, led by young women during the early 1990s, conducted the largest voter registration drive since the Civil Rights days (Baumgardner & Richards, 2000). They are increasingly involved in controversial radical as well as extreme right wing politics, for example, from animal liberation (see Helve, 1997) to neo-Nazism. Younger women are standing for parliaments across the Western world in greater numbers (Sanz, 2001), and those who are too young to stand or vote often look up to female parliamentarians and political figures as role models. For example, in Finland, after former Foreign Minister Tarja Halonen was elected the first ever female president in 2000, she has annually received hundreds of fan-letters from children and young people, mainly girls. One of her fans writes in her letter:

> Hello Tarja Halonen! I am of such an age that I do not have the right to vote yet, but if I could have voted I would have voted for you! I think it's nice that we FINALLY have a woman president in Finland. I would not like [Finland] to join NATO! But I'd like to ask you if you could send me a (real) picture of you and Pentti [the president's husband]? . . . How wide is your power in Finland? I wish you could answer me quite soon, as I eagerly expect for your reply! . . . (Anna-Stina, Finland, quoted in Aapola, forthcoming, translation from Finnish by Sinikka Aapola.)

This evidence of young women's real interest and engagement with formal politics complicates longstanding common assumptions about their apathy. However, it is also important to consider young women's politically motivated reasons for what appears to be 'apathy'. Jacobi (1995, p. 122) suggests that 'girls are unpolitical because politics only provides room for a part of their political interests'. In other words, narrow definitions, rather than the interests or behaviour of young women themselves, often excludes them from politics. Young women who are politically active find themselves challenging conventions of feminine behaviour. For example, Barron's (1997, p. 227) research with young Swedish female disability activists involved in civil disobedience found that 'this kind of action is not only important with regard to reinforcing a common identity as disabled, but also with regard to establishing an identity as autonomous women'.

In much research, however, it is still common to find that young women lack confidence in relation to political matters. Hahn (1998, p. 108), who has surveyed the key studies on youth and politics, says:

> For the most part, researchers have found no gender differences among high school students in levels of political trust and external political efficacy, the belief that citizens can influence policy. On the other hand,

there is evidence that females sometimes express lower levels of political confidence and internal political efficacy – confidence that they can
understand politics – than do males.

When these two pieces of knowledge are put together we build up
a picture of young women sharing with young men an abstracted
belief in the capacity of 'citizens', but on a personal level, lacking
faith in their own individual ability to understand politics and
effect change. This underscores Bhavnani's (1991) point that the
definition of 'politics' is critical in enabling young people and
young women in particular to engage with it. Once 'political
knowledge' is demystified and connected with young people's
own interests and lives, they are far more confident in offering
opinions and making interventions. For example, Australian
research (Vromen, 2003; Bulbeck, 2001) has found that young
women are more engaged in political activity than young men,
especially in terms of membership of activist groups, signing petitions and writing to politicians. This may have something to do
with the ways specific issues are represented and then perceived
as directly relevant to their lives. German research (Boehnke et al.,
2002) has found that young women are more likely than young
men to be actively engaged in left wing causes. Jacobi (1995, p. 122)
notes that because of the localization of their experiences and interests in life that forces girls to take public and private perspectives,
they are political in a different way.

While she does not offer thoughts about the nature of these political expressions, Jacobi does suggest that young women are
uniquely placed in terms of their positioning across two spheres,
the public and the private, and that this has an impact on the
possibilities that exist for them to engage politically (Jacobi,
1995).

> The fire that moves us is deep inside and all around. It is fuelled by
> indignation at injustice, and by the confidence that we are not alone.
> Activism is neither a choice nor a sacrifice for me it's just survival. (Julie
> Devaney, 20, Canada (Devaney 2001).)

Attempts to engage young women as rational and autonomous
citizens, now capable of making political interventions just like
men, cut across equally compelling and enduring interpellations of
girls as mothers, wives and caretakers, responsible for the domestic sphere, as we saw in the constitution of female citizenship in the

Dutch Girls' Memo. Just as with the construction of young women as the ideal multicultural citizen, older modes of femininity are combined with contemporary, post-feminist images to create appropriate forms of political engagement for girls. This can be seen in the enthusiasm for young female role models on parliamentary delegations, transnational NGO committees, youth forums, speak outs and tribunals. This trend suggests that young women represent both caring figures concerned for the global community, and as a newly empowered group who can now speak up and take their place in the public sphere. However, those who argue for a shift away from traditional, formal political engagements towards 'cultural politics', subcultural movements and post-modern protest also see possibilities for the emergence of young women as a new political force beyond the 'role model' position (see Helve, 1997). These new forms of participation do not depend on externally-defined political confidence or the ability to influence government. They stake out political territory in unlikely places, and as Melucci (1996, p. 183) argues, they do not ask, they bring. Many young women utilize these forms of politics to re-invigorate activism and civic engagement at a time when opportunities for youth to be meaningfully involved in their communities and states are diminishing.

Conclusion

Citizenship, and meanings of youth citizenship in particular, have undergone radical changes since de-industrialization and globalization of late capitalist societies. Traditionally, citizenship involved a set of rights guaranteed by the nation state. These related to economic security, personal freedoms, national protections and participation. Today, however, young women grapple with new frameworks for citizenship that devolve responsibility for livelihood onto the individual, that draw on images of girls to allay fears of the unfamiliar, and at the same time rely on young women as a resource in perpetuating a racist and classist global economic order. Further, opportunities for participation and political intervention have diminished for youth, as state power becomes increasingly difficult to separate from corporate interests, and is no longer centralized nor bound to a single nation state. At the same time, young women are visible in the public sphere in ways that are unprecedented, and many remain confident about blending economic self-sufficiency with the responsibilities of family. Young women are at the forefront of a re-thinking of hybrid and mulit-cultural identities and possibilities for improved relationships amongst indigenous, migrant, refugee and majority cultural groups. The picture of contemporary citizenship for young women is therefore complex. The ways in which young women engage with new forms of participation and identity to construct feminist futures for girlhood will be the subject of the next chapter.

CHAPTER 8

Feminism, Power and Social Change

Introduction

So far in this book we have explored the resources available to young women for negotiating their gendered identities in changing times. We have suggested that some of these resources are discursive and some are material. Young women's new opportunities and challenges have been discussed in relation to education and employment, the family, friendship, sexuality and the body, and politics and citizenship. It is clear from our elaboration of these issues that young women do not enjoy unproblematic freedoms in shaping their lives, although much has changed for this generation. Given that there are still barriers to be overcome to enable them to maximize their life-chances, in this chapter we examine the issue of young women's relationship to ideologies and movements to do with power and social change, and in particular, feminism. There has been considerable debate within girls' studies and feminism as to whether young women are still interested in feminist frameworks, and if so, how they are taking feminism forward or creating a 'next wave' to follow the first and second waves of the women's movement. To what extent have the dominant discourses of girl power and crisis influenced young women's relationship to feminism? How have these ideas shaped their ability to utilize feminist discourses and develop a feminist platform in understanding their circumstances? Is there evidence that some young women are developing new kinds of feminisms, more relevant to the socio-economic conditions of late modernity, or are they rejecting feminism altogether? In this chapter we explore these questions in order to come to some conclusions about young women and the future of feminism and social change.

Do Young Women Still Need Feminism?

> Do I feel included in feminism? Yes and no. Yes in the sense that I am
> here and am making the best possible change in my own way in the
> only way I know how, and no in the sense that most feminists and men
> look down on me because I never studied women's studies and don't
> use big words in my arguments. (Yvonne, working class, Australia,
> personal interview, 2000.)

The debate about young women's relationship to feminism has
taken place within a broader context of a back-lash against feminism, a cultural fascination with girlhood, and against a framework
which constructs young women as either 'having everything' or
being in serious trouble. We have already seen how, since the early
to mid 1990s, young womanhood has become a topic central to
debates about culture and society. Two discourses about girlhood
have taken hold as key explanatory devices for understanding
young women's lives. These are the stories of 'girl power' on the
one hand, and 'crisis' on the other. These narratives have also come
to inform the ways that young women are represented in relation
to feminism. In particular, there is an assumption that young
women themselves imagine they do not need feminism any more,
as they are already empowered, or so deeply in crisis that they
struggle to come up with even personal solutions to their problems.
To explore how an issue has developed about young women being
a 'problem' for feminism in these ways, we need to take this wider
context into account. We begin by exploring the assumption that
young women are not interested in feminism, and the ways 'older'
feminists and young women themselves debate this state of affairs.
We do not want to simply reproduce the generational split that has
characterized much of the framing of this debate, but to call it into
question whilst we explore it critically.

We have already seen that young women are growing up in an
environment that supports options for them that are quite unprecedented. Many of these possibilities, such as a professional career,
non-nuclear family arrangements and freer expression of sexuality,
have been feminist ideals. As Sharpe (2001, p. 177) suggests, 'young
women's lives have changed radically over the past few decades.
Social and economic changes, role models and young women's
own sense of growing agency have all led to them "doing it for
themselves".' These changes and young women's responses to
them, have thrown feminism into a crisis of sorts. Currently, young

women encounter a situation where many feminist goals have been achieved, but gender inequity is still deeply embedded in the socio-economic order. How do they grapple with this contradictory circumstance, and what roles do feminist ideology and activism play in their lives today? Often, young women are seen as preferring an optimistic, individual interpretation of their worlds, such that feminism is interpreted by them as an ideology about self-belief and personal effort to overcome difficulties. Therefore, it has become common to highlight their reluctance to describe themselves as feminists, or to find fault with the kind of new feminism they might express. Next, we explore these approaches and see if we might miss valuable information about the complexity and agency with which young women live their lives by subscribing too easily to these views.

I'm Not a Feminist, But?

Within the 'generation debates' about girls and feminism, young women have often been described as being inappropriately disengaged from political analyses of their worlds. For some second wave feminists, girls are seen as complacent because their fore-mothers have already achieved so much for them and they have ceased to see the need for collective action (Summers, 1994). Other commentators suggest that they are in deep trouble, and struggle to find a voice for self-expression, as in the Ophelia discourse (Pipher, 1994).

Regardless of the reasons that are attributed to this situation, it is commonly accepted that young women are not especially interested in feminism as a label or a movement any more. In the Nordic context, it is often claimed that today's young women believe they are equal when they are still in education, but will only start to see the need for feminism when they get older and enter the job market and/or start families (see for example Gemzöe, 2002, pp. 20–1). There is some considerable evidence that many young women are reluctant to use the term feminist to describe themselves although they may espouse feminist ideals, such as equal pay for equal work (see for example Bulbeck & Harris, forthcoming 2004). Researchers have frequently found that young women do distance themselves from the stereotypes of feminists as 'man-haters', lesbians, and masculine-looking women with hairy armpits and big boots. However, it has also been established that even though many young women may feel alienated from or express disinterest in feminist ideology, labels or politics, their identities and world views are deeply shaped by feminist frameworks.

For example, Budgeon's (2001) research with young British women has found that while they do not claim the category of 'feminist', they draw on feminist ideals as resources in their identity formation. Budgeon suggests that young women perceive gender inequities in social relations, and name them as such. However, because of a new emphasis on individualization and personal choice that pervades late modern societies, their solutions to these structural problems tend to be individual rather than collective. Sharpe (2001) draws similar conclusions in her UK research, suggesting that solidarity and cohesion amongst women have been somewhat undermined by an emphasis on individualism and enterprise. However, she also finds that the principles and aims espoused by young women are feminist in nature, if not explicitly articulated as such. She writes, 'the ideas and values they express are still feminist, but by not labelling them as such they miss out on the power and pleasure of shared identification . . .' (Sharpe, 2001, p. 177).

Similarly, in Australian research, O'Brien (1999) suggests that just because young women find the title of 'feminist' problematic does not mean that they are not engaged in feminist practice. She argues that feminism ought not be seen only as legitimate when it takes the form of recognized activism, but that it can have an important place in the 'micropolitics' of young women's everyday lives. Her participants were engaged in developing support, solidarity and a cultural space for young women, as well as constructing a feminist critique of gender inequality. However, they separated themselves from the 'feminist' label. She (O'Brien, 1999, p. 104) says, 'the women interviewed clearly felt that a woman who espouses feminist attitudes becomes "The Feminist", transformed from a temporary aberration into a species.' To avoid being perceived in a negative and one-dimensional manner, the young women simply engaged in local feminist practice without using the title. In this way, O'Brien's research provides a counter-point to Sharpe's, demonstrating how labels do not always bring 'power and pleasure', but sometimes constraint.

> [Young feminists] do exist – we're just hard to find, hard to get to commit to the personal label of 'feminist' even if our philosophies certainly belong to the feminist spectrum. (Naomi Sheridan, 17, Canada (Sheridan, 2001, p. 154).)

There is a problem, of course, when young women are reluctant to 'out' themselves as feminists because of the stereotypes associated with this position. However, some commentators argue that too much of a concern with labels interferes with our perceptions of the feminist work young women are actually engaged in. For example, Baumgardner and Richards (2000, p. 48) say, 'Third Wave women have been seen as nonfeminist when they are actually living feminist lives. Some of this confusion is due to the fact that most young women don't get together to talk about 'Feminism' with a capital F.' And as Jowett (2001) demonstrates, when they do get together to talk about feminism, it becomes apparent that feminism is not perceived as a fixed state that one is either in or not in. Rather, it is a set of complex ideas and practices that contain contradictions and ambivalences, and it is shaped through dynamic relationships.

What is often also missing from this debate about young women's disengagement from feminism is a serious consideration of their critique. Many are reluctant to use the term 'feminist' not simply because of the back-lash's negative attributions to the concept or because it is perceived as unfashionable or outdated, but because it is still seen as non-inclusive. For example, Green (1995, p. 90) argues that

> the movement has come far in acknowledging the diversity of women with respect to ethnicity, sexual preference and economic status. But where the movement still fails miserably is in disability. Women with disabilities are grossly concentrated in the margins. We are women, yet *our* histories and identities are ignored.

The image of feminism as a political movement for white, middle-class, middle-aged, non-disabled heterosexuals has not shifted as fundamentally as many would wish. As Chambers (1995, p. 123) states, 'when it came down to it, I could not trust most white women to have my back'. Thus even young women who are interested and involved in women's rights activism might choose not to call themselves feminists in favour of no labels, or they might utilize other terms such as Alice Walker's 'womanist'. The focus on whether or not young women use labels and feminist monikers has itself been criticized as a way to homogenize their diverse voices. For example, Morgan (1999, p. 62) argues that

> more than any other generation before us, we need a feminism committed to 'keeping it real'. We need a voice like our music – one that

samples and layers many voices, injects its sensibilities into the old and
flips it into something new, provocative and powerful . . . The keys that
unlock the riches of contemporary black female identity . . . lie at the
magical intersection where those contrary voices meet – the juncture
where 'truth' is no longer black and white but subtle, intriguing shades
of grey.

It seems clear, then, that much has been assumed about young
women's relationship to feminism based on the rather blanket
notion that they see themselves as 'not feminists, but . . .' However,
young women who critique the feminist label still draw on feminist resources and strategies, shape its agenda and grapple with its
unfinished business.

Acknowledging but Criticizing Young Feminism

As for young women who do espouse the feminist label, they too
have come to the attention of those who may perceive themselves
as feminist gatekeepers. As Griffin (2001, p. 184) says, 'the discursive context in which many discussions of young women's relationship with feminism is couched, as in so many discussions of
young people's lives, rests on a distinction between "us" (adult
women and "feminism") as distinct from "them" (young women).'
Within this discursive context, some of the 'adult women' want to
acknowledge the feminist practices they feel young women are
engaging in, but they are critical of their new kinds of approaches.
One of the most enduring criticisms has been that being a feminist
must mean being part of a pre-defined political movement, and
that young self-proclaimed feminists sometimes want the kudos,
or the benefits, without the collective work. This argument is consistent with the broader attack on young women for being 'ungrate-
ful' (see Summers, 1994), in that it claims feminism as something
that is owned by the previous generation and can only be passed
on to appropriate heirs. Others have been critical of the specific
ways in which young feminists go about their feminist work. For
example, some feel that they are too keen to see themselves as
victims. Garner (1995, p. 99) writes that young women's feminism
represents the 'creation of a political position based on the virtue
of helplessness.' She suggests that when they enact feminism by
pressing charges for sexual harassment, for example, they demonstrate the problematic development of a feminist identity based on

priggishness, a fear of sexuality and disempowerment. She argues that this kind of activism is a misunderstanding of the politics of feminism, as laid out by the second wave.

Others also suggest that young women have misunderstood feminism; however, this is often perceived from the other perspective; that is, not so much that young women see themselves as victims, but as crowing victors. From this point of view, young feminists are criticized for thinking that feminism means sexually objectifying men and acting like a 'lad' (Greer, 1999; Weldon cited in Griffin, 2001). Germaine Greer (1999, p. 312) has famously criticized 'girl' style feminism for believing that 'equality meant role reversal'. She discusses the Spice Girls, popular girls' magazines and 'pro girl feminist philosophy' as expressed in zines and webpages, and concludes that all of these are damaging to the feminist cause. She suggests that young women have been dazzled by a false language of independence and empowerment that 'conceals utter dependence on male attention' (Greer, 1999, p. 316). Some styles of young feminism sometimes attract these responses because they are perceived to be 'feminism-lite' in attempting to hold on to feminist critique and a feminine image, for example, by a keen interest in wearing make-up, dressing in a sexy fashion and embracing heterosexuality. Baumgardner and Richards (2000, p. 139) also demonstrate how some young feminists' perceived interest in image, sexual expression and 'girlie-ness' has provoked this reaction because it is seen as de-politicizing the agenda around sexuality and the display of women's bodies.

> Sometimes I will just go all out you know. I'll do it just to take the piss and wear the long floating dress and even wear roses in my hair and just be the dead romantic and then I'll wear combat boots because I like the contrast – the idea on surface you can say 'look at me! I'm the girlie type', and then when people actually meet you and talk to you they realise that you're as far from that as you ever could be and I enjoy that. I think that is funny. I may be skinny and weedy and be wearing a floaty dress and roses in my hair but you know I've got a bite. (Anna, 18, Britain, quoted in Budgeon, 2001, p. 24.)

Commercialized forms of feminism, and especially 'girl power', have been the subject of scathing critique because of this tendency towards de-politicization. The alliance between the image of a girlie feminism and the culture industries has been frequently attacked. Young women are seen as victims of a kind of mis-representation of feminism, having been sold the images of pop heroes and celebrities as wealthy, beautiful and successful versions of sexy feminists, whose feminism does not seem politically engaged in any way. As was touched on in Chapter 1, the Spice Girls have been the most common target for having contrived 'success as a cultural phenomenon (out of) the commodification of female empower-ment' (Hopkins, 2002, p. 23). Young women who are fans of this group are often perceived as consumers rather than feminist agents, responding to the Spice Girls call for 'girl power' and 'revolution' through the purchase of merchandise instead of political action. Further, Wald (1998) argues that the Spice Girls demonstrate how feminism is only acceptable when it is infan-tilized, and produced as cute and girlish.

At the same time, many young women report that the Spice Girls and pop heroes like them serve other functions that can be politi-cally grounded and inherently feminist. For example, Lemish (1998) has found in her research with 9–14 year old middle-class Jewish Israeli girls who are Spice Girls fans that ideas about girls' independence and self-worth are some of the strongest messages received and worked through by the fans. Many commentators liken the Spice Girls to predecessors like Madonna, who success-fully combine seductiveness with gutsy independence. However, Lemish also points out that in contrast to Madonna, the Spice Girls work together as a united group, which deepens the contradictions. The female bonding overtly referenced by the singers marks a double resistance: a successful world of women and the dismissal of the myth of bourgeois individualism. Lemish concludes that the Spice Girls can be read in oppositional ways – as independent feminists but also as a disguised version of the conventional 'truth claim' of the centrality of 'the look' in female identity (Lemish, 1998, p. 164).

However, friendship, unity and sisterhood were also seen as important parts of a new female identity that was exemplified by the group. She claims that for the girls in the study, the term 'girl power' was actively interpreted as an expression of strength. One 12 year old girl says, 'It means equality. . . . that girls are strong, each one in her own way.' And another says, 'And the songs, they are the kind that think that we need equality and that girls need strength' (Lemish, 1998, p. 153). Lemish suggests that girl power was mobilized by the girls as ideological support in their everyday experiences of gender inequality, prejudice and as demonstrative opposition to boys. Similarly, Fritzsche's (2001) research with young German fans finds that they use the group's media image as a 'tool box', from which they lift out useful strategies and ideas to apply in their own lives. Specifically, the dominant norm of heterosexuality could be playfully resisted through identification with and reference to the group and its ideologies. She suggests that there is political potential in the empowerment offered by popular girl culture, even though this has been a site typically disparaged by feminist critics.

Young women have therefore been depicted as a problem for feminism, either because they are reluctant to call themselves feminists, or because the feminism they are seen to enact is not familiar to those who may feel they are the true torch-bearers of the movement. Constituting what Griffin (2001) calls the 'discursive context' of the generational debate are those familiar narratives about power and crisis. In response to these images of young women as apathetic or naive, and young feminists as either aggressive and selfish, or victimized and in crisis, many young women themselves have sought to challenge these stereotypes and demonstrate the ongoing feminist activism of a new generation. Although many young women are not engaged in this kind of project, the identification of the 'next wave' of feminism has become critical for many who do perceive themselves as feminist and feel maligned by their critics. In particular, these young women urgently express the need to explain what it means to have some power and some rights, but to still see the need for feminist work; that is, to move forward as a generation for whom 'the legacy of feminism was a sense of entitlement' (Findlen, 1995, p. xiv). There are three major clusters or types of young feminism that we can identify, although of course not all kinds of feminist expressions can fit neatly into a category, and there are also important cultural and national differences in the ways feminism is defined and debated among young women in different countries. Next we discuss these major groupings of 'power feminism', 'DIY and grrrlpower', and 'the third wave'.

Young Feminisms

Power feminism

One of the most significant ways in which the young woman's approach to gender inequality is categorized is through the concept of 'power feminism'. Power feminism represents itself as a completely new approach that breaks dramatically with the tradition of the previous two women's movements. It argues that the gains of the second wave have been underestimated, and that the key issues facing young women are those few lingering formal barriers to equality. It makes a clear distinction between the personal and the political, and tends to display commitment to either individual empowerment or single issue groups rather than a women's 'movement'. A key proponent is Natasha Walter (1998), who argues for a power-based approach in her book *The New Feminism*. She claims that this kind of feminism focuses on increased power and equality for women, is celebratory and optimistic, and is integrated into mainstream society rather than part of a radical fringe. It is made up of a large collection of allied organizations, with a focus on what she deems to be political rather than personal issues, that is, material inequities rather than private concerns, such as sexuality and body image. She says, 'Rather than concentrating its energy on the ways women dress and talk and make love, feminism must now attack the material basis of economic and social and political inequality' (Walter, 1998, p. 4). For Walter, this kind of feminism sees and celebrates the transformation in men, and has no ambivalence about women taking on power.

Naomi Wolf (1994), who actually coins the term 'power feminism' in *Fire With Fire*, also advocates for a feminism that focuses on women's power rather than subordination or victimization, and that distinguishes itself from 'gloomy' feminism by being sexy and fun. She believes that women are very close to equality, and should use their powers as consumers, tax payers and voters to fight for equality. Rene Denfeld (1995) in *The New Victorians* picks up on these themes, articulating the characteristics of power feminism as being against 'male-bashing', or believing that sexual violence, pornography and heterosexuality are modes of men's power, and focusing instead on issues such as childcare, political representation, abortion and contraception. We could also include here Katie Roiphe's (1993) *The Morning After* as another example of an articulation of new young feminism that seeks to restore women's status from victim to agent, and positions itself against previous waves of overzealous, 'anti-sex' feminism. What characterizes power feminism is the rejection of what is deemed to be the 'victim feminism' of the second wave. That is, power feminists are concerned that feminism has become too focused on men's power versus women's oppression, and the ways these are played out in the realm of the sexual and the personal. They are concerned about young feminists getting caught up in this interpretation whereas they should see themselves as strong, sexual, and powerful, and should focus on women's individual strengths.

DIY and grrrlpower

A rather different definition of young feminism is offered through the framework of Do-It-Yourself (DIY) or grrrlpower. Grrrlpower is generally seen to have originally emerged from a combination of punk and feminism in the early 1990s, as discussed in Chapter 1. There are few formal texts that lay out the DIY/grrrlpower agenda, but there are many examples of this approach in less mainstream publications such as fanzines, webpages and music, and these have come to the attention of academics and journalists. These interpretations are found in books such as Karen Green and Tristan Taormino's (1997) *A Girl's Guide to Taking Over the World*, Hillary Carlip's (1995) *Girlpower*, Kathy Bail's (1996) *DIY Feminism* and Marcelle Karp and Debbie Stoller's (1999) *The Bust Guide to the New Girl Order*, as well as Linda Norrman Skugge's, Belinda Olsson's and Brita Zilg's (1999) *Fittstim*. The last book in the list has appeared in Sweden, while the former are from the USA or Australia, but similar publications can even be found elsewhere. All of these books focus on girls as capable, tough, articulate and reflective. DIY/grrrlpower draws on previous women's movements but argues for a new, 'girl-centred' feminism. It reclaims the word 'girl' and sometimes focuses on young women's anger as a feminist tool. It sees that many major issues still face young women, especially regarding the body and sexuality. At the same time, it emphasizes autonomy, sassiness, and is sometimes depicted as sexy and assertive.

Unlike power feminism, it is committed to a view of the personal (sexuality, body image, relationships, the impact of cultural representations) as political. However, it seeks to represent young women as angry, in charge and taking action. For example, Flea reproduces a common quote from the grrrlpower movement in her zine *Thunderpussy*, 'Feminism isn't over, it didn't fail, but something new happened – grrrl power. Next time a bloke feels your arse, patronises you, slags off your body, generally treats you like shit – forget the moral highground, forget he's been instilled with patriarchy and is a victim too, forget rationale and debate. Just deck the bastard'. In a slightly different take on grrrlpower and DIY, Bail (1996, p. 5) argues that young women have embraced this form of 'in your face' feminism because they 'don't want to identify with something that sounds dowdy, asexual or shows them to be at a disadvantage. They don't want to be seen as victims.' Thus both 'power feminism' and 'grrrlpower/DIY' share a desire to mark out a new young feminism that is not based in victim images of girls.

> . . . we want to show that there are girls who have higher goals in life than to be voted for Miss Sweden. We want to show that we exist and that we care. We are cool, good-looking, tough, smart, funny and – first and foremost – we are feminists. (Young journalists, Sweden, Olsson & Norrman Skugge, 1999, p. 7, translation from Swedish by Sinikka Aapola.)

While some of the rather stereotyped basic assumptions about previous waves of feminism held by versions of each of these new young feminisms (power feminism in particular) are questionable, this attempt to reclaim 'power' is worth looking at closely. In the context of the cultural dichotomization of girls as either tough or hopeless, choosing the strong and powerful option makes some sense. To blame second wave feminism for emphasizing the other might be inappropriate, but if generational divide is perceived as partially responsible for the construction of youth as a demographic in crisis, it is easy to see how older feminists have become implicated. This sense of complicity is only fuelled by observations by high profile second wavers such as Beatrice Faust (1996, p. 23), who believes that 'many young women are so naïve that if you spit in their face they'll say it's raining', or Germaine Greer (1999, p. 310), who claims that

> the career of the individual bad girl is likely to be a brief succession of episodes of chaotic drinking, casual sex, venereal infection and unwanted pregnancy, with consequences she will have to struggle with all her life.

In constructing a new young feminism that is sassy and smart, tough and in control, some young women are attempting to answer back to these images of girls' feminist principles as ingenuous, misguided and self-harming. In the process, however, do the oppositional positions of 'powerful girl' versus 'victim' that are currently circulating only become further entrenched?

The third wave

A third example of an elaborated 'style' of young feminism, which sometimes overlaps with girl power, includes those who actively embrace the term 'third wave' to mark their place as the next 'wave' in the tradition of the previous two women's movements. This category perhaps offers the most in terms of working outside the power/victim framework to complicate the picture of young feminism. Some specific examples of those whose work could be classified as third wave would include Rebecca Walker, who founded the Third Wave Direct Action Corporation in 1993 and edited *To Be Real* (1996). In this text she proclaims third wave feminism to be more individual, complex and 'imperfect' than previous waves. It is not as strictly defined or all-encompassing, less punitive and rigid, especially about personal choices (fashion, sexuality), and is keen to avoid easy polarities in identifying forces of oppression in women's lives. Further, she claims it is more ethnically, sexually and economically diverse. Leslie Heywood and Jennifer Drake's (1997) *Third Wave Agenda* follows similar lines. They argue that the third wave elaborates and complicates the second wave critique of beauty, sexuality and power, is diverse in its membership, and focuses on the cultural field as a site of feminist activism (for example, music, TV, magazines).

An Australian example, Virginia Trioli's (1996) *Generation f*, is also consistent with this kind of approach. She identifies this generation as highly pragmatic (that is, they implement their feminism in work places, law courts, and on the street), and particularly wise about using the law to fight sexism. She claims that young women take feminist principles for granted as part of their world, and apply these both unashamedly and subtly. We could also include under this category Barbara Findlen's (1995) *Listen Up: Voices from the Next Feminist Generation* and Jennifer Baumgardner and Amy Richards' (2000) *Manifesta: Young Women, Feminism and the Future*. Kristina Thulin's and Jenny Östergren's Swedish book (1997) *X-märkt* could probably also be categorized in this group. Third wave feminism thus places itself in an historical sequence, seeing itself as building on and expanding previous waves of feminism for contemporary times. It is particularly careful to acknowledge and thank second wave feminists, but argues that there are new issues facing young women today. These are generally associated with either the problems faced by women as they attempt to put second wave gains into action (for example, 'going to the cops', using new laws and policies), or with obstacles that are less structural but just as real, for example, ideological barriers. The third wave considers the politics of issues such as beauty, sexuality, fashion and popular culture with more complexity than is sometimes presented by earlier feminist analyses. In their debates, they attempt to explain what it means to enjoy some previously gained achievements but still fight for others in a world where both the state and political activism have changed radically.

> Feminists. Redstockings. Loud women with boots and big puffs of hair under their arms who stood on the barricades and shouted "Down with men!" Some of them were our mothers. That was then.
> When we grew up girls and boys had the same starting points. Girls played football. And boys had sewing at school. In TV they said that we lived in the most equal country in the world [Sweden] . . . Here the battle was already over. We all had the same possiblities. But then one day we stood there with our first live-in-relationship and washed the dishes after dinner, because it was quicker to do it ourselves than to nag at him. . . . And we realized that we were feminists after all. Red stockings. We too. (Young writers, Sweden, Thulin & Östergren, 1997, pp. 7–8, translation from Swedish by Sinikka Aapola.)

They talk about being 'the first generation for whom feminism has been entwined in the fabric of (their) lives' (Findlen, 1995, p. xv), who 'live their feminism each day' (Else-Mitchell & Flutter, 1998, p. xii); that is, with an ongoing sense of both entitlement and injustice. Consequently, they walk a fine line between displaying their strengths and working on what must still be done. The tendency in this literature to articulate the third wave agenda through personal stories of consciousness-raising is an interesting development that points to some of the difficulties in balancing articulations of both young women's power and the challenges that face them. However, the third wave perspectives point to some important developments in new directions for feminism – diversity, tolerance for difference and contradiction, and multi-level praxis.

These three categorizations have become significant ways in which feminism is being taken up by young women. Each of these positions demonstrates that the ground of 'new young feminism' is hotly contested. However, each is primarily concerned with demarcating a kind of new feminism that sees young women as powerful, but not yet entirely equal. This is a difficult balancing act for young women to maintain. To some extent, the broader context within which these new feminisms are articulated have limited their possibilities. Because young women are so frequently represented as either empowered or in crisis, young feminism itself has had to grapple with these images and find a way through their limitations to engage with the key issues of young women's lives. There has been a lot at stake in the young feminism debate, but this debate itself has perhaps prevented a wider perspective on young women's activism. Importantly, it has often excluded the experiences of many young women who do not access these more formal declarations of feminist theory and practice, but may be engaged in feminist 'micropolitics' in their everyday lives.

> Ever since I was little people told me there was no such word as *can't*. I guess they wanted to motivate me. But when I looked around I saw that people were being told they couldn't do things and I didn't understand why. As I got older I grew more confused and angry. I began to notice the way men looked at women and didn't pay attention to what women said. I wanted to be heard. (Alessia Di Virgilio, Canada (Di Virgilio, 2001, p. 75).)

Di Virgilio illustrates the nexus at which many young women currently live their lives. She is writing specifically from her experience of being physically challenged, but the point is relevant for all girls. As Di Virgilio points out, inspirational, individualized rhetoric is often invoked in relation to young women with disabilities without the concomitant attention to material and social changes that would enhance their empowerment. On the one hand, they are offered girl power-style truisms such as there is 'no such word as *can't*', and on the other, they witness and experience unequal structures of opportunity. This disjunction has led her to pursue a more meaningful, but perhaps more complex feminism, grounded in what she calls 'difference' (Di Virgilio, 2001, p. 75), that moves beyond the young feminism debate.

From a very different starting point, but equally disappointed in the alternatives offered by the various versions of feminism, Swedish writer Nina Björk (1996, pp. 13–14) has also announced her quest for a new strategy. Hers is one that does not want to just re-evaluate femininity but challenges today's feminism to look for ways to loosen up gender identities as based on the feminine and the masculine. The aim is to find a new kind of human being, not formulated by social expectations towards women and men. She claims (1996, p. 12),

Feminism believes in the woman, she is its dearest fetish. Feminism wants to 'liberate' the woman, to 'represent' her, to 're-evaluate her experiences'. Feminism loves the woman. It is a love that has changed her into a utopia, to a dream of another world, a better order. . . . She becomes an exit; if she had been able to decide there would have been fewer wars, less pollution, less frequent racism. (Translation by Sinikka Aapola.)

Next, we explore further possibilities for feminism that can be discerned in young women's praxis, and specifically, those that occur outside of this debate about which version of young feminism should be anointed as the 'real' one. Specifically, we offer some examples of political activism and debate that complicate and move beyond the framework of power/crisis and suggest a real grappling with multiplicity, diversity and dispersal ushered in by socio-economic circumstances of late modernity and cultural conditions of postmodernity. Is there another kind of young feminist activism that cannot be easily contained or summarized, and that may not lend itself to packaging as a style or a text? What about young women who have little to do with feminist books or opportunities to shape policy? What might feminism mean for them, and how do they enact it? It is this kind of feminism we outline next, with the intention of pointing towards young feminist practice and 'micropolitics' that exist beyond the next wave debate, and that might suggest the future of social change politics for young women.

Thinking Beyond Power Feminism, DIY and the Third Wave

Immigrant women, especially teens, feel no connection to someone standing on a podium advocating for equal opportunity because they are more concerned with opportunities, pure and simple. (Azmina N. Ladha, Pakistani-American, USA (Ladha, 2001, p. 141).)

To think beyond power feminism, DIY/Girl power or the third wave as the only categories of young feminism is to see that the young feminist membership is much larger than may be initially imagined, and further, is concerned with a feminism beyond merely claiming girls' power. Central to this perspective are two tasks. First, it is necessary to look at girls' issues and activism beyond the familiar, and beyond the more famous spokespeople for young feminism. The kinds of issues raised by young women outside the formal arenas where feminism is debated draw attention to the limited focus of the 'young feminism' debate and its inability to account for a range of girls' voices. Second, it is critical to look in places often disregarded as sites for feminist work. The role of cultural productions such as zines, webpages, creative writing and performance in allowing 'ordinary' young women to express their views must not be underestimated. As Harris has argued elsewhere, amidst the current flurry of interest in girlhood, real sites and complex discourses for young women's own polit-ical articulations have diminished or gone 'underground' (Harris, 2001a; 2004). Listening to 'other' voices, and looking in 'other' places can help to open up the debate about the next wave and identify some of the features of young feminisms that press beyond the limitations of the existing categories. We suggest that in attending to these tasks, it becomes possible to see an enor-mous potential in new feminist praxis as diverse and open to a range of viewpoints, as exploiting the resources of late modern societies (technology, popular culture, the media) in important ways, and as focusing on dispersed activism rather than a single leader or movement. Here we offer some brief examples of these three features.

> I used to think that activism was letter writing, protesting/marching, sit-ins and sorts of other activities that are most often associated with activism in the media. But I think this is limiting. I think activism is about the belief in change and vision of a better society/environment. It can occur on any level, from how one lives one's life to relationships to actively working towards change in the world/society around oneself. (Rebecca Saxon, member of the young women's Wench Radio Collective, Canada (Wench Collective, 2001, p. 69).)

Diversity and multiplicity

Much contemporary research finds that young women are keen to offer a critique of the standard categorizations of young feminism, or even feminism itself (see O'Brien, 1999; Pallotta-Chiarolli, 1999; Harris, 2001b). Primarily, this is due to a perception of these categories as limited. Speaking about finding an all-encompassing feminist way to address young Black women in the US, Morgan (1999, p. 24) writes, 'How in Oshun's name to capture the nose-ringed/caesered/weaved up/Gucci-Prada-DKNY down/ultra-Nubian alternative-bohemian/beats-loving/smooth-jazz-playing magic of us was something I couldn't begin to fathom'. Her point is that single categories can never capture the diversity of young women's experiences and interests. Young women are much more attentive to diversity and to the need for feminisms that are grounded in multiplicity than they are given credit for in homogenizing categorizations, or than feminists perhaps have been in the past. For example, Maria Pallotta-Chiarolli (1999, p. 75) has found in her research with 'ordinary' girls that young women's feminist praxis is marked by the following features: acknowledging differences within and between groups of people, understanding racism, homophobia and sexism as interconnected, acknowledging shift and flux in definitions and identities, and upholding self-ascribed meanings as opposed to assigned labels. A small example of the ways these features are informing young feminisms can be found in this next example from the UNICEF on-line forum on girls' rights (http://www.unicef.org/). An interest in diversity, difference, and holding complexity manifests itself here in a range of young women's debates around the issues of race, religion and culture. The following discussion takes place amongst young women from Nigeria, the UK and China, who share their insights about the uses and abuses of religion and culture in the treatment and experiences of girls, and what this means for feminist theory and practice.

> The work done in the past and being done now by UN on women and girls is commendable. I am a muslim woman living in the West, and any work on my gender to improve my life must take my belief system into consideration. Any work done on Gender issues pertaining to the Muslim Women cannot ignore 'religion' – otherwise, the project is doomed to failure. (girl, Britain, http://www.unicef.org/)

> In my country, Nigeria, boys are favoured (more) than the girls, in the area of education, boys are allowed to go to school while girls are thrown to one trade or the other, most times they are not allowed to learn any trade but stay at home and do all the work at home and later sent to an old man's house as a wife. This is done in the northern part of Nigeria where they are mostly muslims. This is very bad because this innocent girls end up having V.V.F (HIV) and end up being dumped by the so called husband who has about four of them as wives. Men don't allow their wives to work. I think we children should try to do something about it. (girl, Nigeria, http://www.unicef.org/)

> I think that most of the traditional religions are still imposing some unfair limit and 'rules' on women. In addition, they give the men many

privileges! Since those ideas are already brainwashed in everyone's brain, most of the people, especially the women, is just going to bear them. I am not challenging any religions, which may be worshiped by many people, but it is the time to think of it and ask WHY – why two sexes are not equal in front of most of the gods! To many women in some Asian countries, the beliefs of the local religion is really a great obstacle to their development. Changing such kind of ideas is difficult, and also, females are always taught to be 'accepting' of anything, no matter it is fair or not'. (girl, China, http://www.unicef.org/)

While this discussion does not itself seek to resolve these different perspectives, or suggest ways activism might emerge out of the differences, we can see here that a range of views is opened up without any one being defended as 'more feminist' than another. The three perspectives build up a picture of the complexity of a feminist take on girls, religion, nation and culture. None of this fits easily into pre-constructed categories of young feminism, but suggests an important move forward in feminist analysis. In this example, these young women are expanding the concept of feminism to enable as a matter of course very careful and sophisticated analyses of the meanings of culture and religion that do not deny difference and the complexity of contradictory grounded experience that complicates fixed notions of privilege and discrimination. The careful use of personal knowledge, the potential for different understandings of the meanings of culture and religion, or the degree to which 'traditionalism' dictates the repressive capacity of any religious belief, are all raised here. The ways this translates into political practice, whilst this is not evidenced directly here, is also significant.

In this next example, the US online and grassroots organization *Blackgrrrlrevolution* offers some insights into how diversity and alliances work in their experience. They say

> there's like 20 areas on which we advocate for black grrrls, meaning all girls of colour and many languages – we stand on so many radical frontlines, so I think we're re-focussing our expectations of alliances, we're not going to ally ourselves with the people everyone thinks that we would naturally ally ourselves with. (Personal interview, 2001.)

This organization advocates for a wide diversity of young women, but eschews what might be typical alliances, for example, with some other Black or girls' organizations, because they are perceived to be too rigid and limited in their focus. The fact that their plat-form is diverse and represents a range of differences in lived expe-rience has led to them, as they say, 'shifting paradigms in terms of political organizing and doing business'. However, the subtleties and complexities of this interest in diversity, change and multi-plicity are not often attended to in the official versions of young feminism. In particular, they are not often addressed beyond indi-vidual grappling with difference, or in terms of their implications for feminist praxis, the role and efficacy of women's programmes (for example, within the UN), and the capacity for a range of women to debate, disagree, and work together.

Other sites

> The internet is never going to foment any kind of revolution – except maybe a commercial one (witness the number of businesses exploding on the web) – for reasons of access (it's limited to those with the capital to buy a computer, a modem, and other techno-gadgets), but y'know, when a girl's standing screaming into a hurricane, it's nice to have your friends next to you, shouting and fist-waving too. (Mimi Nguyen, *exoti-cise this!* – website.)

The fact that these debates about culture, religion, feminism and alliances take place in cyberspace is significant. We can see this as just one example of the contemporary sites and strategies for feminism developed or used by young women around new technology, as well as popular culture and the media. Young women who do not have access to publishers and cannot get their voices heard in the mainstream have been responsible for creating new feminist activism and networks through alternative media. Giroux (1998, p. 24) argues that 'when youth do speak, the current generation in particular, their voices generally emerge on the margins of society- in underground magazines, alternative music spheres, computer hacker clubs and other subcultural sites'. This is certainly the case for much young feminist debate, for example, as evidenced in the creation of grrrlzines, girls' webpages and chat rooms. For some young women with disabilities, the internet in particular has become an important forum for community-building and activism. For those whose lives are subject to a large amount of management, whether this be from family, personal careers or social services, the internet offers a virtual private space for agentic expression free from intervention. It is also important that, unlike a physical place, the internet can be utilized for self-expression, community and activist organization without requiring physical access. Meekosha (2002, p. 80) writes

> the virtual community of disabled women activists has made interaction more of a level playing field. Women who feel unable to "speak" in face-to-face situations have "voice" on the Internet. The Internet has provided a relatively cheap means of linking disabled women who are separated geographically, who have been isolated, and who use different forms of communication.

Similarly, zines function as a new site for expression, communication and activism. Short for 'fanzines', zines are independently produced informal newsletters, which usually include reviews, information sharing, editorials and creative writing around issues relevant to young women. They are distributed through wide networks for the purposes of sharing information and building a community of young feminists. Duncombe (1998, p. 3) argues that zines have become an important new locale for young people's political debate and resistance in the wake of the decline of old style social movements. He says 'throughout the 1980's while the Left was left behind, crumbling and attracting few new converts, zines and underground culture grew by leaps and bounds, resonating deeply with disaffected young people (constituting) perhaps the next wave of meaningful political resistance' (see also Leonard, 1998, for an analysis of grrrlzines as new feminist communities). Many young women also use the internet as a place for political action through listservs and chatrooms (see Scott-Dixon, 1999). For example, the zine *Driving Blind*, by Erin, is distributed through an online site which also serves as a meeting point and exchange forum for young people, and especially young women, with disabilities. Zines and the internet often operate in tandem as alternative circuits of communication and distribution of information for young activists.

These kinds of cultural politics – zines, e-zines, comics and webpages – have often been interpreted as girls just 'having fun', but they also hold real promise for feminist work precisely because they constitute 'other spaces' for politics. The three 'next wave' categories tend to concentrate on either demonstrating young women's continued engagement with old style political activism (lobbying government, holding protests, campaigning, civil disobedience and so on), or on their lack of need for this. What is lost in the two sides of this argument is the possibility (and indeed, the very real evidence) that some young women have developed quite new ways of conducting political organization, protest, debate and agitation as a consequence of the perceived co-option of left politics as merely a marketable style, and appropriation of their resistant voices when expressed through traditional protest modes. The trend towards an increased surveillance of youth, the re-discovery of young women in particular as the new consumers, and the cultural fascination with girlhood have all resulted in a deep suspicion of overt activism as the best method for protest and the creation of social change. Young women have repeatedly seen their politics sold back to them as products, and consequently seek other modes for debate and agitation.

Movements without leaders

> I don't see myself as part of any 'wave' really, a lot of the main figures and ideas behind the 'third wave' have turned out to be as disappointing as some of the second-wavers, and while I think both were important and accomplished a lot, I don't know if I fit in with either. There's been a lot of talk lately about 'no wave' feminism as a feminist movement that takes lessons from the past but remains open to critique and dialogue, doesn't create idols whose theory can't be questioned, doesn't excuse oppression in the name of feminism and genuinely tries to be a movement for more than white, middle/upper class women. (Moira, 23, New Zealand, *Moon Rocket* distribution, quoted in interview, http://www.grrrlzines.net)

Finally, another feature of an uncategorized young feminism is that there is not a single leader heading up a single movement. This trend away from the organized, hierarchized movement is a key feature of many forms of social justice action under late modernity (see Melucci, 1996). As Klein (2000) argues, these new practices of resistance respond 'to corporate concentration with a maze of fragmentation, to globalization with its own kind of localization, to power consolidation with radical power dispersal'. The dispersal of the feminist movement is consistent with this broader shift. This has become an important way to enact feminist change within particular communities on specific issues relevant to that place.

Young women are engaged in both specific issues that affect them in their own communities and in wider concerns that reach across the world. These include anti-sweat shop and other labour-related campaigns, health, sexuality and disease awareness raising, environmental and animal rights activism, pro-education and anti-sex slavery work, and so on. All of this is feminist. Swede Lena Gemzöe (2003, p. 172) has argued that feminism as a political movement needs allies in movements for economic equality and for global human rights, but she also claims that the same applies vice versa: no movement towards equality can achieve their goals without also subscribing to feminism.

As *Blackgrrrlrevolution* claims in their case, but arguably in the case of many forms of young feminism, feminism as a framework has become broader. They say:

> feminism is a necessary tool for human liberation, freedom and empowerment: that's broad. What that essentially is saying is that pro black girl feminism, the pro black girl movement is a queer movement, it is a Marxist movement, it is a social movement, it is a labour movement, it is a civil rights movement, it is a gay rights movement, it is every movement. (Personal interview, 2001.)

There is no requirement put on them to choose any one or the other, or to try to homogenize issues into one big movement that might involve silencing or excluding some over others. The three next wave categories have tended to articulate this shift away from the movement by at times denying it, or by overstating young women's desire to express individual needs. None has contextualized this change in terms of the wider trend of left politics, where it can be most easily understood as a re-organization rather than disintegration of feminist alliances.

Conclusion

Young women are imagined as occupying a pivot point in the history of feminism because they are the first generation to have reaped the rewards of the second wave movement. However, as we have seen, this situation is not straightforward, and has been handled in complex and sophisticated ways by young women themselves. They face new opportunities as well as old, and new, barriers to making something of their lives. Whilst a generation debate swirls around, often constituted in terms of the problem they represent for feminism, young women themselves draw on feminist strategies and resources to move forward. These are not always recognizable or typically political, but represent important new ways that women grapple with the contradictory narratives of individualism, personal power, crisis and risk that surround them.

The purpose of offering some suggestions about other kinds of feminisms enacted by young women is to push open the categories currently competing for preselection as the 'real' next wave. We have suggested that the three most common representations of this next wave are stylized versions of 'feminism as girls' empowerment', which have emerged in response to the construction of contemporary girlhood as in crisis, and contemporary young women as troubled, naïve or selfish. However, in this race to colonize the terrain of young feminism, some of the most exciting, if uncategorizeable girls' activism and micropolitics is being lost. The same circumstances which have seen girlhood become a receptacle for social anxieties about change have also seen new possibilities, places and modes for their feminist theory and practice. It is in these other spaces and through these other expressions that may emerge 'a "new feminism" we do not yet know' (Bulbeck, 2000, p. 21).

Conclusion

We opened this book with questions about the discourses that define late modern girlhood, the opportunities and limitations these construct for young women, and how young femininity is positioned within broader socio-economic forces such as globalization, de-industrialization and the trend towards individualization. We have pursued these lines of inquiry by examining girlhood and young women in relation to popular culture, citizenship and politics, education and the labour market, family, friendships, the body and sexuality and feminism.

As Blackmore (2001, p. 128) argues, girls now have a discursive space in which to construct more self-assured identities about themselves as women, as workers, parents and consumers. There is much to be celebrated in the creation of this space, but as we have shown, it is a contested and complex space, and one which is not always accessible to all young women. We have demonstrated that young women are poised between two compelling narratives: one of opportunity and choice, and the other of crisis and risk. We have sought to demonstrate that neither of these represents the real truth of young women's circumstances, but rather that it is these two positions that they must negotiate in order to make themselves in late modernity.

Young women grapple with new material conditions, new possibilities and new constraints. Education and employment have become accessible and important to their imagined life trajectories and economic security. Their relationships to family, friends, sexual partners and their bodies seem far freer than for previous generations. Notions of independence, choice and possibility have meaningfully entered their self-perceptions, backed up as they are by significant changes in law, policy and rights for women.

At the same time that these new opportunities are before them, they are required to take responsibility for their livelihoods and lifestyles in the new economy, manage their way through a risk society, and make high-stakes choices with less structural support than ever before. The need to now make a project of one's life, to manage what Beck (1992) calls a 'choice biography', is perceived by different youth researchers as both positive and agency-enhancing (Du Bois-Reymond, 1998), and as a negative experience whereby lack of options is not acknowledged and risks are seriously underestimated (Rudd & Evans, 1998). Somewhere in between is Peter Dwyer and Johanna Wyn's (2001, p. 12) notion of the 'pragmatic choice', such that young people adjust their ambitions, keep their options open, find new ways to achieve goals and re-define the process of 'becoming an adult' along the way.

We believe that young women draw on the discursive and material resources available to them to make pragmatic choices. Therefore, we have illuminated both these resources and the strategies they make possible for young women to demonstrate how they manage their life projects in between stories of unbounded opportunities and anxieties about increased risk. We have concluded by demonstrating how feminism has provided a previously non-existent analytical framework and language to young women for interpreting their worlds (although these may be taken up unevenly by young women themselves). It is our hope that young women will continue to forge feminist futures for themselves, drawing on and developing this resource in their own ways.

Bibliography

Aaltonen, S. & Honkatukia, P. (eds) (2002) *Tulkintoja tytöistä*, Nuoriso-
tutkimusverkosto, julkaisuja 27, Tietolipas 187, Suomalaisen Kirjallisuuden
Seura, Helsinki.

Aapola, S. (1992) 'Best friends or many friends?', unpublished presentation in *Alice
in Wonderland: The First International Conference on Girls and Girlhood*, Vrije
Universiteit, Amsterdam, Netherlands, June 1992.

Aapola, S. (1997) 'Mature Girls and Adolescent Boys? Deconstructing Discourses of
Adolescence and Gender', *Young: The Nordic Journal of Youth Studies*, 5(4), 50–68.

Aapola, S. (1999a) *Murrosikä ja sukupuoli: Julkiset ja yksityiset ikämäärittelyt*,
Suomalaisen Kirjallisuuden Seuran toimituksia 763, Nuorisotutkimusverkoston
julkaisuja 9/99, SKS, Helsinki.

Aapola, S. (1999b) 'Ikä, koulu ja sukupuoli: peruskoulun kulttuuriset ikäjärjestykset, in T. Tolonen (ed), *Suomalainen koulu ja kulttuuri*. Osuuskunta Vastapaino,
Tampere.

Aapola, S. (2002) 'Pikkutyttöjä vai puoliaikuisia? Tytöt, vanhemmat ja kontrolli', in
S. Aaltonen & P. Honkatukia (eds) (2002).

Aapola, S., Gordon, T. & Lahelma, E. (2002) 'Citizens in the Text? International
Presentations of Citizenship in Textbooks', in C.A. Torres, & A. Antikainen (eds),
*The International Handbook on the Sociology of Education: An International Assess-
ment of New Research and Theory*, Rowman & Littlefield Publishers, Lanham.

Aapola, S. (forthcoming) *Children's and young people's conceptions of citizenship,
politics and power*. Research report.

Abbott, P. & Wallace, C. (1990) *An Introduction to Sociology: Feminist Perspectives*,
Routledge, London and New York.

Adkins, L. (2002) *Revisions: Gender and Sexuality in Late Modernity*, Open University
Press, Buckingham.

Allard, A.C. (2002) ' "Aussies" and "Wogs" and the "Group-in-between": Year 10
students' constructions of cross-cultural friendships', *Discourse: studies in the
cultural politics of education*, Special issue: *Re-Theorising Friendship in Educational
Settings*, 23(2), 193–209.

Allatt, P. (1996) 'Youth, Family and Time: En/countering Exclusion and Inclusion',
unpublished paper presented in the seminar *Unification and Marginalization of
Young People*, House of the Estates, Helsinki, November 1996.

American Association of University Women Education Foundation (1992) *How
Schools Shortchange Girls*, Wellesley, MA.

Amit-Talai, V. (1995) 'The Waltz of Sociability: Intimacy, Dislocation and Friendship
in a Quebec High School', in V. Amit-Talai & H. Wulff (eds) (1995).

Amit-Talai, V. & Wulff, H. (eds) (1995) *Youth Cultures: A Cross-cultural Perspective*,
Routledge, London.

Anderson, B. (1991) *Imagined Communities: Reflections on the Origin and Spread of Nationalism*, Verso, London.

Angwin, J. (2000) 'Researching VET Pathways with Disengaged and Disadvantaged Young People', in J. McLeod & K. Malone (2000).

Anonymous (1999) 'I am scared', in Shandler, S. (1999).

Anthias, F., Yuval-Davis, N., Cain, H & Cashmore, E. (1993) *Racialized Boundaries: Race, Nation, Gender, Colour and Class and the Antiracist Struggle*, Routledge, London.

Arnold, G. (2001) 'Badass girls on film', http://salon.com/mwt/feature/2001/01/22/women_warriors/index.html

Arnot, M. & Dillabough, J.-A. (eds) (2000) *Challenging Democracy. International Perspectives on Gender, Education and Citizenship*, RoutledgeFalmer, London.

Arnot, M., David, M. & Weiner, G. (1999) *Closing the gender gap: postwar education and social change*, Polity Press, Cambridge.

Aromaa, V. (1990) 'Tyttöikä – tuulenpyörre ja tosipaikka', in K. Immonen (ed), *Naisen elämä: Mistä on pienet tytöt tehty, mistä tyttöjen äidit*, Otava, Helsinki.

Associated Press (1999) 'Forget Charlie's Angels the year's ultimate girl power movie is crouching Tiger, Hidden Dragon', 30 June.

Attling, Agneta (2001) 'Lisa Ydring, dramatiker: Mannen står som symbol för det allmänmänskliga.' *Webmagasinet FemKul*, Arkiv. (www.femkul.com/?page=/2/arkiv/1/intervju/ydring.asp)

Australian Bureau of Statistics (2002) *Births*, 3301.0, Australia, Australian Bureau of Statistics, Commonwealth Government, Canberra.

Bagnall, D. (2002) 'Miss Interpreted: The Girlpower Myth', *The Bulletin*, 23 July, 20–4.

Bail, K. (ed) (1996) *DIY Feminism*, Allen and Unwin, Sydney.

Ball, S., Maguire, M. & Macrae, S. (2000), *Choice, Pathways and Transitions Post-16: New Youth, New Economies in the Global City*, Routledge/Falmer, London.

Barron, K. (1997) 'The Bumpy Road to Womanhood', *Disability and Society*, 12(2), 223–39.

Barwick, S. (2001) 'Sex, Boys and Make-Up: Is This What Tweenie Girls Want?', *Daily Telegraph*, 8 February.

Basit, T.N. (1996) ' "I'd Hate to be Just a Housewife": Career Aspirations of British Muslim Girls', *British Journal of Guidance and Counselling*, 24(2), 227–42.

Bates, I. (1993) 'A Job Which is "Right For Me"? Social Class, Gender and Individualization', in I. Bates & G. Riseborough (eds), *Youth and Inequality*, Open University Press, Buckingham.

Baumgardner, J. & Richards, A. (2000) *Manifesta: Young Women, Feminism and the Future*, Farrar, Straus and Giroux, New York.

Beck, U. (1992) *Risk Society: Towards a New Modernity*, Sage, London.

Beck, U. & Beck-Gernsheim, E. (1995) *The Normal Chaos of Love*, Polity Press, Cambridge.

Bellafante, G. (1998) 'Feminism: It's All About Me!', *Time*, 29 June, 54–60.

Bengs, C. (2000) *Looking Good: A Study of Gendered Body Ideals Among Young People*, Doctoral Theses at the Department of Sociology Nr 21, Umeå University, Umeå.

Bessant, J. & Cook, S. (eds) (1998) *Against the Odds: Young People and Work*, Australian Clearinghouse for Youth Studies, Hobart.

Bhavnani, K.K. (1991) *Talking Politics: A Psychological Framing for Views from Youth in Britain*, Cambridge University Press, Cambridge.

Bjerrum Nielsen, H. & Rudberg, M. (1994) *Psychological Gender and Modernity*, Scandinavian University Press, Oslo.

Björk, N. (1996) *Under det rosa täcket. Om kvinnlighetens vara och feministiska strategier*, Wahlström & Widstrand, Borås.

Blackmore, J. (2001) 'Achieving More in Education but Earning Less in Work: Girls, Boys and Gender Equality in Schooling', *Discourse: Studies in the Cultural Politics of Education*, 22(1), 123–9.

Blank, H. (2002) 'Faster, Harder, Smarter: Finding a Political Future for Sex-Positive Smut', *Bitch Magazine: Feminist Response to Pop Culture*, 18 (Fall), 54–91.

Boehnke, K., Ittel, A. & Baier, D. (2002) 'Value Transmission and "Zeitgeist": An Underresearched Relationship', *Samenvattingen Tijdschrift* 3, Tilburg University.

Bordo, S. (1993) *Unbearable Weight*, University of California Press, Berkeley.

Bosma, H.A., Jackson, S.E., Zijsling, D.H., Zani, B., Cicognani, E., Xerri, M.L., Honess, T.M. & Charman, L. (1996) 'Who has the final say? Decisions on adolescent behaviour within the family', *Journal of Adolescence*, 19, 277–91.

Bowlby, S., Lloyd Evans, S. & Mohammad, R. (1998) 'The Workplace. Becoming a Paid Worker: Images and Identity', in T. Skelton & G. Valentine (eds), *Cool Places*, Routledge, London.

Bridger, S. & Kay, R. (1996) 'Gender and Generation in the New Russian Labour Market', in H. Pilkington (ed), *Gender, Generation and Identity in Contemporary Russia*, Routledge, London.

Brown, L.M. (1998) *Raising Their Voices: The Politics of Girls' Anger*, Harvard University Press, London/Cambridge.

Brown, M. (2000) 'Give Us The Pocket Money', *The Guardian*, 29 May.

Brown, W., Ball, K. & Powers, J. (1998) 'Is Life a Party for Young Women?', *The ACHPER Healthy Lifestyles Journal*, 45(3), 21–6.

Brumberg, J.J. (1993) 'Something Happens to Girls. Menarche and the Emergence of the Modern American Hygienic Imperative', *Journal of the History of Sexuality*, 4(1), 99–127.

Brumberg, J.J. (1997) *The Body Project: An Intimate History of American Girls*, Random House, New York.

Buchmann, M. (1989) *The Script of Life in Modern Society. Entry into Adulthood in a Changing World*, The University of Chicago Press, Chicago.

Buckingham, D. (2000) *The Making of Citizens: Young People, News and Politics*, Routledge, London.

Budgeon, S. (1998) ' "I'll Tell You What I Really, Really Want": Girl Power and Self Identity in Britain', in S. Inness (ed) (1998b).

Budgeon, S. (2001) 'Emergent Feminist (?) Identities: Young Women and the Practice of Micropolitics', *The European Journal of Women's Studies*, 8(1), 7–28.

Bulbeck, C. (2000) 'Failing Feminism? What the Generation Debate Does and Doesn't Tell Us About the Future of Feminism', in *Inaugural University of Tasmania Women's Studies Series Seminar*, University of Tasmania, 27 April.

Bulbeck, C. (2001) 'Young Women's Imagined Lives in 1970 and 2000', unpublished presentation in *Casting New Shadows: Australian Women's Studies Association Conference*, Institute for Women's Studies, Macquarie University, Sydney, 31 January–2 February.

Bulbeck, C. & Harris, A. (forthcoming 2004) 'Gender, Youth and Political Engagements', *Journal of Social Issues*.

Bullen, E., Kenway, J. & Hay, V. (2000) 'New Labour, Social Exclusion and Educational Risk Management: the case of "gymslip mums" ', *British Educational Research Journal*, 26(4), 441–56.

Bynner J., Chisholm, L. & Furlong, A. (eds) (1997) *Youth, Citizenship and Change in a European Context*, Aldershot, Ashgate.

Campbell, A. (1991) *The Girls in the Gang*, Basil Blackwell, Cambridge (Second Edition).

Carlip, H. (ed) (1995) *Girl Power: Young Women Speak Out, personal writings from teenage girls*, Warner Books, New York.

Carmichael, E. (1999) 'Fight Girl Power', in S. Shandler (1999).

Carroll, R. (ed) (1997) *Sugar in the Raw: Voices of Young Black Girls in America*, Crown Publishers, New York.

Catan, L. (2001) 'The Role of the Family in Young People's Transitions to Adulthood: Evidence from the ESRC Youth Research Programme', unpublished presentation in European Sociologists' Association Conference *Visions and Divisions*, University of Helsinki, August.

Chambers, V. (1995) 'Betrayal Feminism', in B. Findlen (ed) (1995).

Chesney-Lind, M. & Irwin, K. (forthcoming 2004) 'From Badness to Meanness: Popular Constructions of Contemporary Girlhood', in A. Harris (ed) (forthcoming 2004).

Chideya, F. (1993) 'Revolution, Girl Style' *Newsweek*, 23 November 1993.

Chisholm, L. (1997) 'Sensibilities and Occlusions: Vulnerable Youth Between Social Change and Cultural Context', in J. Bynner, L. Chisholm & A. Furlong (eds) (1997).

Chisholm, L., Büchner, P., Krüger, H.-H. & du Bois-Reymond, M. (eds) (1995) *Growing Up in Europe: Contemporary Horizons in Childhood and Youth Studies*, Walter de Gruyter, Berlin.

Chisholm, L. & Hurrelmann, K. (1995) 'Adolescence in modern Europe. Pluralized transition patterns and their implications for personal and social risks', *Journal of Adolescence*, 18(2), 129–58.

Cooper, C. (1999) 'Mirrors', in S. Shandler (1999).

Cott, N.F. (1977) *The Bonds of Womanhood. 'Woman's Sphere' in New England, 1780–1835*, Yale University Press, New Haven.

Cox, K. (2000) 'Girls Just Wanna Shop', *Sun Herald*, 16 July 2000, 14.

Crawford, J., Kippax, S., Onyx, J., Gault, U. & Benton, P. (1992) *Emotion and Gender*, Sage, London.

Cuneo, A. (2002) 'Affiliation Targets Youngest Female Consumers', *AdAge*, 27 August.

Dale, R., Tobin, W. & Wilson, B. (1998) 'Ganged Up On, Victimised and Alone: Young People and Workplace Violence', in J. Bessant & S. Cook (1998).

Davies, B. (1989) *Frogs and Snails and Feminist Tales: Preschool Children and Gender*, Allen and Unwin, Sydney.

Davis, S. (1999) 'Girl Power', *The Houston Chronicle*, 24 June, p. 104.

De Almeida, J.V. (2001) 'Keynote Address', unpublished paper in the symposium *Youth – Actor of Social Change?*, Council of Europe, Strasbourg, 12–14 December.

Dellasega, C. (2001) *Surviving Ophelia: Mothers Share Their Wisdom in Navigating the Tumultuous Teenage Years*, Perseus Publishing, New York.

Denfeld, R. (1995) *The New Victorians*, Allen and Unwin, Sydney.

Devaney, J. (2001) 'Burning for a Revolution', in A. Mitchell *et al.* (eds) (2001).

Di Virgilio, A. (2001) 'Young Women and Disability', in A. Mitchell *et al.* (eds) (2001).

Difranco, A. (1995) 'Not a Pretty Girl', in A. Kesselman, L. McNair & N. Schnieder (eds), *Women's Images and Realities: A Multicultural Anthology*, Mayfield Publishing Company, New York.

Doren, B. & Benz, M.R. (1998) 'Employment Inequality Revisited: Predictors of Better Employment Outcomes for Young Women with Disabilities in Transition', *Journal of Special Education*, 31(4), 425–42.

Driscoll, C. (2002) *Girls: Feminine Adolescence in Popular Culture and Cultural Theory*, Columbia University Press, New York.

Driscoll, C. (1999) 'Girl Culture, Revenge and Global Capitalism: Cybergirls, Riot Grrls, Spice Girls', *Australian Feminist Studies*, 14(29), 173–93.

Du Bois-Reymond, M. (1998) ' "I Don't Want to Commit Myself Yet": Young People's Life Concepts', *Journal of Youth Studies*, 1(1), 63–80.

Duncombe, S. (1998) *Notes From Underground: Zines and the Politics of Alternative Culture*, Verso, London.

Dunne, G.A. (1999) 'A Passion for "Sameness"?: Sexuality and Gender Accountability, in E. Silva & C. Smart (eds) (1999).

Dwyer, P., Smith, G., Tyler, D. & Wyn, Johanna (2003) *Life-Patterns, Career Outcomes and Adult Choices*, Youth Research Centre, Melbourne.

Dwyer, P. & Wyn, J. (2001) *Youth, Education and Risk: Facing the Future*, Routledge/Falmer, London.

Eder, D., Evans, C.C. & Parker S. (1995) *School Talk, Gender and Adolescent Culture*, Rutgers University Press, New Brunswick.

Else-Mitchell, R. & Flutter, N. (1998) *Talking Up: Young Women's Take on Feminism*, Spinifex, Melbourne.

Epstein, D., Elwood, J., Hey, V. & Maw, J. (1998) *Failing Boys: Issues in Gender and Achievement*, Open University Press, Buckingham.

Erikson, E.H. (1968) *Identity – Youth and Crisis*, W.W. Norton, New York.

Espin, O. (1995) ' "Race", Racism and Sexuality in the Life Narratives of Immigrant Women', *Feminism and Psychology*, 5, 223–38.

Faust, B. (1996) 'Time You Grew Up Little Sister', *The Australian*, 12–13 October, 23.

Ferris, M. (2001) 'Resisting Mainstream Media: Girls and the Act of Making Zines', *Canadian Women's Studies*, 20/21, Winter/Spring, 51–5.

Finders, M.J. (1997) *Just Girls, Hidden Literacies and Life in Junior High*, Teachers College Press, New York.

Findlen, B. (ed) (1995) *Listen Up: Voices from the Next Feminist Generation*, Seal Press, Seattle.

Fine, M. (1988) 'Sexuality, Schooling and Adolescent Females: The Missing Discourse of Desire', *Harvard Educational Review*, 58(1), 29–53.

Fine, G.A. & Mechling, J. (1991) 'Minor Difficulties: Changing Children in the Late Twentieth Century', in A. Wolfe (ed) (1991).

Fine, M. & Weis, L. (1998) *The Unknown City: Lives of Poor and Working-Class Young Adults*, Beacon Press, Boston.

Folds, R. (1987) *Whitefella School: Education and Aboriginal Resistance*, Allen and Unwin, Sydney.

Ford, J., Rugg, J. & Burrows, R. (2002) 'Conceptualising the Contemporary Role of Housing in the Transition to Adult Life in England', *Urban Studies*, 39(13), 2455–68.

Fordham, S. (1996) *Blacked Out: Dilemmas of Race, Identity and Success at Capital High*, University of Chicago Press, Chicago.

Foster, V. (2000) 'Is female educational "success" destabilising the male learner-citizen?', in M. Arnot & J.-A. Dillabough (eds) (2000).

France, A. (1998) ' "Why should we care?" Young People, Citizenship and Questions of Social Responsibility.' *Journal of Youth Studies*, 1(1), 97–112.

France, K. (1993) 'Grrls at War' *Rolling Stone*, July 1993, 8–22.

Fritzsche, B. (2001) 'Spicy Strategies: Pop Feminism and Other Empowerments in Girl Culture', unpublished presentation at the conference *A New Girl Order? Young Women and the Future of Feminist Inquiry*, London, 12–14 November.

Froschl, M., Rubin, E. & Sprung, B. (1999) 'Connecting Gender and Disability', *Gender and Disability Digest*, November, Women's Educational Equity Act Resource Center, Newton.

Frost, L. (2001) *Young Women and the Body. A Feminist Sociology*, Palgrave, London.

Furlong, A. & Cartmel, F. (1997) *Young People and Social Change*, Open University Press, Buckingham.

Ganetz, H. (1995) 'The shop, the home and femininity as a masquerade', in J. Fornäs & G. Bolin (eds), *Youth Culture in Late Modernity*, Sage, London.

Garner, H. (1995) *The First Stone: Some Questions about Sex and Power*, Pan Macmillan, Sydney.

Garrison, E.K. (2000) 'U.S. Feminism – Grrrrl Style!: Youth (Sub)Cultures and the Technologics of the Third Wave', *Feminism Studies*, 26(1), 141–70.

Gavey, N. (1993) 'Technologies and Effects of Heterosexual Coercion' in S. Wilkinson & C. Kitzinger (eds), *Heterosexuality: a feminism and psychology reader*, Sage, London.

Gemzöe, L. (2003) *Bildas Ismer, Feminism*, Bilda Förlag, Stockholm.

Gerson, K. (1991) 'Coping with Commitment: Dilemmas and Conflicts of Family Life', in A. Wolfe (ed) (1991).

Giddens, A. (1991) *Modernity and Self-Identity: Self and Society in the Late Modern Age*, Polity Press, Oxford.

Gilbert, L. & Kile, C. (1996) *SurferGrrrls: Look Ethel! An Internet Guide for Us*, Seal Press, Seattle.

Gilbert, P. & Taylor, S. (1991) *Fashioning the Feminine: Girls, Popular Culture and Schooling*, Allen and Unwin, Sydney.

Gill, R. (2001) 'From sex object to desiring sexual subject: A step forward for media representations of young women?', unpublished presentation at the conference *A New Girl Order? Young Women and the Future of Feminist Inquiry*, London, 12–14 November.

Gilligan, C. (1982) *In A Different Voice: Psychological Theory and Women's Development*, Harvard University Press, Cambridge.

Gilligan, C., Lyons, N.P. & Hanmer, T.J. (1990) *Making Connections: The Relational Worlds of Adolescent Girls at the Emma Willard School*, Cambridge University Press, Cambridge.

Giroux, H. (1998) 'Teenage Sexuality, Body Politics and the Pedagogy of Display', in J. Epstein (ed), *Youth Culture: Identity in a Postmodern World*, Blackwell, Malden.

Giroux, H. (2002) 'Teen Girls' Resistance and the Disappearing Social in Ghost World', *The Review of Education, Pedagogy and Cultural Studies*, 24, 234–304.

Gittins, D. (1985) *The Family in Question. Changing Households & Familiar Ideologies. Women in Society*, Macmillan, Basingstoke.

Godfrey, R. (1993) 'Riot Girls in the Alternative Nation', *Alphabet City*, 3.

Gonick, M. (1997) 'Reading selves, re-fashioning identity: Teen magazines and their readers', *Curriculum Studies*, 5(1), 69–85.

Gonick, M. (2000) 'Canadian = Blonde, English, White: Theorizing Race, Language and Nation', *Atlantis*, 24(2), 93–104.

Gonick, M. (2003) *Between Femininities: Ambivalence, Identity and the Education of Girls*, SUNY Press, Albany.

Gordon, T. (1990) *Feminist Mothers*, Macmillan, London.

Gordon, T. (1994) *Single Women – On the Margins?*, Macmillan, London.

Gordon, T., Holland, J. & Lahelma, E. (2000a) 'Friends or Foes? Interpreting Relations between Girls in School', in G. Walford & C. Hudson (eds), *Genders and Sexualities in Educational Ethnography*, JAI/Elsevier Science, Amsterdam.

Gordon, T., Holland, J. & Lahelma, E. (2000b) *Making Spaces: Citizenship and Difference in Schools*, Macmillan, Basingstoke.

Gray, H.M. & Phillips, S. (1998) *Real Girl/Real World: Tools for Finding Your True Self*, Seal Press, Seattle.

Green, C. (1995) 'One Resilient Baby' in B. Findlen (ed) (1995).

Green, K. & Taormino, T. (1997) *A Girl's Guide to Taking Over the World: Writings from the Girl Zine Revolution*, St Martin's Griffin, New York.

Greenblatt, C. (1996) 'Unwilling Icons: Riot Grrrl Meets the Press', in *Border/Lines*, December, 24–7.

Greer, G. (1999) *The Whole Woman*, Transworld Publishers, London.

Gregory, E. (1993) *Taking a Step Towards Employment*, Ethnic Youth Issues Network, Melbourne.

Griffin, C. (1985) *Typical Girls: Young Women from School to the Job Market*, Routledge and Kegan Paul, London.

Griffin, C. (1993) *Representations of Youth, The Study of Youth and Adolescence in Britain and America*, Polity Press, Cambridge.

Griffin, C. (1994) 'Absences that Matter, Constructions of Sexuality in Studies of Young Women's Friendship Groups', unpublished paper presented at the British Sociological Association Annual Conference *Sexualities in Social Context*, University of Lancashire, March.

Griffin, C. (1997) 'Troubled Teens: Managing Disorders of Transition and Consumption', *Feminist Review*, 55, 4–21.

Griffin, C. (2001) ' "The Young Women Are Having a Great Time": Representations of Young Women and Feminism', *Feminism and Psychology*, 11(2), 182–6.

Griffiths, V. (1995) *Adolescent Girls and Their Friends: A feminist ethnography*, Aldershot, Avebury.

Grosz, E. (1994) *Volatile Bodies: Toward A Corporeal Feminism*, Indiana University Press, Bloomington.

Guidikova, I. & Siurala, L. (2001) 'Introduction: A Weird, Wired, Winsome Generation – Across Contemporary Discourses on Subculture and Citizenship', in A. Furlong & I. Guidikova (eds), *Transitions of Youth Citizenship in Europe*, Council of Europe, Strasbourg.

Guy, L.R. (1995) 'Black Beauty', in Carlip, H. (ed) (1995).

Hahn, C.L. (1998) *Becoming Political*, SUNY Press, New York.

Haikkola, L. (2003) *Ääni ja aikuisuus. Kansalaisuuden ehdot osallisuushankkeeseen osallistuneiden nuorten tulkinnoissa*. Unpublished Master's thesis, Department of Sociology, University of Helsinki, Finland.

Hakim, C. (1991) 'Grateful Slaves and Self-made Women: Fact and Fantasy in Women's Work Orientations', *European Sociological Review*, 7, 101–21.

Hall, G.S. (1904) *Adolescence: Its Psychology and Its Relations to Physiology, Anthropology, Sociology, Sex, Crime, Religion and Education*, Volumes I and II, Sidney Appleton, London.

Hall, S. (1996) 'Who Needs Identity', in S. Hall & P. Du Gay (eds), *Questions of Cultural Identity*, Sage, London.

Hall, T., Coffey, A. & Williamson, H. (1999) 'Self, Space and Place: Youth Identities and Citizenship', *British Journal of Sociology of Education*, 20(4), 501–13.

Halson, J. (1991) 'Young Women, Sexual Harassment and Heterosexuality', in P. Abbott & C. Wallace (eds), *Gender, Power and Sexuality*, Macmillan, London.

Hamilton, S. (1999) 'Subaltern Counterpublics: Feminist Interventions into the Digital Public Sphere' in P. Walton & L. Van Luven (eds), *Popcan: Popular Culture in Canada*, Prentice-Hall, Toronto.

Harinen, P. (2000) *Valmiiseen tulleet. Tutkimus nuoruudesta, kansallisuudesta ja kansalaisuudesta*, Nuorisotutkimusverkoston julkaisuja 11, Nuorisotutkimusseura, Helsinki.

Harrington, B. & Fine, G.A. (2000) 'Opening the 'Black Box': Small Groups and Twenty-First-Century Sociology', *Social Psychology Quarterly*, 63(4), 312–23.

Harris, A. (1996) *Practising Gender: The Subject of Youth*, unpublished PhD thesis, University of Melbourne, Melbourne.

Harris, A. (2001a) 'Revisiting Bedroom Culture: New Spaces for Young Women's Politics', *Hecate*, 27(1), 128–38.

Harris, A. (2001b) 'Riding My Own Tidal Wave: Young Women's Feminist Work', *Canadian Women's Studies Journal*, Special Issue: *Young Women: Feminist, Activists, Grrrls*, May, 27–31.

Harris, A. (2004) *Future Girl: Young Women in the Twenty-First Century*, Routledge, New York.

Harris, A. (ed) (forthcoming 2004) *All About the Girl: Power, Culture and Identity*, Routledge, New York.

Harris, A., Aapola, S. & Gonick, M. (2000) 'Doing it Differently: Young Women Managing Heterosexuality in Australia, Finland and Canada', *Journal of Youth Studies*, 3(4), 373–88.

Haug, F. (ed) (1987) *Female Sexualisation. A Collective Work of Memory*, Verso, London.

Hays, S. (1996) *The Cultural Contradictions of Motherhood*, Yale University Press, New Haven and London.

'Health warnings call for cosmetic surgery', 4 April 2001, *BBC News*, Health. http://news.bbc.co.uk/2/hi/health/1259846.stm

Heath, S. (1999) 'Watching the Backlash: the Problematisation of Young Women's Academic Success in 1990s Britain', *Discourse: studies in the cultural politics of education*, 20(2), 249–66.

Hebdige, D. (1979) *Subculture: The Meaning of Style*, Routledge, London.

Hedengren, U. (1999) *I händelsernas centrum. Samhällskunskap för grundskolans senare år*, Almqvist & Wiksell, Stockholm.

Heinz, W.R. (1995) 'Access to Working Life in Germany and Britain', in A. Cavalli & E. Galland (eds), *Youth in Europe*, Pinter, London.

Helford, E.R. (ed) (2000) *Fantasy Girls: Gender in the New Universe of Science Fiction and Fantasy Television*, Rowman and Littlefield, New York.

Hellsten, V. (2003) 'Uusi politiikka ja poliittisen osallistumisen moninaistuminen: haaste edustukselliselle demokratialle?' in K. Paakkunainen (ed) (2003).

Helsingin Sanomat, Kuukausiliite, August 1999.

Helve, H. (1997) 'Perspectives on social exclusion, citizenship and youth', in J. Bynner, L. Chisholm & A. Furlong (eds) (1997).

Henderson, S., Taylor, R. & Thomson, R. (2001) 'In touch: Young People, Communication and Technologies', unpublished paper at the conference *A New Girl Order? – Young Women and the Future of Feminist Inquiry*, London, 12–14 November.

Herdt, G. & Boxer, A. (1996) *Children of Horizons. How lesbian and gay teens are leading a new way out of closet. With a new epilogue*, Beacon Press, Boston.

Herrmann, M. (1998) 'Feeling Better with BRAVO: German Girls and Their Popular Youth Magazine', in S. Inness (ed) (1998b).

Hesford, W. (1999) *Framing Identities: Autobiography and the Politics of Pedagogy*, The University of Minnesota Press, Minneapolis.

Hey, V. (1997) *The Company She Keeps: An Ethnography of Girls' Friendship*, Open University Press, Buckingham.

Hey, V. (2002) 'Horizontal Solidarities and Molten Capitalism: The subject, inter-subjectivity, self and the other in late modernity', *Discourse: studies in the cultural politics of education*, Special Issue: *Re-Theorising Friendship in Educational Settings*, 23(2), 227–41.

Heywood, L. & Drake, J. (eds) (1997) *Third Wave Agenda: Being Feminist, Doing Feminism*, University of Minnesota Press, Minneapolis.

Hill, R.F. & Fortenberry, D.J. (1992) 'Adolescence as A Culture-bound Syndrome', *Social Science and Medicine*, 35(1), 73–80.

Hillier, L. (2001) ' "I'm Wasting Away on Unrequited Love": Gendering Same Sex Attracted Young Women's Love, Sex and Desire', *Hecate*, 27(1), 119–27.

Hirvonen, E. (2002) 'Nuoren raskaus ja äitiys', in S. Aaltonen & P. Honkatukia (2002).

Hite, S. (1977) *The Hite Report*, Hamlyn, Sydney.

Ho, C. (1999) 'Reviving Ophelia', in S. Shandler (ed) (1999).

Hochschild, A. (1997) *Time Bind: When Work Becomes Home and Home Becomes Work*, Metropolitan Books, New York.

Hoikkala, T. (1993) *Katoaako kasvatus, himmeneekö aikuisuus? Aikuistumisen puhe ja kulttuurimallit*, Gaudeamus, Helsinki.

Holland, J., Ramazanoglu, C., Sharpe, S. & Thomson, R. (1992) *Pressured Pleasure: Young Women and the Negotation of Sexual Boundaries*, The Tufnell Press, London.

Holland, J., Ramazanogly, C., Sharpe, S. & Thomson, R. (1998) *The Male in the Head. Young people, heterosexuality and power*, The Tufnell Press, London.

Holmes, J. and Silverman, E.E. (1992) *We're Here, Listen to Us!: A Survey of Young Women*, Canadian Advisory Council on the Status of Women, Ottawa.

Honkatukia, P. (2000) ' "Lähentelijöitä riittää . . ." Tyttöjen kokemuksia sukupuolis-esta ahdistelusta', in P. Honkatukia, J. Niemi-Kiesiläinen & S. Näre, *Lähentelyistä raiskauksiin. Tyttöjen kokemuksia häirinnästä ja seksuaalisesta väkivallasta*, Nuoriso-tutkimusverkoston julkaisuja 13, Nuorisotutkimusseura, Helsinki.

Honkatukia, P. & Aaltonen, S. (2001) 'Tough Girls in (and behind) the headlines', unpublished paper presented at the conference *New Girl Order? Young Women and the Future of Feminist Inquiry*, London, 12–14 November.

Hopkins, S. (2002) *Girl Heroes: The New Force in Popular Culture*, Pluto Press, Annandale.

Hudson, B. (1987) 'Adolescence and Femininity', in A. McRobbie & M. Nava (eds), *Gender and Generation*, Macmillan Education, London.

Hues (1998) 'Girl Power: What's the Real Deal?', *Hues: Hear US Emerging Sisters Magazine*, vol. 4(3), Genderwatch database, Softlineunformation, Inc. http://home.softlineweb.com/

Hughes-Bond, L. (1998) 'Standing Alone, Working Together: Tensions Surrounding Young Canadian Women's Views of the Workplace', *Gender and Education*, 10(3), 281–97.

Ige, B. (1998) 'For Sale: A Girl's Life in the Global Economy', in S. Inness (1998b).

Illouz, E. (1997) *Consuming the Romantic Utopia: Love and the Cultural Contradictions of Capitalism*, University of California Press, Berkeley.

Inness, S. (ed) (1998a) *Delinquents and Debutantes: Twentieth-Century American Girls' Cultures*, New York University Press, New York.

Inness, S. (ed) (1998b) *Millennium Girls: Today's Girls And Their Cultures,* Rowman and Littlefield, Lanham.

Inness, S. (1999) *Tough Girls: Women Warriors and Wonder Women in Popular Culture,* University of Pennsylvania Press, Philadelphia.

Ittel, A. & Kuhn, H.P. (in press 2004) 'Introduction' in A. Ittel & H.P. Kuhn (eds), Political Socialization and Gender – International Perspectives, Special Issue of the *Journal of Social Issues,* 60.

Jacobi, J. (1995) 'Are Girls Less Political Than Boys? Research Strategies and Concepts for Gender Studies on 9–12 Year Olds', in G. Neubauer & K. Hurrelmann (eds), *Individualization in Childhood and Adolescence,* de Gruyter, Berlin.

Jacques, A. (2001) 'You Can Run but you can't hide: The Incorporation of riot grrrl into mainstream culture', *Canadian Women's Studies,* 20/21.

Jallinoja, R. (2004) 'Familistisen käänteen rakentajat. Arlie Hochschild ja suomalainen mediajulkisuus', in Rahkonen, K. (ed) *Sosiologisia nykykeskusteluja.* Gaudeamus, Helsinki.

James, A., Jenks, C. & Prout, A. (1998) *Theorizing Childhood,* Polity Press, Cambridge.

Japenga, A. (1995) 'Punk's Girls Groups are Putting the Self Back into Self-Esteem', *New York Times,* 15 November, 30.

Järvinen, T. & Vanttaja, M. (2001) 'Young People, Education and Work: Trends and Changes in Finland in the 1990s', *Journal of Youth Studies,* 4(2), 195–207.

Järvinen, T. (2003) *Urheilijoita, taiteilijoita ja IB-nuoria. Lukioiden erikoistuminen ja koulukasvatuksen murros,* Nuorisotutkimusverkoston julkaisuja 37, Nuorisotutkimusseura, Helsinki.

Johnson, L. (1993) *The Modern Girl,* Allen and Unwin, Sydney.

Jones, A. (1991) *At School I've Got a Chance,* Dunmore Press, Palmerston North.

Jones, G. & Wallace, C. (1992) *Youth, Family and Citizenship,* Open University Press, Buckingham.

Jones, S. (1988) *Black Culture, White Youth: The Reggae Tradition From JA to UK,* Macmillan, London.

Jordan, J.V.J., Kaplan, A.G., Miller, J.B., Stiver, I.P. & Surrey, J.L. (1991) *Women's Growth in Connection: Writings from the Stone Center,* The Guilford Press, New York.

Jowett, M. (2001) '"I Don't See Feminists as You See Feminists": Young Women Negotiating Feminism in Contemporary Britain', unpublished presentation at the conference *A New Girl Order? Young Women and the Future of Feminist Inquiry,* London, 12–14 November.

Julkunen, R. (2001) *Suunnanmuutos: 1990-luvun sosiaalipoliittinen reformi Suomessa,* Vastapaino, Tampere.

Kaisamatti, L. (2000) 'Frenditestissä Tiktakin Nea & Tuuli', *Sisters' Club,* 1 May.

Kantrowitz, B. (2002) 'Selling Advice as well as Anxiety: The queen bee best sellers are stories, not science', *Newsweek,* 3 June, 50–1.

Kaplan, E.A. (1992) *Motherhood and Representation. The Mother in Popular Culture and Melodrama,* Routledge, London and New York.

Karp, M. & Stoller, D. (1999) *Bust Guide to the New Girl Order,* Penguin, New York.

Kartovaara, L. (1995) *Life Cycle,* in E.-S. Veikkola & T. Palmu (eds), *Women and Men in Finland,* Statistics Finland, SVT, Living Conditions 1995, 1.

Katz, A. (1997) *The Can-Do Girls,* Department of Applied Social Studies and Research, University of Oxford, Oxford.

Katz, C. & Monk, J. (eds) (1993) *Full Circles: Geographies of Women Over the Life Course,* Routledge, London.

Kehily, M., Mac an Ghaill, M., Epstein, D. & Redman, P. (2002) 'Private Girls and Public Worlds: producing femininities in the primary school', *Discourse: studies in the cultural politics of education*, Special Issue: *Re-Theorising Friendship in Educational Settings*, 23(2), 167–77.

Kehily, M. (2002) *Sexuality, gender and schooling. Shifting agendas in social learning*, RoutledgeFalmer, London.

Kenway, J. & Langmead, D. (2000) 'Cyberfeminism and citizenship? Challenging the political imaginary', in M. Arnot & J.-A. Dillabough (eds) (2000).

Kenway, J. & Willis, S. with Blackmore, J. and Rennie, L. (1998) *Answering Back. Girls, Boys and Feminism in Schools*, Routledge, London.

Kenway, J. & Bullen, E. (2001) *Consuming Children. Education-entertaiment-advertising*, Open University Press, Buckingham.

Kinsey, A.C., Pomeroy, W.B., Martin, C.E. & Gebhard, P.H. (1967) *Sexual Behaviour in the Human Female*, Pocket Books, New York.

Klein, M. (1997) 'Duality and Redefinition: Young Feminism and the Alternative Music Community', in L. Heywood & J. Drake (eds) (1997).

Klein, N. (2000) 'The Vision Thing', *The Nation*, 10 July, also online at http://www.thenation.com/issue/000710/0710klein.shtml

Klein, N. (2001) *No Logo*, Flamingo, London.

Kleven, K.V. (1993) 'In Deadly Earnest or Postmodern Irony – Girls' and Boys' Cultures on a Collision Course?', *Young – Nordic Journal of Youth Research*, 1(4), 40–59.

Knuuttila, J. (1997) *Rockia soittavat tytöt: rockinsoittoharrastus nuoruusiän ja sukupuolijärjestelmän näkökulmista*, Psykologian tutkimuksia. Yhteiskuntatieteiden tiedekunta 19, Joensuun Yliopisto, Joensuu.

Koedt, A. (1973) 'The Myth of the Vaginal Orgasm', in A. Koedt, E. Levine & A. Rapone (eds), *Radical Feminism*, Quadrangle Books, New York.

Kontula, O. & Haavio-Mannila, E. (1993) *Suomalainen Seksi: Tietoa suomalaisten sukupuolielämän muutoksesta*, WSOY, Helsinki.

Krüger, H. (1990) 'The Shifting Sands of the Social Contract: Young People in the Transition from School to Work', in L. Chisholm, P. Büchner, H.-H. Krüger & P. Brown (eds), *Childhood, Youth and Social Change: a Comparative Perspective*, Falmer, London.

Kuczynski, A. (2003) 'She's got to be a macho girl', *New York Times*, 3 Nov, 2003.

Kurki, S. (2000) 'Tanssiaisten prinsessa', *Girls*, 2(13), 4–5.

Labi, N. (1998) 'Girl Power' *Time*, 29 June, 54–6.

Ladha, A.L. (2001) 'Immigrant Young Women as Feminists?', *Canadian Women's Studies Journal*, Special Issue: *Young Women: Feminist, Activists, Grrrls*, 139–41.

Lagerspetz, K. (1998) *Naisten aggressio*, Tammi, Helsinki.

Lagos, M. & Rose, R. (1999) *Young People in Politics: A Multicontinental Study*, Studies in Public Policy Number 316, Centre for the Study of Public Policy, University of Strathclyde, Glasgow.

Lagree, J.-C. (1995) 'Young People and Employment in the European Community: Convergence or Divergence?', in L. Chisholm, P. Büchner, H.-H. Krüger, & M. du Bois-Reymond (eds) (1995).

Lahelma, E. (1993) *Policies of Gender and Equal Opportunities in Curriculum Development: Discussing the Situation in Finland and Britain*, Research Bulletin 85, Department of Education, University of Helsinki, Yliopistopaino, Helsinki.

Lähteenmaa, J. (1995) 'Youth Culture in Transition to Post-Modernity: Finland', in L. Chisholm, P. Büchner, H.-H. Krüger & M. du Bois-Reymond (eds) (1995).

230 BIBLIOGRAPHY

Lamb, S. (2002) *The Secret Lives of Girls: What Good Girls Really Do – Sex Play, Aggression, and Their Guilt*, Free Press, New York.

Lamm, N. (1995) 'It's a Big Fat Revolution' in B. Findlen (ed) (1995).

Lash, S. & Urry, J. (1994) *Economies of signs and space*, Thousand Oaks, London.

Leadbeater, B., Ross, J. & Way, N. (eds) (1996) *Urban Girls: Resisting Stereotypes, Creating Identities*, New York University Press, New York.

Leblanc, L. (1999) *Pretty in Punk: Girls' Gender Resistance in a Boys' Subculture*, Rutgers University Press, New Brunswick and London.

Lee, N. (2001) *Childhood and society, Growing up in an age of uncertainty*, Issues in Society Series, Open University Press, Buckingham.

Lees, S. (1986) *Losing Out: Sexuality and Adolescent Girls*, Hutchinson, London.

Lees, S. (1993) *Sugar and Spice: Sexuality and the Adolescent Girl*, Penguin, London.

Lees, S. (2000) 'Sexuality and citizenship education', in M. Arnot & J.-A. Dillabough (eds) (2000).

Lemish, D. (1998) 'Spice Girls' Talk: A Case Study in the Development of Gendered Identity', in S. Inness (ed) (1998b).

Leonard, M. (1997) ' "Rebel Girl, You are the Queen of My World": Feminism, "Subculture" and Grrrl Power', in S. Whiteley (ed), *Sexing the Groove: Popular Music and Gender*, Routledge, London.

Leonard, M. (1998) 'Paper Planes: Travelling The New Grrrl Geographies', in T. Skelton and G. Valentine (eds), *Cool Places: Geographies of Youth Cultures*, Routledge, London.

Lesko, N. (1988) 'The Curriculum of the Body: Lessons from a Catholic High School', in L. Roman, L. Christian-Smith & E. Ellsworth (eds) (1988).

Lesko, N. (2001) *Act Your Age! A Cultural Construction of Adolescence*, Routledge Falmer, New York.

Lister, R. (2003) *Citizenship: Feminist Perspectives*, Second Edition, New York University Press, New York.

Lloyd, M. (1996) 'Feminism, Aerobics and the Politics of the Body', *Body & Society*, 2(2), 79–98.

Longo, V. (forthcoming) *Something Old, Something New, Something Borrowed, Something Blue: Mothers and Daughters Talk About Their Everyday Lives*, PhD Thesis, Monash University, Melbourne, Australia.

Lopez, N. (2003) *Hopeful Girls, Troubled Boys: Race and Gender Disparity in Urban Education*, Routledge, New York.

Lucas, S. (2000) 'Nike's Commercial Solution: Girls, Sneakers and Salvation', *International Review for the Sociology of Sport*, 35(2), 149–64.

Lundbom, P. (2003) ' "Hei kaveri – millä välineillä äänestät?" Mitä demokratia, vaalit ja poliittisen osallistumisen keinot merkitsevät nuorille?" in K. Paakkunainen (ed) (2003).

Lyon, D. (1999) *Postmodernity*, Open University, Buckingham.

MacDonald, M. (1995) *Representing Women: Myths of Femininity in the Popular Media*, Edward Arnold, A Member of the Hodder Headline Group, London.

Mahoney, M. (1996) 'The Problem of Silence in Feminist Psychology', *Feminist Studies*, 22(3), 603–26.

Malikin, N. (1993) 'It's a Grrrl thing', *Seventeen*, nr. 52, pp. 80–2.

Mann, J. (1994) *The Difference: Growing Up Female in America*, Warner Books, New York.

Marshall, T.H. (1950) *Citizenship and Social Class*, Cambridge University Press, Cambridge.

Martin, E. (1989) *The Woman in the Body. A Cultural Analysis of Reproduction*, Open University Press, Milton Keynes.

Matthews, J. (2002) 'Racialised Schooling, "Ethnic Success" and Asian-Australian Students', *British Journal of Sociology of Education*, 23(2), 193–207.

McDonald, K. (1999) *Struggles for Subjectivity: Identity, Action and Youth Experience*, Cambridge University Press, Cambridge.

McLeod, J. & Malone, K. (eds) (2000) *Researching Youth*, Australian Clearinghouse for Youth Studies, Hobart.

McLeod, J. (2002) 'Working Out Intimacy: young people and friendship in an age of reflexivity', Discourse: studies in the cultural politics of education, Special Issue: *Re-Theorising Friendship in Educational Settings*, 23(2), 211–26.

McRobbie, A. (1987) 'Dance and Social Fantasy' in A. McRobbie & M. Nava (eds), *Gender and Generation*, Macmillan, Basingstoke.

McRobbie, A. (ed) (1991) *Feminism and Youth Culture From Jackie to Just Seventeen*, Macmillan, London.

McRobbie, A. (1991a) 'Jackie Magazine: Romantic Individualism and the Teenage Girl', in A. McRobbie (ed) (1991).

McRobbie, A. (1991b) 'Jackie and Just Seventeen, Girls' Comics and Magazines in the 1980s', in A. McRobbie (ed) (1991).

McRobbie, A. (1996) 'Different, Youthful, Subjectivities', in I. Chambers. & L. Curti (eds), *The Post Colonial Question: Common Skies, Divided Horizons*, Routledge, London.

McRobbie, A. (2000) 'Sweet Smell of Success? New Ways of Being Young Women', in A. McRobbie (ed), *Feminism and Youth Culture. From Jackie to Just Seventeen*, Second Edition, Macmillan, London.

McRobbie, A. (2001) 'Good Girls, Bad Girls? Female Success and the New Meritocracy', unpublished keynote address at *A New Girl Order? Young Women and the Future of Feminist Inquiry Conference*, London, 12–14 November.

McRobbie, A. & Garber, J. (1975/1991) 'Girls and Subcultures', in S. Hall. & T. Jefferson (eds), *Resistance Through Rituals*, Hutchinson, London.

Measor, L., Tiffin, C. & Miller, K. (2000) *Young People's Views on Sex Education: Education, Attitudes and Behaviour*, Routledge/Falmer, London.

Meekosha, Helen (2002) 'Virtual Activists? Women and the Making of Identities of Disability', *Hypatia*, 17(3), 67–88.

Melucci, A. (1996) *Challenging Codes: Collective Action in the Information Age*, Cambridge University Press, Cambridge.

Miles, S. (2000) *Youth Lifestyles in a Changing World*, Open University Press, Buckingham.

Miller, J. (2001) *One of the Guys. Girls, Gangs and Gender*, Oxford University Press, New York and Oxford.

Mills, A. (2001) 'Gee, Your Hair Smells Terrific: Queering the Story of Female Jealousy', *Bitch Magazine: Feminist Response to Pop Culture*, 14, 34–7.

Mirza, H.S. (1992) *Young, Female and Black*, London, Routledge.

Mitchell, A., Rundle, L.B. & Karaian, L. (eds) (2001) *Turbo Chicks*, Sumach Press, Toronto.

Moraby, K. (1998) 'I Am Me: An Australian Muslim Woman' in M. Pallotta-Chiarolli (ed) (1998).

Morgan, J. (1999) *When Chickenheads Come Home to Roost: My Life as a Hip-Hop Feminist*, Simon and Schuster, New York.

Nagel, U. & Wallace, C. (1997) 'Participation and Identification in Risk Societies: European Perspectives', in J. Bynner, L. Chisholm & A. Furlong (eds) (1997).

Nam, V. (ed) (2001) *Yell-Oh Girls!*, HarperCollins, New York.

Nathanson, C. (1991) *Dangerous Passage: The Social Control of Sexuality in Women's Adolescence*, Temple University Press, Philadelphia.

National Information Center for Children and Youth with Disabilities (1990) 'Having a Daughter with a Disability: Is It Different for Girls?, *NICHCY News Digest*, #ND14, October.

NBE (1994) *Framework Curriculum for the Comprehensive School 1994*, National Board of Education, Painatuskeskus, Helsinki.

Niemelä, A. (2003) *Erilainen nuoruus? Varhainen äitiys, ikä ja elämänkulku*. Unpublished Master's thesis, Department of Sociology, University of Helsinki, Finland.

Niemi, I. & Pääkkönen, H. (1995) 'Use of Time', in E.-S. Veikkola, & T. Palmu (eds), *Women and Men in Finland*, Statistics Finland, Living Conditions 1995, 1.

Nikas, C. (1998) ' The Power of Girls', *Ragtrader*, 3–16 April, 20–1.

Noble, G., Poynting, S. & Tabar, P. (1998) 'Lebanese Youth and Social Identity' in R. White (ed) (1998).

Nutter, S. (1997) 'The Structure and Growth of the Los Angeles Garment Industry', in A. Ross (ed), *No Sweat*, Verso, London.

Nykyri, T. (1996) *Naiseuden naamiaiset. Nuoren naisen diskoruumiillisuus*, Nykykulttuurintutkimusyksikön julkaisuja 48, Jyväskylän yliopisto, Jyväskylä.

Näre, S. (1992) 'Liisa Älä! Älä! -maassa. Tyttöjen autonomian säätely', in S. Näre & L. Lähteenmaa (eds) (1992).

Näre, S. & Lähteenmaa, J. (eds) (1992) *Letit liehumaan. Tyttökulttuuri murroksessa*, Tietolipas 124, SKS, Helsinki.

Oakley, A. (1981) *Subject Women*, Robinson, Oxford.

Oakley, A. (1984) *The Captured Womb: A History of the Medical Care of Pregnant Women*, Blackwell, Oxford.

O'Brien, S. (1999) 'Is the Future of Australian Feminism Feral?', in R. White (ed) (1998).

Olsson, B. & Norrman Skugge, L. (1999) 'Förord', in L. Norrman Skugge, B. Olsson & B. Zilg (eds), *Fittstim*, Bokförlaget DN, Stockholm.

Ono, K. (2000) 'To be Vampire on Buffy the Vampire Slayer: Race and ("Other") Socially Marginalizing Positions on Horror TV', in E.R. Helford (ed) (2000).

Orenstein, P. (1994) *Schoolgirls: Young Women, Self-Esteem and the Confidence Gap*, Anchor Books, New York.

Owens, R.E. Jr. (1998) *Queer Kids: The Challenges and Promise for Lesbian, Gay, and Bisexual Youth*, Harrington Park Press, Binhampton.

Paakkunainen, K. (2003) *'Kyllä politiikalle, mutta . . .' Nuoret ja eduskuntavaalit 2003*, Nuorisotutkimusverkosto/Nuorisotutkimusseura, julkaisuja 35. Nuorisoasiain neuvottelukunta, julkaisuja 27. Opetusministeriö. Yliopistopaino, Helsinki.

Paglia, A. & Room, R. (1998) 'How Unthinkable and at What Age? Adult Opinions about the 'Social Clock' for Contested Behaviour by Teenagers.' *Journal of Youth Studies*, 1(3), 295–314.

Pallotta-Chiarolli, M. (ed) (1998) *Girls' Talk. Young women speak their hearts and minds*, Finch, Sydney.

Pallotta-Chiarolli, M. (1999) 'Coming Out/Going Home: Australian Girls and Young Women Interrogating Racism and Heterosexism', *Women's Studies Journal*, 15(2), Special Issue: *Girl Trouble? Feminist Inquiry into the Lives of Young Women*, 71–88.

Palmu, T. (2003) *Sukupuolen rakentuminen koulun kulttuurisissa teksteissä. Etnografia yläasteen äidinkielen oppitunneilla*, Helsingin yliopiston kasvatustieteen laitoksen tutkimuksia 189, Yliopistopaino, Helsinki.

Perho, S. (2002) 'Tyttönä rasistisessa nuorisokulttuurissa', in S. Aaltonen & P. Honkatukia (eds) (2002).

Phoenix, A. (1991) *Young Mothers?*, Polity Press, Cambridge.

Pickvance, C. & Pickvance, K. (1994) 'Towards a Strategic Approach to Housing Behavior: A Study of Young People's Housing Strategies in South-East England.' *Sociology*, 28(3), 657–78.

Pickvance, C. & Pickvance, K. (1995) 'The role of family help in the housing decisions of young people.' *The Sociological Review*, 43(1), 123–49.

Pipher, M. (1994) *Reviving Ophelia: Saving the Selves of Adolescent Girls*, Grosset/ Putnam, New York.

Pitts, V. (1999) 'Body Modification, Self-Mutilation and Agency in Media Accounts of a Subculture', *Body & Society*, 5(2–3), 291–303.

Pohjonen, S. (1992) 'Naiset, väkivalta ja rikosoikeus', in R. Turunen (ed), *Naisnäkökulmia oikeuteen*, Gaudeamus, Helsinki.

Press, J. & Nichols, K. (1997) 'Notes on Girl Power: The Selling of Softcore Feminism', *Village Voice*, Sept 23, 59–62.

Projansky, S. & Vande Berg, L.R. (2000) 'Sabrina, the Teenage . . .?: Girls, Witches, Mortals and the Limitations of Prime-Time Feminism', in E.R. Helford (2000).

Proweller, A. (1998) *Constructing Female Identities: Meaning Making in an Upper Middle Class Youth Culture*, State University of New York Press, Albany.

Pyke, K.D. & Johnson, D.L. (2003) 'Asian American Women and Racialized Femininities: 'Doing' Gender across Cultural Worlds', *Gender & Society*, 17(1) 33–53.

Quart, A. (2003) *Branded. The Buying and Selling of Teenagers*, arrow books, London.

Räthzel, N. (2000) 'Living Differences: Ethnicity and Fearless Girls in Public Spaces', *Social Identities*, 6(2), 119–42.

Rattansi, A. & Phoenix, A. (1997) 'Rethinking Youth Identities: Modernist and Postmodernist Frameworks', in J. Bynner, L. Chisholm & A. Furlong (1997).

Reay, D. (2001) ' "Spice Girls", Nice Girls, "Girlies", and "Tomboys": Gender Discourses, Girls' Cultures and Femininities in the Primary Classroom', *Gender and Education*, 13(2), 153–66.

Rich, A. (1984) 'Compulsory Heterosexuality and Lesbian Existence', in A. Snitow (ed), *Desire: The Politics of Sexuality*, Virago, London.

Rimmerman, C.A. (1997) *The New Citizenship*, Westview, Boulder.

Risman, B. & Schwartz, P. (2002) 'After the Sexual Revolution: Gender Politics in Teen Dating', *Contexts*, 1(1), 16–24.

Robinson, F. (2002) 'Pre-Teen Believers', *The Age*, 9 June.

Roiphe, K. (1993) *The Morning After*, Little Brown, Boston.

Roker, D. (1993) 'Gaining the Edge: Girls at a Private School', in I. Bates & G. Riseborough (eds), *Youth and Inequality*, Buckingham, Open University Press.

Roman, L. (1988) 'Intimacy, Labor and Class: Ideologies of Feminine Sexuality in the Punk Slam Dance', in L. Roman, L. Christian-Smith & E. Ellsworth (eds) (1988).

Roman, L., Christian-Smith, L. & Ellsworth, E. (eds) (1988) *Becoming Feminine: The Politics of Popular Culture*, Falmer Press, London.

Rose, N. (1992) *Governing the Soul: The Shaping of the Private Self*, Routledge, London.

Rousso, H. (1988) *Disabled, Female and Proud!*, Exceptional Parent Press, Boston.

Ruck, M.D., Abramovitch, R. & Keating, D.P. (1998) 'Children's and Adolescents' Understanding of Rights: Balancing Nurturance and Self-Determination', *Child Development*, 64(2), 404–17.

Rudd, P. & Evans, K. (1998) 'Structure and Agency in Youth Transitions: Student Experiences of Vocational Further Education', *Journal of Youth Studies*, 1(1), 39–62.

Saarilahti, J. (2002) 'Nainen ei ole koskaan syyllinen raiskaukseen', *SoneraPlaza –
Ellit*, November 2. (www3.soneraplaza.fi/ellit/artikkeli/0,2208,1990_63769,00.
html)

Sadker, M. & David S. (1994) *Failing at Fairness: How American's Schools Cheat Girls*,
Charles Scribner's Sons, New York.

Salmi, M. (1996) 'Tekno – 90-luvun psykedeliaa ja uutta yhteisöllisyyttä', in L.
Suurpää & P. Aaltojärvi (eds), *Näin nuoret. Näkökulmia nuoruuden kulttuureihin*.
Tietolipas 143, SKS, Helsinki.

Sankari, A. (1995) *Kuntosaliruumis. Kappaleita nuorten aikuisten ruumiillisuuk-
sista*, Nykykulttuurintutkimusyksikön julkaisuja 44, Jyväskylän yliopisto,
Jyväskylä.

Sanz, J. (2001) 'The Shape of Youth Members of the Spanish Parliaments', unpublished paper at the symposium *Youth – Actor of Social Change?*, Council of Europe,
Strasbourg, 12–16 December.

Sassatelli, R. (1999) 'Interaction Order and Beyond: A Field Analysis of Body Culture
within Fitness Gyms', *Body & Society*, 5(2–3), 227–48.

Saxton, M., B. Fiduccia, B.W., Chang, P. & Montañez, W. (1999) 'Reproductive Rights.
Women and Girls with Disabilities' in *Thru the Lens: Women and Girls with
Disabilities*, Women and Philantropy, Washington.

Schaffner, L. (1998) 'Do Bad Girls Get a Bum Rap', in S. Inness (ed) (1998b).

Schalett, A. (2000) 'Raging Hormones, Regulated Love: Adolescent Sexuality and
the Constitution of the Modern Individual in the United States and the Netherlands', *Body & Society*, 6(1), 75–105.

Schlegel, A. & Barry, H. (1991) *Adolescence: An Anthropological Inquiry*, The Free Press,
New York.

Schultz, D. (1991) *Risk, Resiliency, and Resistance: Current Research on Adolescent Girls*.
National Council for Research.

Scott-Dixon, K. (1999) 'Ezines and Feminist Activism: Building a Community',
Women's Studies and the Internet, *Resources for Feminist Research*, 27, (1/2).

Shandler, N. (2001) *Ophelia's Mom: Loving and Letting Go of Your Adolescent Daughter*,
Crown, New York.

Shandler, S. (ed) (1999) *Ophelia Speaks: Adolescent Girls Write about their Search for Self*,
Harper Collins, New York.

Sharpe, S. (2001) 'Going For It: Young Women Face the Future', *Feminism and Psychology*, 11(2), 177–81.

Sharpe, S. (1994) *Fathers and Daughters*, Routledge, London.

Sheridan, N. (2001) 'Beyond Ophelia: Feminism for Girls', *Canadian Women's Studies
Journal*, Special Issue: *Young Women: Feminist, Activists, Grrrls*, May, 152–4.

Silbergleid, R. (2002) ' "Oh Baby!": Representations of Single Mothers in American
Popular Culture', *Americana: The Journal of American Popular Culture (1900–
present)*, 1(2). http://www.americanpopularculture.com/journal/articles/
fall_2002/silbergleid.htm

Silva, E.B. & Smart, C. (eds) (1999) *The New Family?* Sage, London.

Silva, E.B. & Smart, C. (1999) 'The "New Practices" and Politics of Family Life, in
E.B. Silva & C. Smart (eds) (1999).

Simmons, R. (2003) *Odd Girl Out: The Hidden Culture of Aggression in Girls*, Harvets
Books, New York.

Siurala, L. (2000) 'Changing Forms of Participation', in *New Forms of Youth Participation*, Round Table, Council of Europe, Biel, 4–6 May.

Skugge, L.N., Olsson, B. & Zilg, B. (eds) (1999) *Fittstim*, Bokförlaget DN, Stockholm.

Smith D. (1988) 'Femininity as Discourse', in L. Roman, L. Christian-Smith & E. Ellsworth (eds) (1988).

Spelman, E. (1990) *Inessential Woman*, Beacon Press, Boston.

Spirit, (1995) 'What is a Riot Grrrl Anyway?' http://www.columbia.edu/~rli3/music_html/bikini_kill/girl.html

Stacey, J. (1991) 'Backward toward the Postmodern Family: Reflections on Gender, Kinship, and Class in the Silicon Valley' in A. Wolfe (ed) (1991).

Stasuilis, D. & Yuval-Davis, N. (eds) (1995) *Unsettling Settler Societies: articulations of gender, ethnicity, race and class*, Sage. London.

Summers, A. (1994) 'The Future of Feminism – A Letter to the Next Generation', *Damned Whores and God's Police*, Penguin, Harmondsworth.

Svenberg, J. (1999) 'Tack Gud att jag är lesbisk – om homosexualitet', in L. Norrman Skugge, B. Olsson & B. Zilg (eds), *Fittstim*, Bokförlaget DN, Stockholm.

Sweet, R. (1998) 'Youth: The Rhetoric and Reality of the 1990s', in *Australia's Youth: Reality and Risk*, Dusseldorp Skills Forum, Sydney.

Taft, J. (2001) 'Defining Girl Power: The Culture Machine vs. The Girl Activist', unpublished presentation at *A New Girl Order? Young Women and the Future of Feminist Inquiry Conference*, London, 12–14 November.

Taylor, J.M., Gilligan, C. & Sullivan, A.M. (1995) *Between Voice and Silence: Women and Girls, Race and Relationship*, Harvard University Press, Cambridge.

Tegner, E. (1991) 'Dansa min docka', in H. Ganetz. & K. Lövgren (eds), *Om unga kvinnor*, Studentlitteratur, Lund.

Thompson, S. (1995) *Going All the Way: Teenage Girls' Tales of Sex, Romance and Pregnancy*, Hill and Wang, New York.

Thomson, R., Henderson, S. & Holland, J. (2003) 'Making the Most of What You've Got? Resources, Values and Inequalities in Young Women's Transition to Adulthood', *Educational Review*, 55(1), 33–46.

Thorne, B. (1982) 'Feminist Rethinking of the Family: An Overview', in B. Thorne & M. Yalom (eds), *Rethinking the Family: Some Feminist Questions*, Longman, New York.

Thorne, B. (1993) *Gender Play, Girls and Boys in School*, Open University Press, Buckingham.

Thulin, K. & Östergren, J. (1997) *X-märkt. Flickornas guide till verkligheten*, Rabén & Sjögren, Stockholm.

Tolman, D. (1994) 'Doing Desire: Adolescent Girls' Struggles for/with Sexuality', *Gender & Society*, 8(3), 324–42.

Tolonen, T. (2001) *Nuorten kulttuurit koulussa. Ääni, tila ja sukupuolten arkiset järjestykset*, Gaudeamus, Helsinki.

Trioli, V. (1996) *Generation f*, Minerva, Melbourne.

Turner, B.S. (1984) *The Body & Society: Explorations in Social Theory*, Sage, London.

Turner, B.S. (1999) 'The Possibility of Primitiveness: Towards a Sociology of Body Marks in Cool Societies', *Body & Society*, (2–3), 39–50.

Tyyskä, V. (2001) *Long and Winding Road. Adolescents and Youth in Canada Today*, Canadian Scholars' Press, Toronto.

Valentine, G. (2001) 'Coming Out and Out-comes: Negotiating Lesbian and Gay Identities with/in the Family', unpublished presentation at the European Sociologists' Association Conference *Visions and Divisions*, University of Helsinki, August.

Van Drenth, A. (1998) 'Citizenship, Participation and the Social Policy on Girls in the Netherlands', in J. Bussemaker & R. Voet (eds), *Gender, Participation and Citizenship in the Netherlands*, Aldershot, Ashgate.

Vanderkam, L. (2003) 'Teen 'Zines Hawk Fake Girl Power', *USA Today*, 20 February 2003, 13A.

Vanttaja, M. (2002) Koulumenestyjät, Tutkimus laudaturylioppilaiden koulutus- ja työurista, Suomen Kasvatustieteellinen Seura, Turku.

Ventura, M. (1998) 'Warrior Women: Why are TV Shows like Buffy, the Vampire Slayer, La Femme Nikita and Xena: Warrior Princess so Popular, Especially among Teens?', *Psychology Today*, 31(6), 58–63.

Vromen, A. (2003) 'People Try to Put Us Down . . . Participatory Citizenship of Generation X', *Australian Journal of Political Science*, 38(1), 79–99.

Wade, L. (1999) 'Back Talk', *Salon.Com*, website, 15 Sept.

Wald, G. (1998) 'Just a Girl? Rock Music, Feminism, and the Cultural Construction of Female Youth', *Signs*, 23(3), 585–610.

Walker, R. (ed) (1996) *To Be Real: Telling the Truth and Changing the Face of Feminism*, Anchor Books, New York.

Walkerdine, V. (1990) *School Girl Fictions*, Verso, London.

Walkerdine, V. (1997) *Daddy's Girl: Young Girls and Popular Culture*, Harvard University Press, Cambridge.

Walkerdine, V. (1999) 'Girls Growing Up on the Edge of the Millennium', *Women's Studies Journal*, Special Issue: *Girl Trouble? Feminist Inquiry into the Lives of Young Women*, 15(2), 29–50.

Walkerdine, V., Lucey, H. & Melody, J. (2001) *Growing Up Girl*, Palgrave, London.

Wallace, C. (1994) 'Gender and Transition', in K. Evans, & W.K. Heinz (eds), *Becoming Adults in England and Germany*, Anglo-German Foundation, London.

Wallace, C. & Kovatcheva, S. (1999) *Youth in Society: the Construction and Deconstruction of Youth in East and West Europe*, Macmillan, London.

Walter, N. (1998) *The New Feminism*, Little, Brown and Company, London.

Ward, J.V. & Benjamin, B.C. (forthcoming 2004) 'Women, Girls, and the Unfinished Work of Connection: A Critical Review of American Girls' Studies' in A. Harris (ed) (forthcoming 2004).

Wench Collective (2001) 'Wench Radio: Funky Feminist Fury', *Canadian Women's Studies Journal*, Special Issue: *Young Women: Feminist, Activists, Grrrls*, May, 69–74.

Wex, M. (1979) *Let's Take Back Our Space*, Frauenliteraturverlag Hermine Fees, Berlin.

White, E. (2002) *Fast Girls: Teenage Tribes and the Myth of the Slut*, Scribner, New York.

White, R. (ed) (1998) *Australian Youth Subcultures: On the Margins and in the Mainstream*, National Clearinghouse for Youth Studies, Hobart.

Wicks, D. & Mishra, G. (1998) 'Young Australian Women and their Aspirations for Work, Education and Relationships', in E. Carson, A. Jamrozicz & T. Winefield (eds), *Unemployment: Economic Promise and Political Will*, Australian Academic Press, Brisbane.

Wilder, J. (1999) 'Girls got the Buzz', *Win Magazine*, May, p. 34.

Wilkinson, H. (1994) *No Turning Back: Generations and the Genderquake*, Demos, London.

Williams, L.S., Alvarez, S.D. & Andrade Hauck, K.S. (2002) 'My Name is not María: Young Latinas Seeking Home in the Heartland', *Social Problems*, 49(4), 563–84.

Windwalker, B. (1995) ' "Who are We?" girl issues', in S. Shandler (ed) (1999).

Wiseman, R. (2003) *Queen Bees and Wannabees: Helping Your Daughter Survive Cliques, Gossip, Boyfriends and Other Realities of Adolescence*, Three River Press, New York.

Wolf, N. (1994) *Fire With Fire*, Random House, New York.

Wolfe, A. (1991) (ed) *America at Century's End*, University of California Press, Berkeley.

Woollett, A. & Marshall, H. (1996) 'Reading the Body. Young Women's Accounts of the Meanings of the Body in Relation to Independence, Responsibility and Maturity', *European Journal of Women's Studies*, 3(2), 199–214.

Wooden, M. (1998) 'The Labour Market for Young Australians', in *Australia's Youth: Reality and Risk*, Dusseldorp Skills Forum, Sydney.

Wulff, H. (1988) *Twenty Girls: Growing Up, Ethnicity and Excitement in a South London Microculture*, Stockholm Studies in Social Anthropology, Stockholm.

Wulff, H. (1995) 'Inter-racial Friendship: Consuming Youth Styles, Ethnicity and Teenage Femininity in South London', in V. Amit-Talai & H. Wulff (eds) (1995).

Wyn, J. (1994) 'Young Women and STDs: The Issues for Public Health', *Australian Journal of Public Health*, 18(1), 32–9.

Wyn, J. (2000) 'The postmodern girl: Education, "success" and the construction of girls' identities', in J. McLeod. & K. Malone (eds) (2000).

Wyn, J. & White, R. (1997) *Rethinking Youth*, Sage, London.

Yates, L. (1997) 'Gender Equity and the Boys Debate: What Sort of Challenge is it?', *British Journal of Sociology of Education*, 18(3), 337–47.

Yates, L. (2000) 'Representing "Class" in Qualitative Research', in J. McLeod & K. Malone (eds) (2000).

Yuval-Davis, N. (1992) *Nationalism, racism and gender relations*, Institute of Social Studies, The Hague.

Yuval-Davis, N. (1997) *Gender & Nation*, Sage, London.

Zelizer, V.A.R. (1985) *Pricing the Priceless Child: The Changing Social Value of Children*, BasicBooks, USA.

Zhou, M. & Bankston, C.L. III (1998) *Growing Up American: How Vietnamese Children Adapt to Life in the United States*, Russell Sage Foundation, New York.

Ziegler, G. (1997) *Shakespeare's Unruly Women*, Folger Shakespeare Library.

Ziehe, T. (1991) *Zeitvergleiche: Jugend in kulturellen Modernisierungen*, Juventa, Weinheim.

Index